Space
Architecture for Art

Including a directory of arts spaces in Ireland

preface by **Brian O'Doherty**
edited by **Gemma Tipton**

With grateful thanks to the following for their generous support

The National Lottery Programme of the Arts Council of Northern Ireland for their funding of this project

Also to An Chomhairle Ealaíon/The Arts Council, and to our Major Supporters, Associates, Partners and Friends

Edited by: **Gemma Tipton**

Project Research and Development: Liz Aders

Design: Gemma Tipton

Facilitating Editor at CIRCA: Peter FitzGerald

CIRCA Art Magazine

Editor: Peter FitzGerald
International Editorial Adviser: Liz Aders

CIRCA, 43/44 Temple Bar, Dublin 2
Tel/Fax (+353 1) 6797388
info@recirca.com   www.recirca.com

Cover image: Gallery 2, McCullough Mulvin Architects, 2001; at Douglas Hyde Gallery, Paul Koralek, Ahrends, Burton and Koralek Architects, 1978-79; photo and courtesy Christian Richters

Major Supporters

Architecture Ireland

GLUCKSMAN

Lewis Glucksman Gallery, Cork

W & G Baird

Millennium Court Art Centre, Portadown

BUTLER ■ GALLERY

Butler Gallery, Kilkenny

Ormeau Baths Gallery, Belfast

Dublin City Gallery The Hugh Lane

RIAI
Representing Irish Architects

Royal Institute of the Architects in Ireland

Partners

Cooney and Co Architects, Dublin
Crawford Municipal Gallery, Cork
Douglas Hyde Gallery, Dublin
Gallery of Photography, Dublin
Kevin Kavanagh Gallery, Dublin
Limerick City Gallery of Art, Limerick

McCullough Mulvin Architects, Dublin
RHA Gallagher Gallery, Dublin
Roscommon Arts Centre, Co Roscommon
South Tipperary Arts Centre, Co Tipperary
TULCA, Season of Visual Art, Galway

Associates

Belfast Print Workshop, Belfast
Temple Bar Gallery and Studios, Dublin

West Cork Arts Centre, Co Cork
Wilson Architects, Cork

Friends

Ards Art Centre, Co Down
Context Galleries, Co Derry
Custom House Studios, Co Mayo
Dublin Docklands Development Authority, Dublin
Fenton Gallery, Cork
Galway Art Centre, Galway
Golden Thread Gallery, Belfast
Green on Red Gallery, Dublin
Kildare Architects Ltd., Kildare

MacGabhann Architects, Co Donegal
Mackel + Doherty Architects, Belfast
Model Arts and Niland Galleries, Sligo
Origin Gallery and Cill Rialaig Project, Dublin and Kerry
Original Print Gallery, Dublin
Prospect Architecure & Interior Design, Limerick
Sculptors Society of Ireland
The Workroom Gallery, Dublin

Contents

[opposite:] Gerard Byrne:
The End of Architecture is Nigh,
1995, photograph; courtesy the
artist

White Box / Black Cube

Preface by Brian O'Doherty

Each art evolved its signature space – concert hall, movie theatre, stage, museum gallery. Their walls filter out the unmoneyed, the so-called lower classes, the uninitiated, and the indifferent. They let in the opposite of the foregoing. So the walls of these institutions are social regulators, as much mental as physical, subscribing to the rhetoric of inclusion. But paradoxically they announce that the arts aren't for everybody.

These walls protect threatened disciplines (as zoos maintain threatened species) many of which survive with state subsidies. Institutional spaces of every kind evolved in the taxonomic nineteenth century, a century obsessed with categories. They were codified in the twentieth. In the twenty-first, they are being re-visioned. Each revision involves (often involuntary) assumptions. How does this apply to the spaces discussed in this book: museum, gallery, artspace, kunsthalle?

There was, in the latter half of the twentieth century, a rage of museum-building. Every city had to have one. This continues. Each new building, sometimes of surpassing eccentricity, has a double attitude: to the surrounding community and to what it contains. From the imperial Getty Museum in Los Angeles to the dour quasi-brutalist Whitney Museum in New York (which I happen to like), to the baroque-and-roll cosmetics of the Guggenheim, Bilbao; the architecture of museums speaks in several tongues. The contemporary museum's architecture signifies the oft-cited transfer of faith from failed church to the vaguely spiritual emanations of 'art'. It also tends to emphasise the value of the container over the contained.

The post-modern museum has attracted brilliantly inventive architects: Libeskind (who did the reportedly amazing Holocaust Museum in Berlin; most admired while it was yet empty); Eisenmann (his eccentric, even polemical museum in Columbus, Ohio); Gehry, of course; others. What is common to these architectural tours-de-force is that they compete with what they enclose, ironic since many of these architects learned from the art of the minimal/conceptual era. New museum buildings embody paradox and contradiction in ways predicted by Robert Venturi's brilliant polemic[1] (Venturi, by the way, was as hostile to the contemporary art within as Frank Lloyd Wright was with his Guggenheim, New York). There's nothing wrong with such sophisticated architectural enterprises except when they project attitudes (in their interior spaces) that edit the art they enclose. Which brings us, inevitably, to the issue of how to present art.

[1] Robert Venturi, *Complexity and Contradiction in Architecture*, Museum of Modern Art, New York, 1966.

We are accustomed to seeing masterpieces lying in state, which is perhaps where they should reside. But any theory of display depends on a reading of the nature of the art presented. Post-modern and contemporary art also have attitudes to the container, exercising all the wicked ingenuity that sophisticated art is capable of. During the modernist era, art rarely transgressed the etiquette of behaving in its white 'cell'. But now the art sees the spotless gallery as a unit of discourse to be engaged, altered, rejected, ignored. The flexibility of the gallery has been tested by video, film, performance, installations, sound. It has become the versatile cousin of the performing arts' black box. What is surprising, to me at any rate, is the vigorous survival of this so-called neutral gallery space. As one who wished to make its implicit assumptions transparent, and who welcomed 'break-outs' through its walls, the durability of this space has been brought home to me. Such an advanced thinker as Hubert Damisch recently surprised me by pointing out the value and usefulness of the white gallery.

If art needs this 'neutral' space disinfected of all liminal content, we need to think (again) what that neutrality means. Is all art in the classic white gallery, no matter how ingeniously it adjusts, housebroken? Are contemporary art's 'revolutions', tizzies in a white teapot? Does the convention of the gallery de-fang the wild beast within? Do museums and galleries inversely testify to the social irrelevance of art? Have artworks become, as the auction house suggests, emblems of capital, certifying the acceptability of greed, to which a kind of mystical, quasi-spiritual aura is now attached, as it is to the museum itself? Are the trustees of museums, as a visionary bureaucrat once suggested in the mid-sixties, the museum's greatest enemy? Or should we be thinking how to make spaces that make art look good?

This last is not a casual issue. It is where this book springs to the cutting edge of a discourse only recently recognized.[2] Between the artwork and the spectator, falls the shadow, two shadows actually – that of the architect, and that of the preparator. We should not be deceived into thinking that the implications of presenting art are confined within the ghettoes of museums and galleries. For in this presentational intervention, large issues are embedded: how art will be seen, perceived, assimilated, thus made relevant to the inner life of the spectator; which is the challenge for each generation; but never more urgently than now.

I don't think you can contemplate the dividing wall of gallery or museum without pondering the fate of art, its meaning, or lack of it. Such cultural meditations tend to be unprofitable in the abstract, particularly when the next exhibition is imminent. But there is something about a wall, even an invisible one such as Bottom suggested (complete with eye-hole) that immediately raises issues from the benign to the sinister, to the politics of inclusion and exclusion.[3] A conceptual wall, such as Bottom's, exists in the mind, which is plentifully stocked with walls of every kind and dimension.

Brian O'Doherty
New York, August 2004

[2] Victoria Newhouse, *Art and the Power of Placement*, The Monacelli Press, New York, 2005.

[3] *A Midsummer Night's Dream*, William Shakespeare, Act 3, Scene 1, lines 62-66.

Where are the Museums?

Introduction by Gemma Tipton

[1] Quoted on the back cover of *Towards a New Museum*, Victoria Newhouse, Monacelli Press, New York, 1998.

"Guys in suits who can't paint",[1] a remark made by Frank Stella, neatly encapsulates the feelings of many artists about the architects who design the buildings in which they show their work, and in which it is collected. In Stella's case, his dissatisfaction led him, as it did with Donald Judd, to explore architectural designs for museums himself. Judd's conclusion was the Chinati Foundation at Marfa, Texas, a conversion of a disused army barracks in the Chihuahua Desert. Stella's took him in a different direction. "There are millions of square feet of warehouses available for contemporary art where it looks better than in a neutral box, so we need new forms."[2]

[2] *ibid*, p. 129.

Stella is an admirer of Frank Gehry, architectural master of these 'new forms', and Gehry acknowledges the influence of Stella and other artists, such as Claes Oldenburg and Coosje van Bruggen in his work. But under which other influences does the architecture of contemporary art museums fall? From where does today's concept of the art museum derive, and how has its traditions shaped spaces as diverse as Santiago Calatrava's Milwaukee Museum extension (1994-2000), Yoshio Tanuguchi's MoMA extension project (opened November 2004), or Herzog and de Meuron's Tate Modern conversion (1994-2000) – three widely different museum projects, but all ostensibly built for the same purpose?

[3] *Museums for a New Millennium*, ed. Vittorio Magnago Laumpugnani and Angeli Sachs, Prestel , London 1999, p. 30.

Despite this variety, this experimentation, there is still dissatisfaction. "Where are the museums that match my work?" asks Katharina Fritsch in an essay to accompany her 1995 exhibition at the German Pavilion of the Venice Biennale.[3] But as art continues to do its job (at least part of which is to constantly redefine itself, reinventing and breaking its own boundaries), how *can* a museum be made that will match the work of painters, sculptors, performance artists, those with digital visions, situationists, dadaists, futurists, modernists, postmodernists and all their artistic allies and antagonists? And how can a single concept of the ideal museum cater to institutions whose brief is simultaneously to collect, archive, display, commission, surprise, delight, educate – and (these days) act as catalysts for the cultural and economic regeneration of the areas in which they find themselves sited?

While this introduction mainly deals with larger spaces, the architectural issues of space, that are raised hold equally true in smaller galleries. Indeed, within smaller spaces, the

[from left:] Santiago Calatrava, interior: *reception, Milwaukee Art Museum*, 1994-2000; courtesy MAM; Herzog & de Meuron, interior: *Turbine Hall, Tate Modern*, 1994-2000; photo Marcus Leith, courtesy Tate Modern

issues are often intensified.[4] The gallery can be one of the most exciting and creative of architectural spaces, its brief generally more open and receptive to innovation, and yet architects equally find themselves having to contend with the weight of historical baggage attached to the idea of a museum, the inherited architectures and experiences of place. When the *Mona Lisa* was stolen in 1911, in a clear example of the pulling power that presence of absence can exert, thousands of people queued at the Louvre to see the empty space the painting had left behind. In *Stealing the Mona Lisa*, Darian Leader takes this as his starting point to discuss what we are actually looking at when we are looking at art. Art, he concludes, creates a caesura through which the viewer can briefly perceive the larger absence, beyond which one can come to enlightenment, transcendence, God – whatever it is you think you're looking for when you go to a gallery or museum.[5] But the physical context of the *Mona Lisa*'s theft, left largely undiscussed by Leader, is just as worthy of analysis as the particular piece that was stolen. The *Mona Lisa*'s larger frame, the Louvre itself, was the first public art museum, the first treasure house for the masses, the first space to take art out of its context, elevate it to the officially state-sanctioned status of art object, and re-present it to the public as part of a new narrative history of what art is.[6] It is interesting therefore, that this was the space from which Peruggia, the thief, decided to liberate his prize (he later claimed it was an impulse crime, committed 'on spec'). So what caesura do museums create? And what kind of space, or absence do they create for our perceptions?

It is this container, the Louvre, and others which followed it, including the British Museum in London (1823-47, architect Robert Smirke) and the Altes Museum in Berlin (1824-30, architect Karl Friedrich Schinkel), which have given us our paradigms for the display of art. Drawn originally from the 'galleries' connecting apartments and offices in grand buildings such as the Louvre, Vatican and Uffizi, and decoratively hung with portraits and paint-

[4] To clarify terms: museums are defined as having collections, while galleries are the spaces that house them.

[5] *Stealing the Mona Lisa*, Darian Leader, Faber and Faber, London, 2002.

[6] The British Museum was founded in 1759, and therefore pre-dates the Louvre by 34 years. It was at that time a library, and did not appoint a non-librarian director until 1931. The Ashmolean in Oxford (set up in 1683) also claims the title of 'first museum', but it was not an independent public institution. For a full discussion see *The Curator's Egg*, Karsten Schubert, One-Off Press, London, 2000.

[7] Nine days after the French monarchy fell in 1792, the decree was issued to turn the royal palace into a public museum. The speed with which this happened was made possible, however, by the work Louis XVI had already put into the project, work which was naturally left unacknowledged by the new revolutionary government.

[8] See 'Place of Reflection or Place of Sensation', Hans Belting, in *The Discursive Museum*, ed. Peter Noever, MAK, Vienna, 2001, for a discussion of the evolving role of museums in contemporary culture.

[9] *Experience or Interpretation*, Nicholas Serota, p. 7, Thames and Hudson, London, 2000.

[10] Published in an expanded version as *Inside the White Cube*, Brian O'Doherty, University of California Press, San Francisco, 1999.

[11] *ibid* p. 24.

ings, these new museum galleries modelled themselves on their predecessors – either by taking over their premises, or aping their design. These elements of architectural design include impressive entrances, central gathering spaces, ceremonial staircases (signifying ascension to knowledge), and enfilades of regularly-sized and shaped galleries, with prescribed circulation routes. The Enlightenment supplied the didactic impulse of museums, and structured the philosophical aspirations of the model which takes the viewer on a prescribed, generally chronological route through art and cultural history. These paradigms, with only a few exceptions, remained largely unchallenged until the end of the last century and the beginning of this one.

Added to the mix, with the temple-like façade of the Altes Museum (for example), was an element of secular religiosity, an element which continued internally with recontextualised works of plundered ecclesiastical art. That the contemporary art museum is a secular temple, a cathedral-for-our-time, is therefore a cliché almost 200 years old, and yet one continually dusted off and presented with a polish as if something brand new had just been discovered. Yet the history of the museum is relatively brief. Given that the Louvre was only opened to the public on 10 August 1793, it would be wrong to imbue our idea of the art museum with a sense of unalterable timelessness. The late-eighteenth-century Louvre, like its British and German sisters, though it began life as a product of the revolution,[7] developed as a space for colonization of the past, as well as a repository for the fruits of imperialism and colonialism themselves.[8]

For the next hundred years, the display of paintings still resembled the *Wunderkammer* concept – that of the cabinet of treasures, where every available inch of wall space was crammed from floor to ceiling with paintings of every size and shape. Contemporary paintings of the Louvre and the Paris Salons, such as Samuel F.B. Morse's *Exhibition Gallery at the Louvre* (1832-33) illustrate this kind of hang. In 1845, Charles Eastlake (who was to be made Director of the National Gallery in London in 1855) advised his trustees that "it is not desirable to cover every blank space at any height merely for the sake of clothing the walls and without reference to the size and quality of the picture." But it still wasn't until 1887 that the 'single line' hang was achieved at the National Gallery.[9]

Brian O'Doherty makes a persuasive case for the inevitability of this development in his influential series of essays for *Artforum* (written between 1976 and 1986),[10] where he discusses how Impressionism broke and remade existing perceptual laws, and created pictures which seemed to escape from their frames, and so demanded their own discrete conditions of viewing. It was this period, he argues, which also blurred, and then broke, the boundaries between picture and wall. This led ultimately to installation art, and art where the gallery wall became part of, and sometimes subject of, the image.

With this development, the history of art becomes inextricably linked with the history of museum architecture, and of curation and museology. "Hanging," says O'Doherty, "editorialises on matters of interpretation and value, and is unconsciously influenced by taste and fashion."[11] And inevitably the spaces in which art is hung come to shape and dictate a considerable portion of that taste. One of the first architectural articulations of the debate which was going to continue to hover around the building of exhibition spaces for art, took place at the end of the nineteenth century in Vienna. The Ringstraße project there aimed to gather all the major cultural and institutional buildings of the Hapsburg Empire around the curve of a newly created boulevard in what had been Vienna's 'green belt'. Each building was to have its own historical style. Completed in 1891, the Kunsthistoriches

clockwise from top left:
Gottfried Semper and Karl von Hasenauer, exterior:
Kunsthistorisches Museum, Vienna, completed 1891; courtesy
Kunsthistorisches Museum; Joseph Maria Olbrich, exterior:
Secession, Vienna, 1898; © and courtesy Secession; Joseph Maria
Olbrich, interior: Secession, Vienna, 1898; © and courtesy
Secession; Gottfried Semper and Karl von Hasenauer, interior:
Kunsthistorisches Museum, Vienna, completed 1891; courtesy
Kunsthistorisches Museum

Museum (architects Gottfried Semper and Karl von Hasenauer) created a massive building in the style of the Italian Renaissance. The enormous entrance hall of the Museum, with its monumental marble staircases, leaves you in no doubt of the historical weight and cultural significance of the works you are about to see. From 1890 to 1891 Gustav Klimt and his company of artists (the *Künstlercompagnie*) were commissioned to create a series of allegorical panels for the main hall of the Kunsthistoriches, spanning the history of art from ancient Egypt to Cinquecento Florence.

In 1897, only six years after completing this project, Klimt was involved with the creation of a totally different way to experience art, with his selection as the first president of the new *Association of Austrian Visual Artists Vienna Secession*. The aims of the Vienna Secession were to find a totally new form of expression in art, rejecting the traditions of eclectic historicism embodied in the art of the time, and by the Ringstraße architectural project in particular. The erection of its own building was one of the key projects of the Vienna Secession, and was discussed in the inaugural meeting of the society. Joseph Maria Olbrich was commissioned to design the building, and a site had been found on the Ringstraße itself. But when Olbrich's designs were unveiled in the Autumn of 1897, they were violently rejected by the Municipal Council and had to be transferred to the less prestigious Friedrichstraße. The Secession building (1898) is one of the key works of the Viennese Art Nouveau style. It and the Kunsthistoriches Museum embody the dialectic between eclectic historicism and modern architecture. The pure clean forms and unbroken planes of the Secession's interior galleries point towards O'Doherty's 'White Cube', and while the Art Noveau style still called for mythical forms (such as a crown of gilt laurel leaves, and topless dancing maidens in a frieze around the exterior), the clean functionalism of the interior, its glazed roof, with a second internal glazed ceiling, bathing the main exhibition space in diffused light, and the flexibility and adaptability of the main space, make it a revolutionary prototype for contemporary art spaces today.

The Vienna Secession believed in the concept of the *Gesamtkunstwerk*, the 'total work of art', where architecture, interior decoration and lighting combined to create the space in which a work should be exhibited and 'read'. That the space they commissioned for this project should be the precursor of what we would now call a 'neutral' space (the clean white box), forms an articulate part of the argument that there is really no such thing as a space which does not affect what it contains in some way, even if that space is a white cube.

Two further developments must be recognised in the transition from the Louvre/British Museum model of the museum to the contemporary art museum as we understand it today. The first of these was the entry of the United States into the world art market. Initially copying European models, new American museums, such as New York's Metropolitan Museum of Art (from 1880, initial architects: Theodore Weston 1880, and Richard Morris Hunt 1894) were driven by the desire to demonstrate great wealth, legitimise newly-made fortunes, and show evidence of new-world culture by reference to the collection of old-world artefacts. Amassed initially around traditional core collections of antiquities, old masters and nineteenth-century paintings, the Americans also began to add Asian art and the Impressionists.

The ultimate effect of this new axis of purchasing power meant that some areas of art history all but dried up. By the beginning of the twentieth century, a new museum was unlikely to be able to able to pretend to anything approaching an encyclopaedic re-telling of art history, and gradually curators began to consolidate their collections around perceived areas of 'strength'; examples of a particular movement, or the work of a single artist. This (albeit slowly) freed museum architecture from its rigid didactic progressional plan, although it wasn't until Rogers and Piano's Pompidou Centre (The Centre d'Art et de Culture Georges Pompidou, Paris 1977) that the mould was truly broken.

The second development to reshape the course of 'modern' art museums was the Museum of Modern Art (MoMA), New York (1939, architects Philip L. Goodwin and Edward Durrell Stone). Conceived by its first charismatic director, Alfred Barr, as a 'torpedo', its nose "the ever-advancing present, its tail the ever-receding past,"[12] Barr's idea, in indirect answer to Gertrude's Stein's critique that one could either be modern or a museum, but not both, was that the museum would continually de-accession works as they ceased to be contemporary. While there were early attempts at this, it never really happened. But the radical nature of MoMA's project, in terms of contemporary museum development, lay in Barr's famous pronouncement that the architecturally Modernist museum would be "a laboratory; in its experiments, the public is invited to participate."[13]

Museums have an interesting relationship with the new, as Barr's failure to de-accession would suggest.[14] As popular a cliché as is the 'cathedral' one, is that art museums, contemporary and otherwise are both 'dormitories' and more forcefully 'morgues' for the art in their collections. But there is a paradoxically positive nature to the collecting and filing-away of art, in that it liberates us, as makers, from repetition of the past. After the Russian Revolution, when the new Soviet Government expressed concern for the old Russian museums and art collections, Kasimir Malevich wrote a protest to encourage their destruction. "Burn all past epochs," he announced. And if they really wanted to, he suggested storing the ashes of old masters in jars in a pharmacy, where those so minded could still go and finger their charred remains. In an earlier text, Malevich had remarked that it was impossible to paint the "fat ass of Venus" any more, and that something new had to be made. But, as philosopher Boris Groys argues, it is precisely the preserving of the Masters that frees us from having to repeat Venus' ass, and makes the replication of old styles, conventions, and forms unnecessary.[15]

[12] Quoted in Schubert, p. 47, *op cit.*

[13] *ibid*, p. 45.

[14] See Michael Asher's *Painting and Sculpture from The Museum of Modern Art: Catalog of Deaccessions 1929 through 1998*, publication created as part of Asher's project for *The Museum as Muse Exhibition,* MoMA, 1999, for an artistic critique of the Museum's deaccessioning policy.

[15] 'To Collect and To Be Collected', Boris Groys, in *La Fundación Chinati Newsletter*, vol 3, Texas, 1998, p. 4.

Given that today's art museums are the inheritors of traditions of delight, of entertainment, of education, of colonialism and imperialism, of artistic freedom, of paradoxical release from the tyranny of past forms, and increasingly of urban regeneration and social inclusion: to what end – of all these strands – should their architecture be driven? In a reductive sense, according to Vito Acconci, museums are built the way the public stands in front of the art object.[16] But museums also bring you to that art object, and add their own traditions to the aesthetic assumptions and cultural baggage that one brings to the act of viewing. Within the essential architectural vocabulary of art spaces – including controllable natural light, good storage, clean spaces, a certain amount of height, flexible spaces, progression of rooms – a developing new lexicon is attempting to create spaces for all the new forms of art; forms that move beyond the frame and have climbed down off the plinth. Today's art spaces conspire to create freedom and inspiration, rather than merely educational shelter and warmth for art, although, in some cases a confusing new scenario is developing in which "the experience of place is replacing the experience of art".[17]

So where does all that leave the architect of today's art space? As Michel Foucault has pointed out, space is never empty, never neutral, but "always saturated with qualities;"[18] and in terms of the idea of 'presence of absence' which the stealing of the *Mona Lisa* underlined, the white cube's presence of absence all the more strongly calls up the presence of the critical and art-historical apparatus that has determined it over its 200-year history. Attempts in the sixties and seventies to shake off this baggage, by colonising warehouse spaces for art, largely failed as the weight of the museum's history clings more strongly than institutions, like the Dia Center in New York, would want to think. In fact, the weight of the

Frank Lloyd Wright: Guggenheim Museum, New York, 1956-59, interior view; photo David Heald; © The Solomon R. Guggenheim Foundation, New York

historical antecedents of the modern museum often threatens to present architects with a continuum of compromise. In 1943 when Solomon R. Guggenheim presented Frank Lloyd Wright with the brief "that the museum should be unlike any other," the art museum finally broke away from the traditional design of corridors and enfilades, yet even in his radical designs, Lloyd Wright's museum still presented the visitor with a single prescribed route through the works on display. And the strength of the traditions of the Louvre, the Vatican and the Uffizi continue to influence both curators and architects. Richard Meier's J. Paul Getty Museum (1984-97) in Los Angeles had the potential to be one of the most fully realised expressions of the architect's vision for a neoclassical clarity. Yet it is compromised by the Museum's lack of faith in Meier's ability to meet the aesthetic requirements for the collection's display. "We need a museum building that plays skilful accompanist to the collection. The building should subordinate itself to the works of art in the galleries, assert itself with dignity and grace in the public spaces..."[19] Consequently, New York architect and decorator Thierry Despont was commissioned to clad the walls of the gallery in muted fabrics and the floors with parquet, an arrangement which favours neither tradition nor modernity.

[16] Vito Acconci, interviewed by the author at his studio in New York, May 11th 2002.

[17] Belting, in ed. Noever, p. 80, *op cit.*

[18] Michel Foucault, taken from 'Of Other Spaces: Utopias and Heterotopias', quoted in ed. Neil Leach, *Rethinking Architecture*, Routledge, London 1977, p. xv.

[19] Thomas Ford Reese, Carol McMichael Reese, in ed. Laumpugnani and Sachs, p. 47, *op cit.*

[20] Sheila Dickinson, 'A New Model', *CIRCA* 95, 2001, p. 42.

[21] 'Museum Space; Privatising Culture/Imaging Desire', in *Ojeblikket vol 8, The Meaning of Site*, ed Katya Sander, Copenhagen 1998. p. 107. Auyoung notes in an opening quotation, from Robert Venturi, that "a typical 19th century museum assigned 90% of museum space for exhibition uses and 10% for other uses; whereas in the late 20th century, the proportion is more likely one-third for exhibition and two-thirds for other uses." p. 96.

[22] The Lowry, *press material*, 2000.

As architects respond to developments in contemporary art (larger areas balancing intimate spaces, rooms for the exhibition of digital art, installation, etc.), art works are given form and reading by the spaces they inhabit. Architecture impacts on and informs how we experience art, and crucially in site-specific works and specifically commissioned exhibitions, how work is made. Thus in addition to providing a space for the display of art, the architecture of art museums now contributes to its definition. Curators as well as artists and their art can now become characterised by the museum's architectural spaces, as the museum involves itself in the relationship between curator, artist, work and audience.

Artists have often found the architectural presence of the museums where their work is displayed difficult to come to terms with. In 1956, artists including Milton Avery, Willem de Kooning, Philip Guston, Franz Kline and Robert Motherwell wrote an open letter to the Guggenheim trustees saying that the interiors of the New York museum were "not suitable for a sympathetic display of painting and sculpture." In 1958, in his last written words on the subject, Lloyd Wright countered such criticism with the statement that his building was a "genuine intelligent experiment in museum culture." Closer to home, artistic ambivalence about architecture is expressed in a review of the Model Arts Centre (renovation and extension architect: McCullough Mulvin, Sligo 2000): "The seven million pound collection will be left to impress without being outdone by the architecture".[20]

But should a museum be an exhibit in its own right? I. M. Pei's celebrated East Building of the National Gallery of Art, Washington D.C. (1978), created a vast and impressive atrium space after which the exhibition galleries seem small, dark and often confusing. "The East Building itself has become the primary attraction rather than the art on display," notes Poyin Auyoung[21] in a discussion of the general change in the modes of usage for museum space. The Lowry is described as a "must see tourist attraction – not just a venue but a destination,"[22] and in a move even further from an idea of the central role of art in the museum space, Richard Meier (perhaps due to an understanding of the kind of treatment which resulted in the mess of his J. Paul Getty Museum) wanted to officially open his Museum für Kunsthandwerk in Frankfurt before any of the art was installed at all.

Another development affecting the way architecture is perceived is the increasing popularity of the coffee-table architecture book. The rise of new art museums as tourist destinations has accelerated this, signature architecture is seen and understood more frequently in postcards, and in photographs in books and glossy magazines, than in physical reality. As we make artists out of architects, we make architecture into two-dimensional images. Architecture, which has always implied users, is depicted like installation art, without people in its spaces. Famous buildings are deemed successful if they photograph dramatically, rather than functioning well. At its most influential (when it first opened) the majority of people discussing and referring to the Guggenheim Bilbao 'knew' it only from secondary images. This new way of looking at and understanding architecture subjects the spatial, saturated qualities of the museum or gallery to the more impoverished aesthetics of linear perspective. These emotional spaces, where art is viewed, appreciated, and sometimes understood, become pictures in their own right, and the artworks mere figures in the picture plane. A Serra sculpture in Bilbao takes on the same role as an apple in a Cézanne, and only certain forms of art emerge from that process well.

It is unsurprising that there is often an uneasy element to the relationship between architect and artist, both engaged in the visual creation of an aesthetic, both subject to the compromises of site, materials, finance and patronage. The essays, arguments and comments

Michael Wilford: The Lowry, Salford, 2000, exterior view, photo Len Grant, courtesy The Lowry

in this book take up these issues, aiming to illuminate the discussions. They bring closer the disciplines of art, architecture, curation and criticism, which together make up the fabric of the environments we inhabit, respond to and in which art is made. Chapters explore the process of commissioning a building from different perspectives, essays inquire into how space works, case studies investigate what we have, and the *Inspirational Spaces?* section looks at what might be. Concluding the book, a directory of art spaces, from the purpose-built to the *ad hoc*, sets out the architectural backdrop against which these discussions and debates are unfolding.

Until now, these architectural and artistic debates have taken place in parallel, and yet they are contingent upon one another. Changes in architectural materials mirror changes in artistic media and scale. The creation and the realisation of the Guggenheim Bilbao would have been impossible without the development of computer-aided design programmes (made originally for the construction of fighter planes), responding to the architecture, its vast spaces house commissions by Sol le Witt, Richard Serra, Jenny Holzer and Francesco Clemente. The Bilbao Guggenheim accommodates work on a scale that it would be impossible to show in all but a few museums worldwide. And it is this symbiosis which points to the potential of the challenges, which both art and architecture offer each other. Each discipline making spaces and creations whose notional limitations are constantly called into question by the developments and interventions of one another, called into question, proved false, raised and reset until the boundaries are broken again.

Architects have always played a key role in the development of this debate, both through writings and discussion of theory, and through their creation of spaces in which these discussions take place. By widening the field of participation in architectural criticism, and by bringing the writings of curators and critics, artists and architects together in this book, the aim is to explore some of the hows and whys of art and architecture, and to create further discussion among those who build, use and inhabit our art spaces. Whether they wear suits, and whether or not they can paint.

The Process

Introduction by Gemma Tipton

Some spaces for art grow, opportunistically, from a mixture of availability, pragmatism and a coincidence of space and time. A semi-derelict space is available at a negligible rent; an existing building is offered for conversion and use; an historic building carries a preservation order, but no one seems to have found a viable role for it; a performing arts venue has some spare space near the foyer, by the bar or in the basement. All these scenarios have given rise to art spaces, with varying degrees of success. Sometimes the characteristics of the existing building work in harmony with the agenda of the curators of the space; and the results are galleries with that elusive (and impressive) sense of synchronicity; of *Gestalt*. In other instances, the building seems to wage perpetual war with both the curatorial practise, and the art, going on inside. In these instances, it would seem that building-from-scratch would be the best solution, for it offers the opportunity to get everything 'right' from the outset. And yet examples of new-build galleries, abounding with problems and spatial irritations, exist around the world; costly white elephants whose difficult scales, geometries and volumes would seem to send the planners of new projects hastily back to the relative safety of the historic or industrial conversion.

Do we view art differently in different spaces? The answer, of course is 'yes', as the essays and discussions in this book tease out and underline. Given that the container undeniably affects the contained, in an imaginary ideal world, where would one begin? How would one start the process of creating the ideal space for art? Initial considerations have to take in location and context. They also have to address the question of what, exactly, the art space is expected to *do*. In a community-focused gallery project, an arts centre needs to be integrated into the community which it is intended to serve. Using an existing, and well-known building is a way of 'knitting' the art space into the fabric of its locality. In a major, or capital, city, siting a flagship gallery, or contemporary art museum, in an historic building sends the signal that the government, (and the country itself) is both forward-thinking, yet still grounded in a rich cultural tradition. "It's a revelation to break out of the white cube time warp," said Charles Saatchi, of his gallery's move from 98A Boundary Road to the historical splendour of London's County Hall. "If art can't look good outside the antiseptic gallery spaces dictated by museum fashion of the last 25 years, then it condemns itself to a worryingly limited lifespan."[1]

[1] Charles Saatchi, quoted in *Time Out Guide to the Saatchi Gallery*, ed. Sarah Kent and Cathy Runciman, September 2003, p. 8.

Brand-new buildings are a riskier proposition. They speak of a cultural confidence that has shaken off the grasping tentacles of tradition, that has utter faith in the future. Yet they run the risk of implying that there is no tradition at all, and of becoming alienating and alienated spaces, where art is cut off and removed from the cultural roots, and the general activities, of the population. In either instance, if the flagship gallery is to be a tourist draw, it must be easily accessible for visitors. Those discussing the dramatic effect that the Bilbao Guggenheim had on tourism to the Basque city often forget that in addition to building the massive museum, Bilbao also commissioned Santiago Calatrava to design a new airport with handy access to the city, and Sir Norman Foster to build a metro system for Bilbao. Not only is Bilbao easy to get around, it is easy to get to.

After considerations of context and 'use', the choice of which 'type' of building to opt for brings its own architectural and financial issues to the discussion. Architects adapting existing buildings have a template from which to operate, a framework within which to work out the challenges of exhibition space, commercial space, education space, access, circulation, climate control, and services, which go to make up the modern museum or gallery. As with many creative practices, the constraints of a template can challenge and stimulate ingenuity. On the other hand, the resulting building can also provide a template for art which is too great (or limiting) a challenge for *artistic* ingenuity; with rooms and doorways that are simply too small for the installation of sizeable works of art, or interior walls and fittings that cannot be drilled into or painted over.

Depending on the circumstances, conversion can sometimes (but not always) be a less expensive option. Charles Saatchi made this argument when opting to lease a large chunk of County Hall. "Instead of spending millions on creating identical, austere modernist palaces in every world city, they could actually use the money to buy some art."[2] The director of the Dia Art Foundation in New York, Michael Govan also offers a financial argument for converting existing buildings, although not overtly 'historic' ones. He quotes Donald Judd, "so much money spent on architecture in the name of art, much more than goes to art, is wrong, even if [the] architecture were good, but it's bad." Govan goes on to add himself, "A utilitarian existing building… unlike so many architect-designed new museums, where the building itself is intended to have the qualities of a sculpture – does not impose its own overriding artistic signature onto the art."[3] But without a strong tradition of heavy industry, Ireland has less choice when it comes to industrial conversions. Void in Derry, and the Temple Bar Gallery in Dublin, are both housed in former shirt factories, but the massive-scale post-industrial spaces simply do not exist here. Also, industrial spaces may well be ideal – but ideal for a particular kind of art only, finding their supreme expression in the kind of art that Dia Art Foundation collects and exhibits, which is the large-scale minimalism of the 1970s.

[2] *ibid*, p. 8.

[3] Michael Govan, 'Dia in Context', in *Dia: Beacon*, Dia Art Foundation, New York, 2003, p. 28.

Entering the debate, Frank Gehry, an architect who has designed art spaces as diverse as the industrial conversion, Temporary Contemporary (now Geffen Contemporary) in Los Angeles (1983), and the Guggenheim Bilbao (1997), tells a story in which a group of artists changed his mind about how spaces for art should look and feel: "My discussions about museums with artists began in the late 1970s, when I was confronted by a group of artists. It was Michael Asher, John Knight, Benjamin Buchloh, and Daniel Buren. They asked, 'Okay Mr. Gehry, you love the artist and the work, what kind of museum would you make for us?' And I said what architects have said for a long time and what architects keep saying, 'Well the building is for art, so the art should stand out. The building should be very neutral and should not intrude, it should not in any way compete with the art or become visible. We should be that invisible puppeteer, like in the Japanese dances.' I said all of that, and when I finished my holier-then-thou statement I got attacked like I've never been attacked before. I was told, 'Goddamnit, you're so stupid. Don't you understand that when we finally get our work to be shown in a museum, we want it to be an important place? If you give us a neutral damn thing it ain't gonna be very important. It's not going to be important in the city, it's not going to have any presence in the community.'"[4]

[4] Frank Gehry, from 'Recent work', a lecture delivered at the *Art and Architecture Symposium*, hosted by the Chinati Foundation, April 25 and 26 1998. Proceedings published as *Art and Architecture*, the Chinati Foundation, Texas 2000, p.166.

Interestingly, Michael Asher disputes this conversation.[5] Asher's own practise is primarily concerned with the making of site-generated work, and with institutional critique, so it is unlikely that he would have led a call-to-arms for the creation of distinctive spaces, which stamp their personality on the art they contain. In defence of Gehry's argument, whether

[5] Michael Asher, in correspondance with the author, 15 April 2004.

based on an actual conversation or not, there *is* an undeniable extra sense of 'excitement' in approaching an innovatively and interestingly designed space; a feeling that here you are going to experience art that will challenge, stimulate and inspire. Nonetheless, the way in which Gehry justifies the creation of spaces, such as the Guggenheim Bilbao, is telling. His implication, that artists require, and desire, a building that will speak for them and for their art, in terms of impact and presence, is actually symptomatic of a desire more often held by those commissioning and funding the new arts spaces themselves.

Too often, it seems, the basics of a new art space are dictated by a committee, who each lay down the fundamentals of their requirements. Here is where the desire for drama can come into play – relying on staples such as a big atrium, an impressive entrance, lots of social space, and a monumental staircase. As Michael Govan put it, "projects are driven by client decision, civic imperative and money. If Bilbao want a Sydney Opera House, they're going to get a Sydney Opera House, they're driving it. Given that imperative and that structure, what Gehry did in Bilbao has some very interesting features. From the outside it's one of the most important buildings of the 20th century. And from the inside it may not be the most hospitable for every kind of art, but certain pieces, like Jenny Holzer's at the opening, have looked fantastic in it. But it's a whole different starting point..."[6]

This idea, of a variety of points from which to start, may lead to fundamental differences of opinion as to where, and how, to engage with the creation of spaces for art. While the architect, or a member of the committee may want the grand gesture, the sweeping entry, the dramatic façade, these ideas may be tempered by the presence of other members of the committee more interested in less aggressive spaces, or with an entirely different aesthetic in mind. In general, new arts buildings will be the result of the (often conflicting) drives of Arts Council and Local Council policy, the influence of a sponsor or benefactor, the input of the Director or Curator of the new space, local and community interest groups, board or advisory members who may be artists or architects, and of course, the project architects themselves.

The dangers of this design-by-committee approach have been wittily exposed by the Russian conceptual artists Komar and Melamid in their *The Most Wanted Paintings on the Web* project (begun in 1995 in association with Dia), in which an online poll asked a list of detailed questions about what people liked to see in a work of art. Collating the answers

[6] Michael Govan, interviewed by the author, 22 July 2003. Michael Govan was deputy director of the Guggenheim at the time of the Bilbao project, before taking over at Dia and establishing Dia: Beacon.

[7] *The Most Wanted Paintings on the Web, 1995-98,* by Vitaly Komar and Alex Melamid, in association with Dia New York. The project, including the questionnaire and results, and images of the web's most and least wanted images, broken down by country, are online at http://www.diacenter.org/km.

[from far left:] Frank Gehry: Geffen Contemporary, 1983, interior and exterior views, photo: Squidds & Nunns, courtesy Geffen Contemporary; Guggenheim Museum Bilbao, 1997, exterior and interior view showing installation by Claes Oldenburg, photo Erika Ede, courtesy Guggenheim Museum Bilbao

from 3001 respondents, Komar and Melamid then painted a series of banal, utterly inoffensive, yet singularly uninspiring, pastoral scenes dictated by the results.[7] And yet, in architecture, the needs of a new building's constituency do need to be taken into account, and this is particularly the case when creating a space for the exhibition of contemporary art. A gallery or arts centre that incorporates a community-focused agenda will also need to include the work of local arts groups into its programming, and the arts spaces will need to accommodate these. A new gallery positioned to function in an international context, on the other hand, will need to have spaces which conform to stringent standards of climate control and security. The spaces, storage and loading access will also need to be large enough to accommodate large-scale work.

So what does work? What has worked (and not worked) in the past? What elements are crucial? And which buildings have that ineffable 'extra' which makes them great? Even when starting from scratch, the various considerations that come into play begin to dictate the way a space is created, often before the actual 'rooms' for the art are even addressed in the plans. The *Solutions* chapter at the end of the first part of this book looks at various issues in this process, which are the often-unseen elements of space, such as storage, access and technical services. Returning, however, to that imaginary ideal world, how are we to make the choice of where and how to site our new contemporary art space? What is going to inform our decision? What influences are at play? And how is that decision going to affect the art that's not just shown, but also *made* in relation to it for a long time to come. The essays in this chapter look at what underpins this process, from an architectural as well as a curatorial perspective. They describe the background to policy, and to best practise, recommending the role of project-adviser to give coherence to the arts-build process.

Where we go next is a complex question. It's like Goldilocks and her porridge; we don't want too old or too new. Too big to dwarf smaller works, or too small to exclude bigger ones. We have been building art spaces at an alarming rate, in Ireland and around the world, and in only a few instances do we seem to be getting it right. Given the constraints and challenges of funding and context, new arts spaces in Ireland will always have to include compromises: between old and new, between visitor-friendly and art-friendly, between extravagant and basic. But we also have to be careful with those compromises, or we will end up with more and more of those architectural white elephants which serve the purposes of neither art, nor architecture well.

Space and Time:
Commissioning a Building

by Ruairí Ó Cuív

There has been a dramatic increase in the building of arts centres and other specialised buildings for the arts in the last decade, and in the last five years in particular. However, many of the new exhibition spaces which have been part of these developments have been criticised by both artists and curators. I have been amongst these. What particularly upsets me about the design of these specialist facilities is that, in many cases, major finance has been spent on these buildings without the detailed consideration of their function and of those who need to use them.

It is easy to be simplistic and blame the architects. While architects can be headstrong, I believe that much of the fault lies with the commissioners of these spaces. Architects need to be multi-disciplinary in that they are expected to be adept at designing a range of private, public and commercial buildings which have, by necessity, to fulfil very different technical requirements. All of this demands a deep knowledge of the end use of the building and of the users, and architects cannot be expected to come to the initial stages of a project with such a detailed knowledge of these requirements. This is the role of the commissioner. Often the commissioners of arts facilities, however, do not themselves have a clear understanding of the complexities involved in establishing or running arts organisations; and there are many examples of arts buildings, and exhibition spaces in particular, which have been developed without consultation with the required experts, or even without an organisation in place to run the activities intended for it. This focus on the building, rather than the development of a vision for the space, is a classic example of putting the cart before the horse. Or is it the illusory myth that if a building is put in place, the activities will suddenly begin or evolve to the design of the building?

Arts organisations rarely get an opportunity to define their own destiny when it comes to buildings. Too often they are designed *for* them rather than *with* them. There are two particular approaches which can cause problems if not thoroughly thought out. The first is when an existing building is identified and then designated for an arts organisation. The adaptation of a building can be attractive for commissioners, such as local authorities or state agencies, in that they often have historic buildings for which they no longer have a use. Often the motivation for acquiring them is the laudable one of ensuring the preservation of a major landmark. However, the simple decision to turn such a landmark into an arts centre or gallery tends to overlooks the specialist requirements of the client organisation.

The second approach is where arts buildings are developed in the abstract, and without a defined organisation in mind. To develop a building without the end user being identified is like developing advance factories. Where possible an existing client should be identified who will operate the space, and the client should be consulted in the shaping of the building. Where an organisation has not been established, it is important to initiate a parallel development to the building, during which time the arts organisation is established and the resources are provided to manage and operate the building when it is developed. At the same time, the arts organisation should be preparing for the impact of running a brand new space.

Commissioning bodies can be complex organisations and they often have many functions, responsibilities and layers of administrative structures. This does not necessarily lend itself to sequencing the development in a manner which will maximise the available resources. While they often have worthy intentions, they tend to be pragmatic in their ways of fulfilling their intentions. It is my experience that architects are given a sketchy brief of major facilities such as theatre, gallery and café with attached service areas such as toilets, dressing rooms, etc.; and that they are expected to identify the required experts to advise them on the design. Too often visual-arts experts are not consulted. I wonder is this a case of the architect being presumed (or presuming) to have the required visual expertise to design a gallery? As a result the end users, be they curators, artists or the public, can find that visual art spaces do not meet the demands of the programming or indeed have quirky and idiosyncratic architectural features which impede the ability to function well. Many visual-arts spaces turn out to be limiting and unforgiving, with the architecture inhibiting creativity rather than enhancing it. In many cases the exhibition space is designed as an add-on to the theatre foyer or café rather than being a defined and dedicated space. It is therefore essential that commissioners understand why they are engaging in the development. It's not just good enough to identify a pot of money and spend it. It is necessary to develop a clear vision which will include the policy and function of the space. This is where specialised expertise is required.

Without definition of the policy for the space and its function, architects are unfairly abandoned to their own devices. Therefore, research and development is a critical phase of the commission. This process is about minimising the risks and maximising the potential of the budget. It is essential to have specialist advice, and a project adviser should be appointed to manage this process. The role of the project adviser is to liaise with the commissioners and the architects, making sure that the interests of the clients and end users is maintained throughout the development. This should begin with defining the vision (if necessary), and then developing a clear and detailed brief for the architects. The project adviser should work closely with the architects and should be engaged to 'proof' designs as the project develops, and even to be on site to work with the architects, ensuring that the construction follows the details of the design. The project adviser should have specialist knowledge of the visual arts and it is important that they should have an understanding of architecture, and experience of working with architects. They should be able to identify required experts if necessary, (these can be artists, lighting designers, workshop facilitators, etc.), who will offer specialist insights into how specific spaces should function.

The project adviser can be a member of the arts organisation for which the building is being designed, though this experience is not always available within an organisation. In such cases, and especially where the organisation has not yet been established, it is important to appoint an outside expert to act as project adviser. It is essential, if the project adviser is not a staff member of the arts organisation for which the building is being developed, that they liaise with the organisation, or in the case of a new organisation, regularly consult with those who are developing it. Only then can the brief be properly defined and the architects appointed.

This is the stage when the creative engagement with the architect should begin. Watching an architect begin to define and sketch out rough ideas for three-dimensional space is exciting and, as with any artist, the architect should be given scope to bring their identity and expertise to the project. Appointment of the architects can be undertaken in three different procedures: direct commissioning, open competition, or limited competition. This really depends on the scale of the commission and on legal requirements such as government or EU regulations concerning the offering of contracts. These regulations apply not only to state departments and agencies but also to local authorities. There are plusses and minuses to each of these commissioning procedures. While the quality of the brief for the architect is vital to the success of a building, it becomes critically important in a competition where architects are invited to present detailed designs and visual concepts for the building. In any case, I believe that, apart from choosing an architect whose work elsewhere is found to be inspiring, it is essential that the architect and commissioner have a shared vision for this building.

The architectural adage that 'form follows function' is relevant to the design of places for creativity. While individuality of design is important, this should take place within the context of the use of the space. There is something wonderful about discovering a gallery which has its own character but which functions well as an exhibition space. Galleries which I have always appreciated in this way include: the Butler Gallery, Kilkenny, opened in the 1970s; the recently designed exhibition space in the City Gallery, Limerick; and the Model and Niland Arts Centre, Sligo, which includes both adapted classrooms and the newly built galleries for the Niland Collection. One of the joys of touring an exhibition can be to experience how the different dynamics of space can affect your understanding of the artworks. Each of the mentioned spaces has very different characteristics but they all work to enhance the display of artworks. Adapting an exhibition becomes rewarding in these cases but is difficult when the space is badly designed. One example of badly designed space is the exhibition space in the Dunamaise Arts Centre, Portlaoise, where the triangular void is an unnecessary architectural feature. Without this it could be a much more useful space. A different problem is posed by the exhibition space in the Mermaid Arts Centre, Bray. Here, the gallery is really an extension of the first-floor theatre foyer and is not a coherent space for the exhibition of artworks. A glass screen wall dominates the space and the remaining available wall space is broken by corners and doorways. It is notable that neither of these arts centres had organisations in place before their development. Nor was a visual-arts expert employed to advise on their design.

The function of any exhibition space should be of primary consideration, whether it is a specialised facility or one which is expected to be used for the display of a range of visual-arts media. For example, the exhibition of works in national collections requires particular conservation standards such as controlled light, temperature and humidity conditions, which are not necessarily required for the display of most exhibitions on temporary display throughout the country. A space intended to receive international touring exhibitions will also often have to meet these standards. Different contemporary artforms in themselves require specialised conditions. It is obvious that multi-media work such as projections require darkness; that paintings require light and flat wall space; and three-dimensional works require floor space which should also be capable of bearing heavy loads. It is amazing how many galleries do not provide these conditions.

Difficulties don't only relate to the aesthetic considerations. Adequate and dedicated storage facilities to accommodate equipment as well as artworks and crates are often inadequate or non-existent. Practical issues such as wall and floor surfaces, load-bearing capabilities, availability of services such as electric power, internet/broadband and audio connections are also vital to the operation of the space. Amazingly, loading access to galleries, especially for bringing large or heavy works, is often difficult. Most important is that exhibition spaces should be dedicated spaces and that they should not be shared with cafés or for that matter, theatre foyers. This is not only for security or conservation considerations, it is for respect for the artists and their work.

Installation view at the Model Arts and Niland Gallery, photo Christian Richters, courtesy McCullough Mulvin Architects

Commitment has also to be made to architects. It is not good enough to say "here's the brief: now work away". Along the way, as the architectural designs develop, there will inevitably be difficult choices. This includes matching the available resources, be they spatial or financial, with maximising the potential of the building. Matching resources with ideals is not only a question of compromise. It is often an issue of prioritisation and problems can be overcome by giving time to the architect, and to the project adviser, to come up with creative solutions to them. The most precious resource is time, and too often buildings are rushed, adhering to a timescale which neglects the fact that the space is meant to operate for many years.

Key Points: to note in planning an arts space

Vision It is necessary to develop a clear vision as to why the exhibition space is being developed.
Research and Development It is essential to understand that a building is a vessel in which activities happen. Therefore it is important to develop the policy for the exhibition space, and to establish the nature of exhibitions and activities which are to take place there.
Expert Advice Galleries are specialised spaces, and commissioning bodies should appoint an arts-expert to act as project adviser. The project adviser will provide ongoing advice and help to draw up the brief for the architects.
Appointment of the Architects The appointment of the architects should only take place after the previous tasks have been completed. The architects should share the vision for the building.
Liaison The architects and project adviser should work closely together.
Time The most important commodity is time. Given time, creative solutions can be found for most problems which might arise.

New Arts Facilities: In Design

The Arts Council of Northern Ireland's Approach **by Paul Harron**

«Art museums are pulled four ways: by the differing demands of their patrons, their public, their architects, and their curators. From a curatorial point of view, what matters most – apart from space, space and more space – is carefully controlled daylighting, precise atmospheric controls, gallery design that allows easy display of a huge variety of different art forms, and all the relevant back-up facilities in terms of restoration workshops, storage, office space and so on. The patrons of such buildings are less concerned with the technicalities, and crave the cultural landmark, frequently as a means to urban regeneration. They may desire educational facilities such as lecture theatres, which curators are seldom interested in. Aesthetically, the patrons tend to be more conservative than their architects. Meanwhile the public – apart from the few visitors who are going for the art rather than the "experience" – wants soundbite-sized cultural entertainment and a good café. The upshot of all is that, in all but a few cases, the modern art museum is effectively a multi-use building."[1]

While the term 'art museum' is not exactly right for this context (in fact Pearman uses it as a catch-all to include galleries and exhibition spaces of all descriptions), and I would, of course, mildly protest at his slightly cynical take on the 'patron' if applied to the Arts Council, Pearman's observations above do illustrate that the commissioning of new arts facilities is a process of covering many bases. The Arts Council of Northern Ireland has, with the benefit of National Lottery funding since the mid-1990s, been involved as a key partner funder with a variety of commissioning bodies ranging from local authorities to significant arts organizations, in the creation and large-scale refurbishment of eight quite major multi-use arts buildings across Northern Ireland, with four more in receipt of funding and in the process of current development (not to mention several somewhat smaller scale capital projects finished or ongoing).

By neat coincidence, the Arts Council (as the result of the Clive Priestley Review) was given the formal remit to promote architecture and design quality simultaneously with the opportunity to distribute the first National Lottery awards to arts-focused capital projects in 1995. While an Arts Council policy on architecture and the built environment took some time to develop (the policy document was launched in 2003), from the outset the Council sought to follow best practice in design and commissioning terms in the building and refurbishment of these key infrastructural arts spaces. Prior to Lottery funding, there had been a

[1] Hugh Pearman, *Contemporary World Architecture,* Phaidon Press, 1998.

general lack of capital investment; the advent of these new funds literally changed the landscape.

The Council's approach as 'patron' has been demonstrably superior in attitude to Pearman's notional patron: rather than being essentially 'conservative', at the heart of its approach was the desire to get good architects to produce good, imaginative buildings through fair but demanding competition. So the process may not have yielded any Bilbao Guggenheims, Tate Moderns or 'landmark', 'iconic' buildings (and that is arguably no bad thing in our context), but several of the buildings have made strong architectural statements and have been noted in national awards for it – the Market Place Theatre in Armagh (Civic Trust Centre Vision Award 2001 and nomination for the Stirling Prize amongst other plaudits), as well as the Verbal Arts Centre (Civic Trust Award 2001 and RIAI Regional Award 2001) and Millennium Forum (Civic Trust Award 2003 and RICS Award for Excellence 2003) which are both in Derry, for example.

The Council's 'best practice' approach has required applicants to its capital programme to go through a rigorous (and, yes, perhaps somewhat daunting) staged application process of feasibility and design development before the main building and fit-out application. This process requires applicants to ask crucial questions of themselves from the outset: What is the vision? Does a new (or refurbished) building actually meet a need? What is the market? What kind of building and what facilities are desired? Is the scheme viable and thoroughly costed? How will the capital scheme work – who will take it forward and manage it? How will the building operate when it is completed? When all of this has been examined and agreed, the actual process of drawing up the design brief, appointing a design team and making the vision a reality gets underway. The rationale is, of course, that having gone through these stages of analysis the 'white elephants' (or dysfunctional elephants, to strain the metaphor) should be avoided.

Quality of design and construction has, as I've already outlined, been a pre-eminent concern. In the guidance notes to the application forms, the Arts Council sets out its stall: "We aim for the highest standards of architectural quality and building design … You should: avoid short-term savings which would obscure the positive benefits of good design and fitness for purpose; ensure that new buildings and refurbishments are environmentally-friendly and energy efficient; ensure that the style of buildings and refurbishments complements the character of the locality; ensure maximum independent access for disabled people – attenders, artists or members of staff." In short, good facilities are viewed as those which put design excellence above financial short-cuts; are sustainable; respect their context; and are universally accessible. These were prescient concerns when originally articulated, finding echoes later in the Government's *Better Public Buildings* document of 2000

[below, from left:] interiors: Flowerfield Arts Centre, Millennium Court Arts Centre, Island Arts Centre, [overleaf:] exterior, Market Place

(which, as if to emphasise the point, featured the Market Place Theatre and Arts Centre prominently).

In terms of getting the design team as well as the procurement process right, the Arts Council has sought the advice of the relevant professional bodies – such as the Royal Society of Ulster Architects (RSUA) and Royal Institute of British Architects (RIBA) – and followed European Union procurement requirements. Design teams and construction service providers are appointed through openly and widely advertised tendering, and design teams have been appointed competitively (selected on the basis of the design quality of their proposals), and, where the commission has been of a sufficient scale, through architectural competition. Mindful of the fact that designing buildings for arts usage is a specialized field and no two arts buildings are the same, the Arts Council states that Design and Build – and variations of that procurement process – are not considered suitable approaches. Moreover, the design team should, of course, include a key representative of the actual users and programmers of the space, with an eye to the specific needs of the facility who can advise on such specifics as access, the right colours for exhibition walls, finish, the lighting requirements and need for blinds and so on (Pearman's 'curatorial' point of view). The Council has also sought to develop and articulate good practice through the funding of handbooks, the guidelines of which it in turn attempts to follow. These handbooks include, for example, Mike Sixsmith's *Designing Galleries* (1999) and the Clore Duffield's *Space for Art* (2003) and *Space for Learning* (2004).

Over and above the commitment to the appointment of a competent and visionary design team, the Council has also placed a strong emphasis and requirement on the involvement of artists and craftspeople in the creation of capital arts projects. Not only does it seem obvious that an arts space should involve inter-disciplinary discourse between artists and architects, but – especially if they are involved from the very earliest stages of design development, which is the ideal – artists can also bring new and unique dynamics to thinking through the needs and aesthetics of a place. While a per cent for art scheme has not actually been mandatory to date, priority has been given to projects which take this cross-disciplinary approach and the application guidelines encourage applicants to earmark an appropriate percentage of capital costs for the commissioning of new work in unrestricted media – in other words, tangible works of art or craft are eligible costs in a project.

Space does not permit an account of every project that has been funded, so brief descriptions of a few of these multi-functional spaces will have to serve to illustrate what the Arts Council has attempted to achieve and promote. The, already mentioned, Market Place Theatre and Arts Centre Armagh was one of the first major spaces, receiving a substantial award in 1995. The building was completed in 2000 and houses a 400-seat auditorium, a 150-seat studio theatre, art studios, an art gallery exhibition space, workshop spaces and refreshment facilities. Designed by Glenn Howells Architects, it nestles into the hillside beneath the Church of Ireland Cathedral, successfully enclosing one side of a civic square. An impressive yet restrained new building, the Civic Trust's judges in 2001 commented: "This is a brave modernist building like no other in Northern Ireland."

On Derry's City Walls, the Verbal Arts Centre also received one of the first major Lottery grants towards the refurbishment of a listed Victorian primary school to make it fit for new, multi-functional purpose. The Centre now houses gallery, workshop, studio, exhibition and performance spaces and a café. Refurbished by Hall Black Douglas, it is a model of sensitive and imaginative re-use of a building on the one hand and of the integration of artwork on

interior view, Verbal Arts Centre

the other, with commissions by a number of artists such as Rita Duffy and Carolyn Mulholland.

In a similar vein, the Lagan Valley Island Arts Centre (Consarc Design Group) received an award for the arts elements of this major new civic building which transformed a previously ghastly, derelict site. Now, the regenerated river banks and weir are attractive public amenities and the building and its surrounding public space incorporate a wide range of permanent art works by a variety of national and international artists. This project also received a Royal Society of Arts Art for Architecture Award, bringing in an artist to inform and collaborate in the development of the multi-purpose civic and arts spaces.

The Millennium Court Arts Centre in Portadown, meanwhile, was awarded a major grant in 1996 for its transformation by Harry Porter Architects from a former market building to a visual, multi-media and verbal arts centre in the heart of the town. The Centre includes two galleries, rehearsal and studio rooms and a multi-media suite, providing new facilities and opportunities in this area.

Finally, the Flowerfield Arts Centre in Portstewart forms the centrepiece of Coleraine Borough Council's art provision in the north of the province. Completed in 2004, it is a multi-functional arts and crafts facility with a 150-seat flexible auditorium space. The building (Consarc Design Group) combines sensitive refurbishment of a period property and the addition of a contemporary, modernist extension – well handled through the use of complementary, high quality materials.

In conclusion, the Arts Council seeks and has sought as a funder – or 'patron' – to ensure that these new arts facilities are primarily fit for function but equally that they are inspirational and visionary buildings which delight as well as work (the spirit of Vitruvius lives on). Of course they must be well built, but even before they get built they need to be thought through (not to mention abide by Green Book principles). Good architects need good clients; good artists ought to be involved throughout, while design professionals equally need to be respected as 'artists' in their fields; and everyone needs a good brief to follow. In short, the desire is to produce architecture rather than building. This cannot always be achieved all of the time, but the best of these new buildings and refurbishments do achieve design quality and create meaningful, usable, beneficial spaces. They add significantly to Northern Ireland's architectural portfolio.

Readings:

Architectural Competitions: A Handbook for Promoters, Department of the Environment and Department of National Heritage, 1996

Arts Facilities: Preliminary Guidance, Voluntary Arts Network, 1994

Better Public Buildings: A Proud Legacy for the Future, HM Government, DCMS, 2000

Pearman, Hugh, Contemporary World Architecture, Phaidon Press, 1998

Sixsmith, Mike, Designing Galleries: the complete guide to developing and designing spaces and services for temporary exhibitions, Arts Councils of England, Northern Ireland, Scotland and Wales, 1999

Space for Art: A Handbook for Creative Learning Environments, Artworks/Clore Duffield Foundation, 2003

Space for Learning: A Handbook for Education Spaces in Museums, Heritage Sites and Discovery Centres, Clore Duffield Foundation, 2004

From Neoclassical to Contemporary

Conversation: Barbara Dawson, Des McMahon, Gemma Tipton, August 2004

Gemma Tipton: In planning new gallery spaces, one of the debates is whether to renovate an historic building or whether to build new. An extension might seem to offer the best of both worlds, but can also bring its own problems.

Des McMahon: We began this project with a lot of research. In Europe there are so many great and established museums and galleries, and they tend to define what museums and galleries look like.

Patrick Scott, retrospective exhibition at the Dublin City Gallery, the Hugh Lane, 2002, installation view, photo courtesy Dublin City Gallery

Barbara Dawson: One of the challenges of marrying the old with the new is, as Des noted from the outset, making a credible circulation route through the buildings. By 'circulation' here we are talking about physical transition, about visitor participation, visitor experience, and about the presentation of the collection. What we have arrived at, on the plans, is one central circulation route with additional outer tangents. Maximising the visitor experience, you are nudged and encouraged along, which is particularly helpful if you don't know the collection. This emphasis on circulation is vital. Even with somewhere as huge as the Louvre there is a basic route, with additions, so you come out feeling that you have had a good visitor experience.

That's why I find the Metropolitan Museum of Art in New York to be such a mess. Because everyone who endowed it wanted their own 'bit', there is no clear route through and you get vaguely panic stricken that you've missed out on something, which isn't actually important, it just feels important when you're lost there.

This is something I discovered from looking at different museums, it is a simple point but it is absolutely essential. You have to start from a single place, go around, and come back to the same place. It's a simple format and one which can be developed. As your collection grows you can create a series of spaces off the main circulation. These can be connected if you want. In this way, you have secondary, what I call 'selective', spaces, and yet you still have this very simple, legible, sequential route, which brings you right back to where you began. You can also introduce the element of narrative, the pauses and punctuations that make the sequence work.

This simple circulation takes care of everyone, the family who come every Sunday, the specialist, and the person who is coming to see a specific piece. And it eliminates the problems which the gallery experience has given rise to – like exhaustion, or that feeling that you have missed something. I think almost every question about gallery design goes back to that basic format, because that format can absorb the different uses of a gallery. You can ask: is a gallery about looking? About shopping? About eating in the café? You can look at a gallery as a mixture of a sacred place and a supermarket. You begin in a supermarket, you go through a sacred place, and you come out again through a supermarket.

The supermarket analogy is interesting in that so much more work has gone into how supermarkets are designed and laid out, into how people use them than into galleries. There is an entire science (called atmospherics) devoted to it.

This not only concerns architecture in a gallery, but also how the collection/exhibition is presented. Do you hang from right to left? What is the best way to approach an installation, bearing in mind how the room is approached architecturally? This can create the difference between fluidity and that staccato which, when not deliberate, is disconcerting. Supermarket elements, the bookshop, the café, the non-contemplative elements, have

Gilroy McMahon Architects, drawings for circulation routes and plans: extension to Dublin City Gallery the Hugh Lane, 2002-06, courtesy the architects

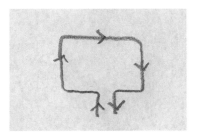
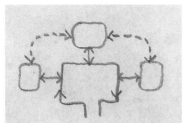
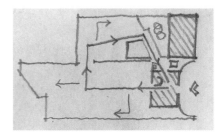

become a part of the modern museum. These were facilitated in the existing Hugh Lane with difficulty. There will be better arrangements for both in the new building because they also help the visitor to spend an optimum time amount of time in the gallery. You can spend time looking at the art and, as a hiatus or a 'time out', go to the coffee shop or the bookshop.

One of your problems in extending and developing your building is that people love it. They love it for its quirkiness, for its beauty, for its juxtapositions – say of a Kathy Prendergast or an Eilís O'Connell – with the older architecture of the entrance hall. Is there an issue in 'tampering' with that? There is also a potential area of difficulty with the transitional spaces, between the old and the new, both architecturally and curatorially.

It is beautiful and you are right, people love the Hugh Lane. It is the city's art gallery. It is a hybrid, with all of the attractions and oddness that that brings. It isn't easy to tamper with, as you say, or to extend a Neoclassical building like Charlemont House, but then again that's the challenge, and Des has come up with an excellent solution with this contemporary extension. There will be no mistaking the different architectural expressions.

Things are changing here. Twenty years ago, anything built in Ireland not fronted with a faux Georgian façade was greeted with derision or dismay. We're at last starting to embrace the excitement of new buildings. And that's a sea-change in the way we think about how new buildings, or contemporary extensions to older buildings, fit in.

We've started to acknowledge international influences, and have stopped accepting traditional limitations.

True. And with the art we are understanding that internationalism and local expression are not mutually exclusive. There is the question of an Irish sensibility, Irish artists who have lived abroad, from the Irish impressionists to Sean Scully, have retained a distinctive sensibility. Sometimes it is very subtle but it is recognised.

Using that to jump ahead, there will be a dedicated Sean Scully room in the new building. How different is it to design for a known quantity than it is to create spaces for works that haven't even been made yet?

It is so much easier. It's a collaborative process, Sean Scully knows exactly what he wants, he can walk into a room and know if it would work for one of his paintings or not. He knows which of his paintings would work best in a space. I spent a day in his studio in New York, and when I came back I knew, within three inches, the dimensions of the Sean Scully Room in the new galleries.

To expand on that, Scully is giving us eight paintings in all, including two very large works; an extremely generous donation for the city. And because we have the dimensions and have seen the works, the architecture of the space is exactly in relation to the hang of the room.

You can also see, when you look at his abstracts, why the spaces in which they hang are so important, even the door openings can disrupt the geometries.

Seán Shanahan, from *Vidar* exhibition at the Dublin City Gallery, the Hugh Lane, 2002/03, installation view, photo courtesy Dublin City Gallery

That is why someone like Donald Judd's work is so interesting as a commentary on gallery architecture. The spaces between his works are as important as the space they occupy. And they are disrupted by things like intrusive floorboards, heating vents, windows, doorways. It's the same as with a Scully, when you're dealing with works that use the geometries of the square and the line, the lines and geometries of the spaces themselves become part of the work.

It's not very often that you get the opportunity to work collaboratively with an architect and an artist, it is very interesting and it is one of the reasons that makes this donation at this time so significant. Scully was born in Dublin, and the Scully Room will become another of the gallery's significant focal points (or idiosyncrasies!) which make the collection unique. The collection is eclectic but renowned; we have Hugh Lane's splendid French Impressionist paintings, the Irish Impressionists, the superb twentieth century collection and the recently-acquired collection of Francis Bacon paintings which complement the Bacon studio. And Bacon too was born in Dublin.

Which brings us onto the question of how you handle the transitions when extending existing spaces.

Speaking purely as an architect, and looking at the word, it's a transit from one state to another. You have two choices: you either make it as seamless and invisible as possible, or you acknowledge it and make your transition a point of emphasis. You might introduce windows, and maybe punctuate with a glimpse of water outside. That has been done very beautifully in the Beyeler Foundation building in Basel by Renzo Piano. One thing about Piano is he's a wonderful builder, his father was a building contractor, he comes from that background and you see that in the way he crafts his spaces. The harmony in his buildings comes from his understanding of how the elements fit together, unlike Gehry who throws them up on a computer.

Now at first glance the Dublin City Gallery might seem a very different kind of space, but the essentials are the same. The inner galleries are sacrosanct, but when you're transiting you look out over this beautiful pool. We did a similar thing at Collins Barracks, transiting from one wing to another you go over a glass bridge and look over the square. The square isn't just landscaping, it becomes part of the whole thing. It's a complicated process, but it has to be organic in that it has to be related to the curator and their curatorial programme and outlook. You also have to feel, even though you're moving from one part of the building to another, that you're in a totality. I think it's handled well in the National Portrait Gallery in London, and also in the Picasso Museum in Paris. That's the architectural point of view, but I think Barbara also has very strong views on what transits mean for the collection.

As we've already said, we're not in a green-field site, we're in one of the oldest parts of Dublin, and we're tied in on both sides so that shapes our decisions architecturally. The transition to the new extension will be obvious, it's a new building as opposed to a 1765 one. The simple drama of light and shape created by the architecture, coupled with the presentation and juxtapositioning of the art works will create its own impact. On the first floor the existing temporary exhibition space will be physically linked by a bridge to the new spaces so artists could have their work on display in the Neoclassical building as well as in the contemporary space.

Gilroy McMahon Architects, montage showing proposed new link for the extension to Dublin City Gallery the Hugh Lane, 2002-6, courtesy the architects

Are you incorporating any physical references to the existing building?

That kind of thing can be very patronising too so we're avoiding that.

Definitely. There are different elements to our building already; there is the original 1765 building designed by William Chambers, the 1929 extension designed by Horace T. O'Rourke, and David Chipperfield's Francis Bacon Studio.

While dealing with the physical aspect of building a museum the architect also has to try to make it as invisible as possible, it can't compete with the collection.

But you can't get away from the fact that the space in which you see the collection is subtly altering how you see it. The route you take to get to the gallery, in this case up

Parnell Square, is already conditioning your mood when it comes to look at the works. Back inside, however, one thing that can happen when an old building is extended is that the new spaces provide the opportunity to show larger works, and that then dictates your curatorial practice, so that the experience of visiting the gallery becomes compartmentalised into the old and the new.

In fact the new rooms are fairly close in size to those in the existing gallery, but their height and scale and feeling will be quite different.

Was that a deliberate decision to keep the size relatively comparable?

Gilroy McMahon Architects, view of courtyard to resource facilities pavilion; Dublin City Gallery the Hugh Lane, 2002-6, courtesy the architects

It's partly what we were talking about in terms of transition, and also as a result of discussions about how Barbara would hang the spaces, how she would curate them.

We will continue to curate a variety of exhibitions. The existing galleries have worked well for both classical and contemporary exhibitions. I find artists love these spaces. So while there was an element of wanting more of the same, we couldn't do that as the new building is an architectural expression in itself. There are also restrictions as it is a museum and its function and responsibility is to create an environment, which informs and encourage participation and engagement with visual arts expression. The environment has to have the ability to exhibit art work, be it video, painting, sculpture mixed media… There might have been occasions when you'd think that's a really good architectural idea, but that doesn't mean it would work here.

That's why so often art spaces that are commissioned and built before a Director is in place can go so wrong. I'm thinking here of something like the Museum of Modern Art (MUMOK) in Vienna. But what were those really good ideas that didn't work?

You can come up with all these really glossy architectural spaces, when the most important thing to get right is focal distance, the distance and the way you stand in front of the work. If you think of a space like the main space at the RHA Gallagher Gallery in Dublin I have felt their main gallery made it difficult to have that relationship with a work, lately though they've done a few things to subdivide it and it works better.

Proportions are important even in monumental spaces otherwise the work can suffer.

We didn't go for those huge spaces, both because of the constraints of site, but also because of that excessive contrast with the existing spaces.

They will be very different and, whilst not monumental, the heights are as good as we could get! The extension will provide us with better facilities for example to display video works, which has been difficult up to now. It is not very visible outside so the delight will

Janet Mullarney, from *The Perfect Family* exhibition at the Dublin City Gallery, the Hugh Lane, 1999, installation view, photo courtesy Dublin City Gallery

be in the approach, like entering a secret garden. Then there are also considerations like plant rooms, fire safety, health and safety, stairs. I appreciate they have to be there, but they are also constraints to developing your ideal aesthetic space.

Well, everything can't be "Wow". In the Saatchi Gallery in London, for example, you have Chris Ofili's quiet inks (hung in the corridor when I saw them) and a "Wow" is going to kill them. They are small works which demand quiet time.

We've been trying to avoid corridors, the layout is a variation of the notion of an enfilade of galleries and approach is all. We want to maximise the best walls. But talking about "Wow", I always think of Noel Sheridan discussing space saying there are two ways of looking at a space, there's the "Wow… Hmmm", or the "Hmmm… Wow". We'd prefer the latter.

You have two approaches, one is the desire to innovate, and yet you also have the idea that what actually works are plain white rooms. Yet if nobody innovated we would never have got even to the white rooms themselves. In your research for this project, and in the course of your work anyway, you've travelled the world looking at amazing spaces (and otherwise). So how do you balance your desire to create something uniquely different, to test ideas that haven't been done, and your experience of what actually works?

Advances in technology have made it very easy to provide the 'cardiac arrest', but the greater challenge is in how do you create spaces for somebody to undertake this deeply personal act of engaging with a work? I've tried to do as much research as possible and to listen closely to Barbara. One of the best ways to assess gallery architecture is to have had the experience of how the same exhibition can have a totally different impact in different spaces. For example, I remember seeing the Patrick Scott retrospective at the Hugh Lane, and then at the Crawford in Cork (in 2003 and 2004), and it was interesting to see how it was changed in the second venue. I've also taken ideas from the failures I have seen.

One immediate example of that, which I can think of is Tate Modern in London. After the Turbine Hall, the galleries themselves seem small and mean, like afterthoughts. You've been given this huge drama of scale, and then you have quite narrow escalators then these rather mean galleries which wouldn't feel mean at all if it wasn't for the Turbine Hall. The harmony is gone.

I agree, I came away from Tate Modern deflated. Architecture that is designed to impress is quite different from architecture that is designed to inspire.

There is also something in that idea of inspiration about the way art galleries make you feel. Perhaps it's for this reason that I'll enjoy a coffee more in a gallery café than elsewhere. There is a Georges Bataille quote about how "every Sunday crowds flow through the museum […] coming out purified and fresh."[1]

[1] Georges Bataille, taken from 'Museum', quoted in ed. Neil Leach, *Rethinking Architecture*, Routledge, London, 1977, p. 23.

I think a successful gallery will do that…and a cup of coffee doesn't go astray. Cafés are important in their way, and so too is the bookshop. Every gallery now has to look at all of their operations in a hard-headed business way. These operations should be contributing to the overall dynamic of the gallery's operations.

If the way people visit and use a gallery has changed, so has the kind of works which are to be displayed. You have to look at what are the needs of contemporary art as opposed to, say, pre-1950 works.

That's one of the areas where Brian O'Doherty is so interesting in the *White Cube* essays, when he talks about Impressionist art breaking away from the frame. You need the frame to define the parameters of these pictures as they are not perspective-driven. That need for a framing space changes the whole dynamic of the gallery, as the wall and the space become framing devices too.

A lot depends on the geometries of the works themselves. Francis Bacon worked to a particular set of shapes and forms, which lend themselves to spaces in which you would have more difficulty with, say, an Ellsworth Kelly. I would say, however, that great works of art are timeless and so unless there is a geometric problem or a media problem they should work in old buildings as well as new. But what has changed is the visitor, the audience. This is why you can't recreate the past. You couldn't build the Louvre today, but do you think, perhaps, there's room for a Guggenheim in Dublin?

There is a fine line between the internal architectural climate of a city, and the cultural temperature of the moment. I would be generally in favour of signature buildings, but personally I like the Renzo Piano, Beyeler-type of building; signature architecture with sensitivity to the site. A Gehry or a Meier building in Dublin, well why not? The Guggenheim in Bilbao is spectacular to look at. But you need to look at what the city would best accommodate.

I agree, to a point, a signature building yes, a signature building for art, no. I've yet to see one that is really kind to art. People assume that the space for innovation has to be cultural, but why? You don't have to reserve your innovation for galleries. There's Frank Gehry's 'Fred and Ginger' office block in Prague, or Tom de Paor's water pumping station in Clontarf.

That is a very good point and they are two excellent examples. I would like to see some more renowned architectural statements in Dublin and not necessarily for art.

Definitely not for art.

Notes on Building for Art

by Valerie Mulvin

What is an appropriate architectural space for art? Who decides? How should art and architecture interrelate – if at all? Does it depend on the type of work to be housed – temporary installations vs. permanent collections? How does modern architecture, with all its necessary weight and finality, deal with a constantly changing and evolving (if fashion-bound) art practice? Who is facilitating whom? If one thing is certain, a simple cry for 'flexibility' is an inadequate answer.

As arts practice fragments into a multiplicity of directions, a space for modern contemporary art may be a shop window, a warehouse, a derelict housing complex, or the street; it may also be a purpose-built cathedral of art. With the increasing congruence of art and architecture (some would say art in trouble, seeking a useful lifeboat) it may be the space itself, or exist only in cyberspace. With such diversity, should designed (i.e. not 'found') spaces become more, or less, specific?

Buildings for art have achieved new iconic status and there is a lot riding on their success. Things were politer in the mid-twentieth century and less heatedly articulate. A rich patron or enlightened state commissioned a new building, a cathedral for the elite, displaying art for the education of the public while securing their own position in the annals. As a by-product we got a series of masterpieces by the likes of Louis Kahn (the Kimbell in Fort Worth, Texas, 1967-72, and the Museum of British Art in Yale, 1969-74), and Mies van der Rohe (the Berlin New National Gallery 1965-68). These static beautiful buildings were the direct inheritors of a nineteenth century mantle: the temples of culture housing cultural touchstones, collections of early twentieth century art in danger of becoming establishment chic. Younger artists were moving beyond the gallery walls altogether to challenge perceptions of what art was and where it should be shown, branching out in directions involving landscape, real/violent life and popular culture (which often paradoxically demanded the context of a gallery, a Warhol Campbell's Soup would be lost in a supermarket).

The Pompidou in Paris (Renzo Piano and Richard Rogers, 1974) was a conscious critique of this elitist model in studied casual, post-1968 garb – art building as political statement – and aspired to locate art for ordinary people within an approachable neutral framework. Escalators, essence of modern shopping culture, moved consumers effortlessly into an art world, wittily serviced by an exoskeleton of coloured pipes and ducts. Everything could be beautiful if you knew how to look.

Today, global architecture has fractured into nearly as many directions as art, but this does not necessarily mean innovation. Some would say the debate among architects, like the debate in the art world, has become internalised and self-referential, less focused on making appropriate spaces and more on the creation of star events. Perhaps this is the consequence of information-sharing and, thus, extensive emulation through electronic means and magazine culture. Undoubtedly the increased internationalisation of both art and architecture has had an impact on cultural tourism, shopping and fashion. The Bilbao effect – flagship buildings for competing city states – finds a parallel and a symbiotic universe in the globalisation of art: buildings as prize bulls: Gehry in Bilbao, Nouvel in Paris, Hadid in Cincinnati; paired with blockbuster shows: Bourgeois in Tate Modern, Miyake and Armani in the Cartier and Guggenheim. Fashion meets art in a winning combination. The phenomenon has generated a spiral of increasingly anxious validation by curators and regional governments competing for tourism numbers, which consumes the art building and exhibition budgets of entire regional economies. Is it productive? Does it widen the appreciation of art or architecture? Like any form of advertising, the crude answer must be yes – but only in one way and at a cost. Fewer architects are building bigger buildings (in a Darwinian sense, tough but fair), and some of the best architectural minds of this generation have focused on building for art, throwing up new solutions based on reinterpretations of the problem. Relatively untried materials are extending the repertoire of choice, perhaps altering the perceptions of those who come to look at art, rather than extending the range of artists and curator. Maybe that is just what is needed to gain new audiences, but the downside is the 'top-down' consumer nature of this culture – innovation is stifled at the lower end with endless repetitions of the successful motif. There are probably fewer original ideas floating around in the making of architecture than ever before.

[clockwise from top left:] Louis I. Kahn, Architect (1901-1974) Kimbell Art Museum, Exterior: North portico, reflecting pool and waterfall; Interior: South gallery, Copyright © 2005, Kimbell Museum; Interior and exterior, Kunsthaus, Graz; Cook and Fournier, 2003, photo: Kunsthaus Graz / Zepp-Cam 2004 and Kunsthaus Graz / LMJ / Eduardo Martinez, May 2004.

What are the current approaches? Architecture is obsessed by issues of participation vs. observation. It is also involved with developing an architecture of land and landscape, and with the re-use of places and spaces, which, at some level, is an intellectual response to environmental needs. It is also concerned with hybridisation, a blurring of edges and demarcations that can be productive (Art and Shopping or Art and the City). At its simplest, a gallery space is through a door off a street with no mediation whatsoever; most commercial galleries in New York and London speak the language of the shop window, using the directness and familiarity of the retail model. Economic necessity to sell the artist's work impacts on the gallery form, offering immediacy and direct appeal. Non-commercial galleries have also learned from this model. A recent project (the de Young Museum in California, 2000-5) by Herzog & de Meuron places large frames in the entrance which literally ask the visitor to become involved in the reciprocal process of viewing and being viewed. For shock tactics, take the Kunsthaus in Graz (Cook and Fournier, 2000-3), an Archigram idea of the 60s, repackaged as a blue blob on legs, glued to the back of an unsuspecting group of historic houses in the city. Inside, the Graz building is by no means a radically different way to display art, but it does introduce a new audience to the idea of venturing in, simply because it looks different and irreverent: the rather quaint language of pop-art meets advertising. It interests the visitor, but perhaps no more than once. However, bold ideas in the world of art building can give promoters in smaller places the confidence to support risk-taking by less well known architects, so ultimately we all benefit.

Rem Koolhaas' Kunsthalle in Rotterdam (1993) enlisted an aesthetic of cheap, commonplace materials reminding us that art, like architecture, was a lens to see the extraordinary in everyday situations. More recently still, Palais de Tokyo in Paris has ripped out all its finishes (Lacaton and Vassal, 2003) in an attempt to create a 'found' space, full of trash appeal. Here, chance/random organisations are intended to function in a way that is more interesting and immediate than the more traditional planned architectural promenade. There is a parallel here with the intensity of personal choice (albeit kept at arm's length) derived from interactive TV shows, e-mail and electronic shopping. The logical direction for art buildings for a consumer age may be towards the Schaulager (Show Storage) model in Basel, again by Herzog and de Meuron (1998-2003). Here is the gallery as warehouse: no didactic messages, but a tiny exhibition space with huge areas of storage for private collectors. An appointment can be made to view a particular work for personal research, and while the isolation and privacy of the individual is complete, a new opportunity exists to view works previously held in private hands. From a (French-) intellectual idea about large, state subsidised buildings bringing art to the masses, to an introspective search for personal, consumable satisfaction, the arts centre is changing its nature.

'Found' spaces and reclaimed landscapes provide an antidote to the perceived over-packaging of purpose-made art buildings. These are places redolent with weight and meaning, heavy with memory and association. The renaissance of the historic city has been underpinned everywhere by recycling of this kind, as buildings with strong identities but obsolete functions are re-used for art; factories, barracks, power stations: Tate Modern, Duisburg Steelworks, Baltic Mills, Ormeau Baths, Neuss missile base; the unexpected transformations opening new audiences to the work. These buildings must be handled with spontaneity, with enjoyment of juxtaposition, with acceptance of their scale and ambition. Like a second-hand bookshop, they offer an alternative to preconceived ideas, and they can reveal chance jewels – but they have to be encouraged to yield up their secrets. Adding to them requires a strong concept, a positive, even destructive, contribution. It cannot be a neutral, weak thing. Neither can it be fossilised: it must be made new and passionate.

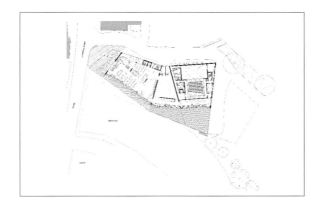

Thurles Arts Centre, ground plan, and digital image, McCullough Mulvin Architects; digital image by ARC Consultants

Intervention invokes all the fantastic juxtaposition of a cubist painting in a Baroque carved and glided frame. Buildings such as Tate Modern's Turbine Hall or the industrial parks/steel mills of the Ruhr offer a destruction of old readings with their vast spaces and obsolete machinery. They are perfect havens for the scaleless manifestations of shows like Olafur Eliasson's *Weather Project* (Turbine Hall, Tate Modern, 2003). The scale and subject matter of work by artists like Joseph Beuys and Anselm Kiefer similarly demands the not entirely clean air of a bunker or abandoned industrial process. These are spaces beyond human gesture for a post-catastrophe world view.

A counter-cultural equivalent is the art/landscape Museum Insel Hombroich (1987) at Neuss, near Düsseldorf, where sculptor/architect Edwin Heerich located a series of very spare, beautiful, salvaged brick boxes across an abandoned missile base. Each box makes a gallery of a different size, shape and lighting, linked by casual paths through a tangle of wild vegetation, or hidden by tall hedges. There are no labels, no interpretation; the juxtaposition of ancient pieces of sculpture with modern, without attribution: the determination of the route between them calls on older responses buried in your genes. As an opposite, Donald Judd's Chinati installation(s) at Marfa (begun in 1979) places his obsessive, perfect collection of fixed objects in an abstract landscape abandoned by the military, and takes control to a degree impossible in spaces for changing exhibitions. Judd's single vision, his fixed and unchanging brief creates a total place. Its exclusion is its power, and its clarity and singularity an example to owners, users and makers of art space everywhere.

How do these ideas relate to architecture about art in Ireland? Some of the buildings for art we have had the opportunity to make offer some examples. Temple Bar Gallery & Studios and Black Church Print Studios (Dublin, 1994) are very urban buildings where the art is on view through large windows to the street. Once inside, the exhibition space opens into the atrium/stairwell, a multi-level meeting space shared by all the artists' studios, with a large void in each floor for raising art. The artists themselves saw more potential in this bright utilities space and promptly developed it into an extension of the gallery, loose fit in the scheme allowing for growth in other directions. In Gallery 2 in the Douglas Hyde (2001), a small art space carved from a storeroom was closed by a new door with sliding panels, allowing the artist to frame work and control entrance and exit (the visitor may potentially have to bend down or turn sideways to get in). Hybridisation is common too, a similar blurring occurs where different functions are wrapped into the same building volume: the library and arts centre, the civic offices and theatre, all increasingly common mixes in the Irish context as shared spaces reduce capital and staff costs. These hybrids aim to grow new audiences through adjacency, through casual contact, through a gradual breaking down of barriers – and they are admirable for that: you came to borrow a book, saw a challenging exhibition and your perceptions shifted. Symbiotic relationships of compatible functions put new communities together and a civic building can acquire presence with a critical mass of functions. In Thurles, Co Tipperary, we are building an art space (of 145 Sqm) shared between a library and arts centre/theatre. It is internalised and roof lit, a secret space inside a stretched form of glass, folded into a sheltering metal roof along the banks of the river Suir. The art space depends on its neighbours, one function flowing into the other. The plan shape provides irregular walls, creating a non-square room, treading a line between perspective and abstraction.

'Found' space has a deep resonance: the old Model School in Sligo (original building James Owen, 1855; McCullough Mulvin, 2000) offered a unique opportunity for intervention, working with and into the building fabric, using its geometry to complete an incipient pinwheel plan. The brief required a modern gallery to house a municipal collection of great importance, releasing a series of old rooms for contemporary exhibitions. Rear yards were cleared to generate a roof lit central atrium, around which all activities are organised, while a zinc and cedar clad box of new space closes the north side of the newly-created atrium. A crabwise circulation pattern links old and new , a rising series of diagonal movements set against boardmarked concrete or cedar walls. Indirect light guides a journey from the old (and now new) entrance through to the new gallery spaces. There are west-facing roof lights in the atrium (evening sun), switching to north-facing roof lights in the gallery itself (shadowless daylight). The building is about the inter-relationship of absolutely modern architecture and traditional form (a difficult, but rewarding, sympathy to establish, whose quality is founded on the careful and exact conservation of the old).

What are the lessons and ideas that derive from all this? Today, most artists and curators will say that gallery space must just be flexible, but this is actually a way deferring issues, not thinking about them. Total flexibility is a myth difficult to dislodge from public perception, and it can be counter productive, with spaces stretched without sufficient budgets to achieve their aspirations. There has to be more of a dialogue, which can release the more beautiful things a piece of architecture offers. For the architect (and the promoters of the building) choices have to be made about light, about what balance of space should be devoted to gallery use and technical fittings, and what other functions (if any) are to be included in the container. In reality, spaces can be designed which are good for most artistic interventions; so it is essential that artists, curators and promoters are clear about what arts practices are they promoting, what budget is available and how it should be disposed of throughout the building. They should also be aware that architecture can have a strong character, or give rise to a most particular light, and that these are not necessarily bad things. In Ireland, the building can sometimes be completed before a curator is appointed, or the brief changed late in the process to take on new curator's ideas, leading to additional costs or delays on site – or disappointment that a new element cannot be incorporated.

From one end of the telescope of the design process, one must start with the function; it is usually a reasonable strategy to start with the gallery and make it as big in plan, as well lit, as high in section, and as structurally capable as the budget allows. From the opposite end of the telescope (and at the same time) the architect must devise a concept which places the experience of that art space at the core of the building's meaning in a way that will release the richness of the art located there. The art spaces are of prime importance for the artist, but this is an interactive world. We are all – artist, curator, audience – involved in a part-

Atrium at Model Arts and Niland Gallery; Niland Gallery, Sligo, McCullough Mulvin, 2001, photos Christian Richters, courtesy the architects

nership of reciprocal viewing intended to change perceptions. The building can help or hinder this exchange: the spatial experience of the audience generates a need for light, depth, intimacy or drama, creates conditions where the work is viewed, bringing the audience on a journey, enhanced by both the work on view and the building itself. Requirements to move numbers of people through a series of spaces (which might be a fixed or a random route) generate an organising device which can enhance appreciation of the art by making memorable, emotionally charged and physically intense spaces in which to place the work.

The architect should compose space in a way similar to a composer of music or a novel, using a range of elements to explore and define spaces, but controlling all elements so a dominant theme is clear. There can be any number of sub-plots: it is not a static pursuit, even thought it may have great static quality or monumental calm, but (as with the music analogy) it depends on the additional dimensions of space and time. To make a plan, as Le Corbusier said, is to determine and fix ideas. The clarity of that plan in three dimensions must translate into an articulation of volumes underpinned by structure and modulated with light. This is the syntax of architecture. The way the volumes are punctured to allow daylight in, or to indicate a route which navigates the building clearly while allowing exploration of inlets and channels; the qualities of the building (heavy/light, solid/void) achieved with the smallest palette of materials; the context of the building (urban/rural/suburban), its story and its memories; the screen or filter of its external skin, set between the outside world and the interior world of the imagination; these are the vowels and consonants.

The real world will and should interpose itself, shaping and directing future years of building art spaces, but we should keep a space in our imaginations for the intensity and power of a singular, unmediated vision.

How Space Works

Introduction by Gemma Tipton

One of the problems with architectural criticism is that you don't really know what you are going to get until the building is built. And by then it seems a little late. Of course there have been architects' models, technical drawings and (in the case of art spaces) a long process of consultation, compromise and consideration, but until you are actually faced with the building itself, a sense of the space is impossible to imagine. And once the building is built, it's a bit of a fait accompli. There's a big gala opening, and mindful of the millions that have been spent, and how much the future reputation of the space will be founded on the efforts of those who work, perform and exhibit within it, one is encouraged to focus on the good points. A little later, when the fuss has died down, you can start to think about the dodgy lighting, the unsympathetic hanging space, the intrusive atrium... Perhaps, then, the real key to objective architectural criticism is time.

[1]Donald Judd, 'Complaints: Part II', in *Donald Judd, Complete Writings 1959-1975*, quoted in Kynaston McShine, *The Museum as Muse*, MoMA New York, 1999, p. 225.

[2]Pablo Picasso, 'Conversation with Picasso', 1935, in Alfred H. Barr, Jr. *Picasso: Fifty Years of His Art*, quoted in *ibid*, p. 208.

[3]Philip Johnson, quoted by Victoria Newhouse, *Towards a New Museum*, Monacelli Press, New York 1998, p. 14.

[4]Le Corbusier, 'Other Icons: The Museums', 1925, quoted in Kynaston McShine, *op. cit.*, p. 205.

[5]Donald Judd, interviewed by Lawrence Alloway, *Artists on Museums*, 1967, quoted in *ibid*, p. 217.

[6]Quoted by Deyan Sudjic in 'The Architecture', in Alison Roberts (ed.), *Saatchi*, a supplement to the *Observer* in April 2003, p.19.

Artists have traditionally had a problematic relationship with the museums and galleries that collect, sell and exhibit their work. Donald Judd said that "museums patronise, isolate and neutralise artists,"[1] and according to Picasso, "museums are just a lot of lies, and the people who make art their business are mostly impostors." Architects can feel somewhat differently, "Museums satisfy... a deep natural want... as deep and as natural as sex or sleeping," says Philip Johnson[3], a view which is challenged by Le Corbusier's suggestion that "the museums are a recent invention; once there were none. So let us admit that they are not a fundamental component of human life like bread, drink, religion, orthography."[4] While these quotes relate directly to the institution of the museum, the issues go beyond and encompass the shape of the gallery space. Both museums and galleries are areas where control of how an artwork is viewed has passed from the artist, who has envisaged and created it, into the hands of an architect, gallery designer, museum director, and art curator.

Asked how he would like to see his work exhibited, Judd did have some more positive suggestions to make. It should be: "a large rectangular space with a fairly high ceiling... There shouldn't be any mouldings or grooves. The walls and floors should be smooth and square, not flagstones... the floor shouldn't be patterned. Ideally, the architecture of the building should be good outside and inside. That excludes the elegance of most new galleries and museums."[5]

Adding to the issue of how the art is seen in their galleries is the way in which museum collections, and private collections, contextualise new additions. Saatchi's art collection is a case in point here, for it is a defining collection. Being acceded to it was always to be subsumed into the YBA (Young British Artists) phenomenon, associations and aesthetic. Interesting for the purposes of this discussion is the Saatchi Gallery's move in 2003 from Boundary Road (conversion of a garage and motor repair shop, architect: Max Gordon, 1984) to the Edwardian splendour of County Hall on London's Embankment (architect Ralph Knott, 1911). 98A Boundary Road lurked off the beaten art-track in St. John's Wood. Notoriously hard to find, it was nonetheless named, in an international poll of artists, the "British Gallery in which they would most like to exhibit,"[6] giving the lie to the idea that accessibility is a prime requirement (you even had to take a bus to get there…). Gordon lined the interior of the original building to create top-lit, windowless, aggressively white galleries, whose industrial origins were revealed only in the steel trusses of the shed roof. Art shown in 98A Boundary Road was 'out there', the difficulties in finding the galleries mirroring the effort expected of the viewer in engaging with what was being presented as the absolute avant-garde. The unrelieved whiteness of the exhibition spaces (with no creature comforts like seating or bookshops and cafés) demonstrated that the art was centre-stage, that the art was about nothing, and cared about nothing – except itself. It was a self-referential world, and created the necessary self-regarding insularity to turn a collection into a phenomenon.

The interior of County Hall is listed, and while Saatchi has subverted some of its grandeur with the placement of exhibits, such as Damien Hirst's *Spot mini* (2002) careening down the marble entry staircase, and Duane Hanson's *Tourists* (1998)[7] lurking in the lobby, the architecture and historical resonances of the building now announce that Saatchi's collection is no longer the art-outsider, the Salon des Refusés, it is now the Salon itself. Artworks and museum collections sited in historic buildings place the art in the inexorable stream of history, emphasising its significance in the unfolding of the cultural heritage of the city or country. This subtle alteration of a work's meaning through context does not just happen in overtly 'historic' buildings like the new Saatchi Gallery, or the Irish Museum of Modern Art (conversion architect Shay Cleary, 1991).

[7]At time of writing these works had been temporarily removed for security reasons.

Asked what he thought the ideal space was, artist Barnett Newman's view was "that my work be shown, as closely as possible, the way it looks in my studio where it was created."[8] Newman's ideal is taken up and embodied in art spaces housed, like the studios where Newman and his contemporaries were making their work, in renovated industrial buildings, retaining their industrial aesthetic and characteristics. The location of art objects in a setting similar to that of their making definitely works for a particular kind of art. Not only that, but siting art works from other conditions and periods of making in industrial conversions exerts as much of a contextual layering of references as does their location in classical historical buildings. An example is *Matisse Picasso*,[9] where the familiar images of these art heavyweights are first redefined by juxtaposition, and then again by context. At MoMA QNS in New York (as well as at Tate Modern), images that had seemed, in the more hushed galleries of Tate Britain, or in the Musée Picasso in Paris, quietly brilliant, now jumped off the walls as shockingly challenging newcomers to the art scene. While it should be noted that this reading would be closer to that of their first viewing, it also demonstrated the historicising effect of our venerable art spaces.

[8]Barnett Newman, interviewed by Lawrence Alloway (1967), quoted in Kynaston McShine, *op. cit.*, p. 217.

[9]*Matisse Picasso*, Tate Modern, London, May-August 2002; Galeries Nationales du Grand Palais, Paris, September 2002-January 2003; MoMA QNS, New York, February-May 2003.

Tate Modern, the Baltic in Gateshead (conversion of a flour mill, architect Dominic Williams, 2001), and the Lingotto Exhibition Spaces in Turin (former Fiat factory, conver-

Exterior and interior views, Saatchi Gallery, County Hall, London, images courtesy Saatchi Gallery

sion architect Renzo Piano, 1983-1996 phases 1 and 2), are all conversions of former industrial buildings. These conversions are beloved of governments and city planners as they provide a use for irritatingly listed buildings, and demonstrate that while manufacturing industry may have all but collapsed, the sexy new leisure industry, with its concomitant tourism, is a welcome replacement. Art is located firmly as an alternative industry, beginning also to accede to the demands of industry as business, in terms of targets, financial returns and visitor numbers. Art in these buildings is telling you that the greatness of the nation has moved beyond making things to creating; art here is a sign of cultural maturity rather than a testament to historical significance.

The apotheosis of this type of art space is Dia: Beacon in New York (conversion of a printing factory, designed by Robert Irwin, in collaboration with architects OpenOffice, 2003),[10] while, at another extreme, Rem Koolhaas took on the conceit to create an industrial space where before the only industry had been gambling and, as the Americans would put it, 'vice', in his Las Vegas Guggenheim (2001, now converted to a theatre). Koolhaas even went as far as to choreograph carefully placed ersatz oil spills on the gallery floor.

Given that whether you choose to build, or to renovate recent or historic buildings, you are placing works of art in inescapable contexts, what do artists themselves choose? Claes Oldenburg suggests, "I believe museums should be austere and dignified, and packed with experts completely in love with art and detached from everything else," immediately adding, "but the rare times when a museum relaxes and risks the penetration of life can be sublime."[11] And that, unfortunately is the issue with architecture: barring buildings which were obviously set to be disasters from the outset, you only know how a space is going to work when it's finished.

So what do we really think we want from those finished spaces? Crazy inspirational shapes and spaces? 'Neutral' white cubes? Architecture that whispers? Architecture that declaims? With so many words spent and ink spilt on what art museums could and should look like, Peter Eisenman suggests a little 'going back to basics'. "Perhaps one of the problems with museums is that we in architecture are in fact stuck with a tradition which I would call theorizing form… We are at the end of a dying line. That line is a line that has always thought that form took care of everything and that space really was what happened."[12]

Eisenman goes on to advocate taking another look at the void, considering the shape of the space that the art will inhabit, rather than focusing on the constructions that surround it, and it is here that the art of architecture (if there is such a thing) lies. Beyond the mathematics of space, it is the essential understanding of the dynamics of volume that creates the memorable white cubes (and white other shapes) where works of art can find the space to speak on their own terms. The pursuit of this is realised, of course, in Donald Judd's Chinati Foundation at Marfa, isolated in the middle of the West Texas Chihuahua desert, the museum he created for the permanent installation of his (and other) artworks. "It takes a great deal of time and thought to install work carefully. This should not always be thrown away. Most art is fragile and some should be placed and never moved again."[13]

Of course it's a rare artist with the time, money or inclination to create their own museum, but conversely, museums and galleries do plenty of creating of their own. The 1999 exhibition, *The Museum as Muse*, at the Museum of Modern Art New York (architects Philip L. Goodwin and Edward Durrell Stone 1939), placed the role of the museum as inspirer and instigator of art, centre-stage. From the museum-in-a-box experiments of Marcel Duchamp

[10] Thanks to the US system of private funding and endowments, Dia: Beacon is luckily freed of the necessity of actually having to earn its keep. For a full discussion of the Dia: Beacon space and project, see my article, 'Whispering architecture', *CIRCA* 105, September 2003, pp. 42-47.

[11] Claes Oldenburg, interviewed by Lawrence Alloway, *Artists on Museums*, 1967, quoted in Kynaston McShine, *op. cit.*, p. 217.

[12] Peter Eisenman, quoted in John Elderfield (ed.), *Imagining the Future of the Museum of Modern Art*, MoMA New York 1998, p. 40.

[13] Donald Judd, quoted by Charles Derwent in Barbara Minton (ed.), *Writers on Artists*, Dorling Kindersley, London 2001, p. 336.

and Joseph Cornell, to the renditions of the Guggenheim's rotunda in fibreglass relief, running from white to black to gold to rainbow by Richard Hamilton (1965-66), to Komar and Melamid's *Scenes from the future: the Guggenheim* (1975), showing the Guggenheim in ruins, the exhibition demonstrated artists' long-term fascination, and discomfort, with the ideologies and architectures of the museum. As it did this, however, it also inescapably underpinned the museum and gallery's central role in art-making.

The essays in this section address these issues. They ask how spaces work, and they take a look at what architecture does to art. Negative impacts of architecture, such as lack of sufficient access excluding artworks or projects, are discussed, as are the sometimes intrusive aspects of the architectural flourish that can leave one wondering *was that art, or was it just part of the building...?* On the other hand there are also the occasions when the resonances of a space lend something 'extra' to an exhibition; or those particularly interesting instances when curator, artist and architecture all seem to collaborate and the space becomes part of the work itself.

Of course, artists working towards commissioned exhibitions will take account of the gallery's size, shape and aesthetics, even if only subconsciously. An example of a more conscious method is to be seen in the way in which an artist like Mike Nelson will take on the space, actively using its architecture to become an integral part of his installations. *Tourist Hotel* at the Douglas Hyde (architect Paul Koralek, Ahrends, Burton and Koralek, 1978-79) in 1999 used the awkward tunnel and triangle areas of the gallery to construct a creepy flophouse environment where the visitor was lured from the openness of the main space into strangely intense encounters with the objects placed in Nelson's dimly-lit rooms. At the 2001 Venice Biennale, Nelson created *The Deliverance and the Patience* in a disused brewery on the Giudecca. Discussing the installation, Jonathan Jones remarks, "As Nelson's architectural installations become ever more grandiose you begin to wonder if it is his ultimate intention to build a work of art so vast that it consumes the reality around it."[14]

In considering this idea, it soon becomes apparent that the massive size of some of our most recent art spaces is influencing the creation of art installations so large that they in turn could perhaps be considered to become architectural. Anish Kapoor's 2002 installation at Tate Modern, as part of the Unilever Series, saw a vast structure stretched through the Turbine Hall. Part massive sucking trumpet, part enormous jungle-like plant, *Marsyas* attracted the attention of city authorities in Italy, who have asked the artist to turn architect and create the entrance to a metro station in Naples.

Another Tate Turbine installation, Olafur Eliasson's *The weather project*, is an interplay of light and mist which uses mirrors to dissolve the ceiling, and creates an unearthly space where the heavy-handed forms of the hall miraculously disappear. While Eliasson's project dissolves the architecture, Kapoor's slugs it out with the constraining walls. Nonetheless, Kapoor will be the first to resist the label 'architectural'. Instead, he insists he is "toying with form at architectural scale but they are not buildings, I loathe making anything practical whatever."[15] In fact Kapoor is so insistent that architecture is not art, and art is not architecture, that he describes a discussion on the topic with Frank Gehry when he was showing his plans for Naples:

"I had dinner with Frank and he did a little benediction on me and said: *I now declare you an architect.*" What was your response to that? "Fuck off."[16]

[14]Jonathan Jones, quoted in *The Deliverance and the Patience* at http://www.peeruk.org/projects/nelson1.html.

[15]Anish Kapoor, quoted by Marcus Fairs, in "They don't know what they've let themselves in for", *The Guardian*, 6 May 2003.

[16]*ibid.*

The case of My Paradise is Here by Fergus Martin & Anthony Hobbs

by Vittorio Urbani

Fergus Martin & Anthony Hobbs, *My Paradise is Here*, 2003; giclée on water colour paper, installation views at Oratorio di San Ludovico, Venice, and at Green on Red Gallery, Dublin

The purpose of this essay is to discuss how, or if, architectural spaces affect artworks. This may seem an obvious question, especially if one thinks of the Galerie de Rubens at the Louvre, or the Sistina, but more about exactly how and why can be seen from looking at the issue in the light of a specific art work, which has been exhibited in two very different spaces.

A man clothed in white wanders in a clear space. He looks as if he is wearing pyjamas, or perhaps it is the uniform of a psychiatric hospital inmate? His attitude seems serene. He walks, or better, makes gestures like one who is mimicking a walking person; moving very lightly. Although the figure is not particularly slim, his movements are gentle and silent. Is he a sleep-walker? The space itself in which the white figure is set lacks architectural features like windows or mouldings. Its colourlessness gives no hint of the location in which the figure is moving, or is maybe recluse. Its pale, gloomy white light doesn't even tell the position of the body in space. The figure could well be upside down. If it weren't for the visible effect of gravity on the tails of the white shirt, one wouldn't know.

Let's now take a step back. This figure is not alone. A series of them, in slightly different attitudes, all of them in a same pensive, melancholic but serene mood, is hung on the walls of two different spaces.

One is the Oratorio of San Ludovico, a little shadowy church in Venice; the other one is the well-lit space of the Green on Red Gallery in Dublin (conversion architects Michaél and Simon O Drisceoil).

The church is primarily a place dedicated to prayer, or at least to quiet conversation and reflection. Not conceived as an exhibition space in the conventional modern way, this chapel was built under the influence of Tuscan architect Andrea Sansovino at the end of the sixteenth century, the period which was both the peak and the end of Venice's Golden Age. The building that now houses the Green on Red Gallery has its own former history too. An old hay loft for a set of commercial stables in Dublin's city centre, its well proportioned and high hall has been 'white-cubed' by the insertion of free standing white walls, which draw that sort of clear space conventionally chosen for contemporary exhibition, while still leaving the evidence of the building's different history and character.

Artist Fergus Martin and photographer Anthony Hobbs have worked together on the realization of this work, which was originally conceived as an installation in the church in Venice. The photographic technique, *Giclée*, produces prints of images from a Digital Scan Camera in pure pigment onto watercolour paper. Here, the images have such a depth, such a wealth of visual information, that they are able to challenge the acuity of the human eye and create interesting 'visual traps' for the viewer. The rich but smooth surface of the resulting image is deceptively simple to see, but it is simultaneously challengingly elusive. Richness of detail has always called for a closer inspection. When one is looking closer and closer at something, one expects to see more… details enrich the general picture with an additional narrative, sometimes in contrast to, or even critical of, the main one. Martin and Hobbs' work escapes this destiny, because the detail is achieved by excess of visual information: consequently this can be compared to a fluxus of visual material, as it seems to make a fool of our accepted visual conventions.

If visual art has any meaning, it may be considered in its capacity to bear a message in a non-verbal form. To get this message, one has to read the image, and to do that it is necessary to know the grammar of this language. Things become more complicated when the art object is set in a context. It is not possible to escape the 'frame' that the environment makes around the art work, not even in the case of the white cube. Reading images in a context means considering the frame-environment as being as significant for the interpretation of the image as the image itself. Space commands that a different description of the art work would be given by the visitors of different spaces; and the frame provided by these two places is utterly different.

In the Venetian church the little man floats, stumbles, lies down. In the Dublin art space instead, he pensively walks. In the church we see one set of individual images, different in shape, spread on the walls with attention to the symmetry of the pediment and the columns of the altar – like those paintings with stories of the saints that one expects to see on church walls. In the gallery, the same series of work is presented as a set of vertical images, regularly paced like a horizontal frieze. The different figures, one after the other, create a fluent rhythm that makes one compare them to the repetition of frames in a film.

Fergus Martin & Anthony Hobbs, *My Paradise is Now*, 2003; giclée on water colour paper, installation view at Green on Red Gallery, Dublin, photo courtesy Green on Red Gallery

The different influence of the two buildings on the artworks comes from their own ineluctable histories.

The church – as Catholic churches in particular, but all places of prayer of Christian influence may do – has a tradition of showing art. Western figurative art was born as religious art. In showing 'art' in a church, one has always to confront the problem of being provocative, or conversely, the problem of not being provocative enough. This dilemma is not futile, and it sometimes runs the risk of dwarfing the content and relevance of the exhibited art. Another character of the church space is the symmetry created by the presence of many architectural features like mouldings, windows; and mainly by the altar. The altar immediately establishes a hierarchy and presents degrees of importance proportional to closeness and relationship with it. A church is a Manichean space, aware of moral responsibility. Contemporary culture can look to these attitudes with compassion and maybe a nostalgia for a wholesome system of values, but that brings its own unease.

The space of the gallery on the other hand seems apparently simple. It may be considered to be less loaded with ideology, and to be easier as an exhibition space than a church. But this is not true. Spatially clear, properly lit with state-of-the-art spotlights; the 'indifferent' space of contemporary galleries like Green on Red is born out of a nineteenth century scientific approach to cultural items, and out of Positivist thinking. The rational space of the gallery is the true and ideal *theatrum anatomicum* in which art corpses can be examined in a cool, clinical way. From the very origin of its having been the hay loft for a stables, which would have served the nearby docks with transport, the gallery building is related to the practicalities of commerce and business. These economic issues are present also in the work exhibited in the church, of course, but in that case, given the original purpose of the building, spirituality was a starting point: in the case of the show at the gallery, spirituality seems to be an additional value of the art work as purchasable commodity.

I have reflected on this matter several times, yet I still feel reluctant to draw a conclusion, even now that I should. Maybe my conclusion is that there isn't one possible conclusion, but a multiplicity of solutions and contradictions.

Life is interesting because it cannot be fully described with words.

(scritto a Venezia, 13 luglio 2004)

Inhabiting Space

by Peter Richards

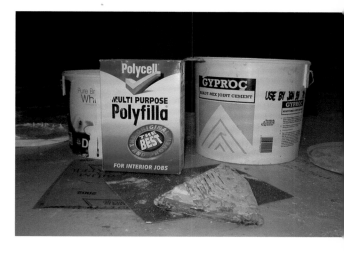

Peter Richards, *Between Shows*
2004; photo, courtesy the author

As the nature of contemporary art changes over time so do the demands placed on the gallery space. No longer is it practical to envisage that an exhibition will take the form of a number of 2D works hung on a white wall. In fact it is almost impossible to make any assumptions as to what an artist may wish to do or present.

I came to Belfast in 1994, and around that time I became involved with presenting my own work as an artist and organising exhibitions as a curator/facilitator. Both of these activities have led me to gain some understanding of how the gallery space can be used and abused (inadvertently of course).

Through the following text I will not attempt to set out a model of what an ideal gallery space could be, rather I will try to illustrate some of the demands that it could face. In doing so I will raise some points for consideration and advocate flexibility as the single most important factor that an architect, designer, engineer should embrace when working on the construction/refurbishment of future gallery spaces.

From 1996 a key element of my own practice has been the construction of a camera obscura/pinhole camera and using this construction to document an activity, such as a performance or social event. At the same time I have been a co-director of Catalyst Arts, a Director of The Golden Thread Gallery, Belfast (for the last three years) and worked to facilitate a number of artist-run exhibitions and events. Whilst at Catalyst, many of the exhibitions and events could not possibly have taken place in the gallery space that we had at Exchange Place due to practical reasons, such as access. One of the more extreme examples of how significant an issue access is to a gallery space, is the performance by Anthony Howells that took place as part of *Fix* 98.

For his performance Anthony Howells was asked to provide a brief description of the event/activity and a list of technical requirements needed, several months prior to the event. The acquisition of this type of information was a standard practice that was applied to all the activities we programmed, from exhibitions of paintings to installations.

Anthony simply stated that he intended to create a series of minuets, using his (naked) body, which he thought might be found entertaining or engaging by a live pig; and also that the event would take approximately half an hour. His sole technical requirement was the live pig. The story attached to finding a live pig that did not have to be killed after the event is not really relevant, so I will skip it on this occasion, suffice to say we managed somehow to conjure up a live pig that could be borrowed and returned to where it came from, in the same condition we found it.

For those of you who had never visited Catalyst Arts when it was at Exchange Place, there were three ways of accessing the gallery space, the first being the front entrance, a doorway approximately four feet across followed by a very steep staircase. The second led from an enclosed courtyard at the back of the building. The doorway was of similar width to the first though the staircase was less steep. The third access was through the neighbouring unit that had a lift; however, this was never an easy option to utilise, as the landlord used the unit for his clothing company.

Access had always been a major issue and limiting factor, and it impacted on our programming significantly in terms of what we could actually show. For example, no large-scale sculptural works were possible, unless they could be reassembled in situ.

Half an hour before the event was scheduled to start, the man with the pig arrived at the courtyard entrance. He brought the pig to the bottom of the staircase and announced that the pig could make it up the stairs, but there was no way it would come back down, alive.

Plan B: you always need a plan B (it is usually a good idea to have plans C, D & E as back up) especially in relation to festivals. I had previously discussed the project with the director of the Proposition Gallery, a street level (window fronted) space in North Street Arcade, and provisionally secured permission to use the gallery if any problems with the pig arose. A phone call later and we were all making our way around to the Proposition Gallery to set up for the work.

Although access was no longer a problem a new issue did present itself. The handler was concerned about the very large windows, as was the gallery director, and thought we needed to do something to stop the pig walking straight through them. At this time an audience began to gather. They were our solution. We guided the audience into the space, stood them along the windows and requested that they all link arms to create a human barrier, and told them that under no circumstance would they be able to leave the event before it had finished.

Interestingly a completely different type of problem concerning access arose to the ones we were accustomed to: the gallery had too much access. A passer-by had called the police and complained about seeing a naked man standing on his head (or in the lotus position or some such pose). This, along with the 'artrage' front-page coverage in the Sunday World, is a whole other story.

Seriously though, access to a venue is such a significant factor in the whole programming of a space, and yet I do not believe it is always considered fully. I acknowledge that many newer galleries I have worked with do, at the very least, now cater for disabled access. However, trying to place large crates of artwork into a disabled lift can never be described as good practice. I believe accessibility regarding the unloading / delivery of the artworks and installation materials is often not fully considered at the design stage.

Apart from access, other key factors that a gallery needs to have considered at its inception include lighting and finish. Unfortunately (or fortunately!) I do not have the space left to illustrate these concerns in quite the same anecdotal way.

With regard to lighting, good natural light / daylight is always a good thing (as long as the windows / skylights are fitted with UV protected glass) – apart from when it comes to showing video projections and the like. Work that requires a black-out space is ever more common, and comes with an expectation that black out can be achieved. This is often easier said than done and is an area that I do specialise in. The amount of silver foil and gaffer tape that I have personally used in recent years would probably justify an investigation in terms of the environmental impact.

Finally I would like to look at 'finish' as this is a particular subject that is becoming more and more problematic in terms of practising as an artist. Why would somebody wish to renovate or refurbish a building to be used as a place for showing artwork and then set in stone that you cannot drill into the walls, floor or ceiling? This really is the inspiration of many nightmares. Galleries should accept that they will, before too long, exist mainly as a mass of polyfilla, and accept this or do not bother to show artwork at all. Instead, the venue should just focus on presenting a space that can be hired out for private and corporate functions.

Whilst at the beginning of this text I stated that it is almost impossible to predict anything about the nature of the artwork, the drilling of holes is as close to being a constant as you will find. New hanging systems and picture rails are all very nice for something I'm sure, but just what, I have yet to fathom. And why are gallery spaces being finished with design features such as coloured areas of wall or other such paraphernalia? Some artists paint directly onto the walls, floors or ceilings and others need the whole space to be a particular hue for the art to work.

Anybody who has worked or shown in a gallery knows that the only thing hiding the fact that the building is mostly made up of polyfilla is the amount of paint on the walls. It should also be noted that galleries do become smaller with the passing of each exhibition; a common and generally necessary practice in almost every gallery is that the space is repainted between each exhibition.

So – here are my conclusions: gallery spaces need to be flexible if they are planning to host exhibitions of the ever-evolving diversity of practices that make up contemporary visual art today. The nature of a gallery space implicitly impacts upon the nature of exhibitions or events that it can present to the public. I would therefore strongly recommend that any company or organisation that is planning a new-build, or the refurbishment of a building into a gallery, have a very clear set of aims and objectives that will not only set out what is expected of its curator, but will in the same way inform the design brief. In my opinion the best gallery spaces to work with are those that can serve the particular needs of the exhibition being presented within them at the time. These spaces in general only look the way the designer or architect finished them when there is no art in it, for example when the gallery is closed between shows.

Specific Places

by Declan Long

[from left:] Verne Dawson, *Big Bear*, 2002, Oil on canvas; Robert Adams, *Long Beach on Signal Hill*, 1983, Gelatin silver print; photos courtesy Douglas Hyde Gallery

In April 2004, two exhibitions at the Douglas Hyde Gallery, Dublin, offered contrasting visions of 'place'. In the main gallery space, a selection of paintings by the American artist Verne Dawson evoked the realm of Arcadia: these were bucolic scenes that were at once idyllic and strangely unsettling. Dawson's imaginary places were comprised of past, present and possible future worlds, the vibrantly depicted pastoral imagery making reference to a rich assortment of mythology, folklore and fantasy. In Gallery 2, a different exhibition took as its subject specific real-world localities: the suburban districts and rural territories of modern-day California. These lonely places had been captured by the lens of the influential photographer Robert Adams and were here seen in the form of understated, small-scale, black and white studies.

The contrasts between the works of these artists were, therefore, vivid and engaging. The fields and forests of Verne Dawson's utopian settings appeared to be all the more verdant, for instance, once time had been spent with the arid realities of Adams's desolate American landscapes. And where in Dawson's work the activities of humankind tended to take place beneath starry skies – setting the efforts of communities in a universal context – in Adams' photographs, the hazy polluted atmosphere of these edge-city regions obscured the sky, limiting the horizons. Such immediate contrasts were, however, given additional sharpness by the relation of the works to the architectural characteristics of the galleries: the high-ceilinged main space was a fitting environment in which to encounter Dawson's grand visions, while Gallery 2 served as a suitably intimate context for the contemplative gaze of Robert Adams.

In viewing these separate visions of place, then, it seems valid not only to identify aspects of a relationship between the two but also to consider how the spatial dynamics of *this* place, the Douglas Hyde Gallery, might influence understandings of the work. In designing Gallery 2 (opened in June 2001), the architects McCullough /Mulvin had created what they termed "an intense counterpoint" to the "much larger volume"[1] of the existing gallery, and this architectural argument had evidently become matched by a curatorial approach concerned with making connections and revealing contrasts between disparate forms, themes and spaces. Perhaps it was as a result of this approach that further elements of the Douglas Hyde's architectural distinctiveness – and their relation to the works on display – became heightened. At intervals when making one's way around the gallery for example, external views could be glimpsed through the slender floor-to-ceiling windows, one view offering

[1]Quoted on the website of McCullough Mulvin: Architects and Urban Planners, http://www.mcculloughmulvin.com/pages/type_f1.html

garden scenes, another a combination of exterior concrete walls, overgrown shrubbery and the street beyond. Alongside artworks which principally explored different ways in which nature and culture become intertwined, it was (from certain positions) possible to see low-key exterior scenes showing either nature in 'cultivated', form or disciplined cultural forms being disrupted by unruly nature. This hint of a dialogue between inside and outside was therefore a potential means of thinking beyond the internal points and counterpoints, conceivably broadening the range of ways in which we might seek to understand how gallery spaces contextualise artworks.

For Hal Foster the 'fundamental reorientation' which was to place lasting emphasis on an artwork's context was inaugurated by minimalism. Donald Judd's 'specific objects', for instance, prompted the ongoing exploration of what Foster has described as "the perceptual consequences of a particular intervention in a given site"[2]. At the centre of Judd's work was a desire to understand 'space', an interest which, he believed, was new in art (but certainly not in architecture). In Judd's view, space was not to be thought of as neutral; rather it was "made, indifferently or intentionally" and in his work he developed this concept both by concentrating on the way in which, as he said, "the smallest work of art creates space around it"[3] and also by establishing specific locations for the work in, for instance, Spring Street, New York, or Marfa, Texas. With these specially adapted environments, Judd was attempting to set and fix the spatial terms on which the work would be encountered, aiming for a spareness of detail in the surroundings which was, as Nicholas Serota has written, "a means of ensuring that nothing should interfere with the prime focus of attention, works of art installed in the rooms themselves"[4]. A high value was therefore placed on the notion of contemplation and in certain places, Judd would position chairs or benches in order to encourage a particular kind of relation with the work and the space. In the case of the Chinati Foundation in Marfa, in particular, however, it seems inconceivable that any response to Judd's work could be understood merely in such limited, immediately phenomenological terms – finding one's way to Marfa, after all, involves many hours of driving through rural Texas. The weary pilgrim's response to Judd's works may therefore be as much conditioned by interior arrangements as by time spent in the Chihuahua Desert.

This question of time, it should be added, is one which is identified by Foster as being of specific significance with regard to the innovations of minimalism. Minimalism, Foster says, places a stress "on the temporality of perception"; the meanings of minimalist artworks are, he argues, "produced in a physical interface with the actual world, not in a mental space of idealist conception" and by necessity this involves the positioning of the viewer

[2] Hal Foster, *The Return of the Real*, Cambridge, Massachusetts: MIT Press, 1996, p. 40.

[3] Donald Judd, "21 February 1993", *Donald Judd: Large Scale Works*, exh. cat., New York: The Place Gallery, 1993.

[4] Nicholas Serota, "Donald Judd: A Sense of Place", in Nicholas Serota (ed.) *Donald Judd*, London: Tate Publishing, 2004, p. 107.

[from left:] Exterior, Venetian-Resort-Hotel-Casino, Las Vegas; Rem Koolhaas (Office For Metropolitan Architecture) Guggenheim, Las Vegas, at the Venetian (now closed), showing *The Art of the Motorcycle*, photograph David Heald, © Solomon R Guggenheim Foundation, 2001; Whitney Museum of American Art, 945 Madison Avenue, New York, N.Y., architect: Marcel Breuer and Hamilton Smith (1963-1966), photograph Jerry L. Thompson, N.Y.

[below:] Exterior view of artillery shed housing permanent installation of Donald Judd's *100 untitled works in mill aluminum*, 1982-1986. Collection the Chinati Foundation, Marfa, Texas. Photograph by Florian Holzherr, 2001. © Judd Foundation, licensed by VAGA, New York, NY.
[far right:]Donald Judd, *100 untitled works in mill aluminum*, 1982-1986, detail. Permanent collection the Chinati Foundation, Marfa, Texas. Photograph by Florian Holzherr, 2002. " Judd Foundation, licensed by Vaga, New York, NY.

[5]*Art News* 65, no. 6, October 1966, p. 29.

[6]Marcel Breuer, 'Comments at the Presentation of the Whitney Museum project,' 12 November 1963, reprinted in *Whitney Museum of American Art* by Ezra Stoller, New York: Princeton Architectural Press, 2000, p. 82.

not just in space but in time. 'Time', of course, is also a way of referring to 'history' and a key interest of Foster's is in understanding ways in which the experience of viewing art is historically constituted and situated. A related point might therefore be that in the case of Judd's permanent displays at Marfa, certain historical conditions (the changing realities of "the actual world") are implied by the use of buildings formerly occupied by local residents, businesses and the military – this decline in prosperity created the circumstances for development of the Chinati Foundation and so it must inevitably have a bearing on the 'meaning' of the works.

The flux of history is of course always in the background when we consider how artworks are contextualised by exhibition spaces, and invariably the pressures or possibilities brought about by rapidly changing social and economic conditions produce particular conventions with regard to how art is located in – or separated from – the contemporary world. In certain cases, for example, there has been a manifest determination to situate galleries or museums away from the contingency of life in cities, perhaps in an effort to seek cultural associations of permanence in natural surroundings (Judd at Marfa or Dia:Beacon in upstate New York; even the siting of the Irish Museum of Modern Art in an historic building at the fringes of Dublin city). But also within cities there has been a need to address how the experience of looking at art may be impacted upon by the conditions of the public realm. In designing his Whitney Museum in New York during the 1960s, for instance, Marcel Breuer aimed to create a defensive structure that stood in strict opposition to the frenetic commercialism of its upper East Side location ("a black Crusader Castle among the tearooms and boutiques of Madisonia"[5] as one contemporary review of the building put it) while at the same time making contact with the passer-by. For these reasons Breuer's structure was designed to reach out over the street "[receiving] the visitor before he actually enters the interior of the building"[6], but it also featured stern concrete walls and a 'moat' which would separate the building from the street. Breuer was taking a stand against an unwelcome tide of cultural commodification and he sought to contrast what he termed "the sincerity and profundity of art" with the frivolousness and decadence of the commercial popular culture that defined the building's immediate surroundings. The Whitney Museum, Breuer said "should not look like a business or office building, nor should it look like a place of light entertainment"; the central idea, as the architectural critic

K. Michael Hays has suggested, was for the Whitney to be "a refuge for Art."[7] The Whitney's galleries also subtly demonstrated Breuer's attitude to the modern city through an emphasis on spaces that were on a domestic scale (Breuer believed that the "greatness of art was best apprehended in a parlour") and by the addition of regular visual reminders of the fast-paced world beyond this 'refuge' – the building's distinctive windows were there only "to establish a contact with the outside".

For some contemporary architects and curators, however, such rigidly 'oppositional' dynamics would appear to be a redundant means of establishing an artwork's 'place' in the world. Hans Ulrich Obrist, for instance, has written of how exhibitions have traditionally "emphasised order and stability... but in our own lives, in our social environments, we see fluctuations and instability, many choices and limited predictability."[8] Rather than imagining the gallery space as a refuge, therefore, Obrist advocates "unstable environments" and "connective possibilities" – a position which is perhaps not unrelated to the Douglas Hyde Gallery's tendency to play on possible connections between the exhibited artworks and 'peripheral' elements of the viewing experience. For Obrist, there is a need to "embrace contradictions, to escape from paralyzing categories" and he cites the practice of Rem Koolhaas as an exemplary instance of an architect seeking to meet these challenging requirements. In the museum projects developed by Koolhaas and his Office For Metropolitan Architecture (Guggenheim, Las Vegas; Kunsthal, Rotterdam) a significant interest has been in facilitating "the co-existence of the equivalent of urban noise experiences, and experiences that enable focus and slowness"[9]. This is a combination of inside and outside, public and private, which is in Obrist's view a vital consideration for contemporary curators; and equally therefore, it is an indication of the "expanded field"[10] within which contexts for viewing art must now be understood.

[7] K. Michael Hays, *ibid.*, p. 5.

[8] Hans Ulrich Obrist, 'Battery, Kraftwerk and Laboratory (Alexander Dorner Revisited)', in Carin Kuoni (ed.) *Words of Wisdom: A Curator's Vade Mecum on Contemporary Art*, New York: Independent Curators International, 2001, p. 128

[9] Rem Koolhaas, quoted in *ibid.*, p. 129.

[10] Rosalind Krauss, 'Sculpture in the Expanded Field', in Hal Foster (ed.), *The Anti-Aesthetic: Essays on Postmodern Culture*, New York: New Press, 1998.

Working with an historic space: the Scuola San Pasquale

by Patrick Murphy

When asked to serve as Commissioner for Ireland for the Venice Biennale 2001, I was confronted with the issue that tends to dog most non-Western countries: no national pavilion in the Giardini. With the proliferation of satellite projects around the main event exhibition, space is at a premium on the islands of San Marco and Dorsoduro. Initial scouting by Vittorio Urbani identified three possible sites. The one I chose was selected because it offered two very distinct architectural spaces, though I didn't completely recall their character until I revisited the space in autumn 2000.

I first saw the Scuola one evening in 1998, when the British Council opened an exhibition by the (then-termed) YBAs. The space was darkened, relying on the strong chiaroscuro of theatrical lighting to add shock and impact to a work by the Chapman Brothers. Under the staircase an 8mm projector whirled away showing a Jaki Irvine film. Upstairs, black-outs concealed the physical nature of the room which featured one of Douglas Gordon's epileptic works. Now there was probably a dozen other artists there, but that was all I did (and do) recall. Thinking back, it was the way the Scuola had been used by the British Council, that very professional outfit, that had given me the predisposition to select it.

Grace Weir, *Distance AB,* video, 2000, 4'30", stills courtesy the artist

Meeting the Scuola in the afternoon, with a view to its reservation as a National Pavilion, was a very different matter. Boxed up against the south side of San Francesco della Vigna, it is a very undistinguished building. One enters through an internal porch owing more to DIY than to professional building. The ground floor is a square room, harbouring four pillars that create a further inner square and framing an altar. It is an ecclesiastical room; processional to the altar it then rises to the altarpiece and onward, to a religious painting of a heavenly ascension scene. Flanking each side of the altar are staircases leading to a room of similar dimensions (square on square) but here dedicated to discussions and lectures. Fitted out with chairs, dais and amplification systems, it had been secularized; only small traces of its once-painted ceiling remaining as evidence of its former religious use. One of my strategies for selection of the artists for the Biennale was not to opt for the single participant, but to combine two: one well known the other less so. I was fortunate that this process paralleled the securing of San Pasquale with its double spaces, and even more lucky that the two artists would create work addressing their spaces; work that amplified the architectural and historical character of each of the two areas of the Scuola.

Siobhán Hapaska, installation at the Scuola San Pasquale, Venice Biennale, 2001, courtesy Kerlin Gallery

Siobhán Hapaska immediately connected with the religious nature of the ground floor. She was ambitious to tackle the entire space. One of the problems of working in an historic building is the care one must take when interfering with the fabric. Hapaska's concept was to infill the center square created by the pillars with a forest of hanging, upside-down, Christmas trees. This necessitated the commissioning of engineers to design, fabricate and install a frame of steel I-beams that rested on the ledge of the capitals of the pillars. Then, using steel rope, we were able to suspend over one hundred trees from the lattice work of lines. Hapaska then addressed the altar. In the space of two months, she conceived, shot and edited a ten minute film which was shown on a 50inch plasma screen. Mounted on the altar, it sat perfectly in the center of the space once occupied by the tabernacle.

In the film, two stylised middle-aged and middle class individuals travel to a forest to procure tree trunks, which are cut to the scale of their bodies. They move on to a beach, undress to black body suits, lie along the length of the tree trunks, and then produce a slick plastic curved object that emits a red flashing light – a beacon of sorts. The camera pans from their prostrate bodies over the waves and up into the sky. Following the sight-line created by the camera-pan, took the viewer's eye beyond the plasma screen, bringing the gaze to the ascension painting, and into the clouds that surrounded the feet of the depicted saint. With her upside-down Christmas trees (which literally turn over a sentimental Christian symbol), and her ritualized film (an ironic statement on our unanswered need for divine contact), Hapaska skillfully, and beautifully, toyed with the essential design and former function of the ground floor of the Scuola.

Moving up the staircase, away from the religious space, the upper floor was engaged by Grace Weir. Weir, who mainly works in video, derives much of her material from the philosophy and speculation of cosmic physics, from Newton to Einstein. She also has a more minimalist strategy in her approach to installation. The upper room of the Scuola is about eight meters high, its four walls punctuated with tall windows. For the installation we needed to black out each window, providing suitable conditions for projections. Thus the construction of this secularized space was rendered unseen, its architectural definitions obliterated. Here the idea reigned: ideas as expressed in the moving image of video projection and video screen. At the entrance, Weir presented a ten minute video displayed on a plasma screen. The piece dealt with Einstein's theory of relativity, as expressed through a specific problem detailed by Einstein – how best to measure the distance from a particular point on earth (Potsdammer Platz, Berlin), to a cloud passing above.

Weir's main projection was two-screen, again dealing with the philosophical impossibility of static points of view. A puff-ball cloud floating in the summer sky was filmed from a helicopter. One screen showed an exterior revolution of the gaseous mass – looking in, the other a revolution with the camera pointing away from the cloud – looking out. The vertiginous atmosphere underlined the democracy of viewpoints that is associated with the philosophy of contemporary physics. The clouds also nicely referenced the final sky shot of Hapaska's video. Together the two artists created a site specific narrative: after religion, science. And with science, finite comprehension and endless possibility.

The rationale of the dual spaces of the Scuola and their application to the two separate artists' practices seems very pat from the above description. But it was just that, it may have been serendipitous, but it was nonetheless an entirely appropriate intervention into the architectural character of the two spaces. And yet these things are always planned at some level. Perhaps it had been during that first reconnaissance visit that I began to understand the notion of how each selected artist could adapt and adopt each space, or that within the 2001 Irish participation in the Venice Biennale we had all teamed up together: artists, space and curator.

Grace Weir, *Around Now*, two simultaneous films, 2000, 5'each, stills courtesy the artist

John Gerrard, installation view at the Gallery of Photography, *Viewing Platform, 2003;* lambda prints on aluminium, courtesy the artist

Space for (Digital) Art

by John Gerrard

Zaha Hadid presented a lecture to the Art Institute of Chicago in 1999 in which she showcased and explained some of her celebrated designs for, among others, a fire station, art centre and transport hub. Startling in their fragmented silhouettes and sinuous layouts, one of these works, the art centre, was discussed in relationship to the role of the architect in 'staging' art. In Hadid's own words the architecture offers "a new freedom in the curators' palette, this in turn digests and recomposes the experience of art spectatorship as liberated dialogue with artefact and environment".[1]

[1] From the architects website: http://www.zaha-hadid.com.

As an audience member I was both impressed by the work presented and by the vivacity and clarity of vision of the architect herself. I was also not just a little concerned as to the challenge to artistic autonomy that was being uncritically presented. These buildings are strong buildings, muscular buildings. They are made up of lots of windows, angles, turns, complexity, strange long spaces. They are interesting, sure, but how can I possibly park the lorry

John Gerrard, installation view at Gallery of Photography, *Portrait Diptych* 2003; mixed media

I want to drive into the space to power my upcoming show… bolt the twenty seven hand-made cast-iron speakers to the wall and project my looped DVD???

[2] *ibid.*

There is a strange discursive disjunction between architects and the future, and ongoing, tenants of their buildings. I am not surprised that Hadid's ideas relating to "liberated dialogues between artefact and environment"[2] are directed towards curators, for curators are much more likely to be making instrumental decisions about new art buildings than artists. Artists may well want to create liberated dialogues. Their own liberated dialogues in which the exhibition environment may or may not get a look in. Artists frequently do not want to share the space with anyone, let alone with a fashionably scrubbed wood finish. They want to control the spaces that they show work in utterly. They are energetic. If they need a wall, they will build one.

Think of the approach as 'ideal art space as hangar'. One interesting departure from this is during collaborations between architects and artists when installation strategies are informed by the divergent sensibilities of each party. This is an area of exhibition and gallery design that could be expanded upon. (Anish Kapoor's 1998 Hayward exhibition was a good example of this potential.)

A trip through Chelsea in New York is an edifying experience as to what contemporary artists desire and what perhaps shows contemporary art in all its myriad forms to its best advantage. Maybe it is that dose of cold hard commerce that hones these spaces down to some extreme of functionality. Galleries such as Matthew Marks or Andrea Rosen are, quite literally, cathedrals to contemplation: large, empty and simple, monastic almost. I think of galleries such as these as some of the very few public spaces for quiet contemplation and thought that we have. And what are they? Expensive white boxes, exquisitely produced, with floating walls, polished and floated cement floors, and with high ceilings and recessed windows for natural light. These buildings were mostly concrete garages and warehouses and retain a large measure of that origin in functionality, simplicity and frugality.

A case in point: the Gallery of Photography, Dublin (architect O'Donnell + Tuomey), is a fine gallery. The main gallery, balcony space and small exhibition rooms challenged me somewhat to create works that would work well during my solo exhibition in the gallery in late 2003. It was, luckily, an interesting and not overly weighted challenge. I was surprised however that when showing documentation of the show, a frequent question was to explain why I placed the dark half circle across the floor of the main space. My piece (pictured) *Portrait Diptych* was an interactive work minimally installed on its own (bar one other smaller work on another wall) in the main gallery. Surely the large half-circle on the floor was the gesture, Richard Serra-esque, that completed the work?

But no, that 'work' predated me and is an unnecessary metal track for a hinged wall which swings out to spilt the gallery in two. A rubber wheel could have rendered it redundant. It is an architectural flourish, one so strong as to affect the reading of artworks in the space. Thus the saga of 'open brief' and 'signature building' art galleries goes on. Stunning buildings, lighting up architects' portfolios like mini infernos, and all too often making life difficult for contemporary artists that must work with and in them.

But what about the digital? When fitting in the digital, firstly it is important to remember that every contemporary space worth looking at will be showing all manner of media: photography one month, digital animations the next. Adaptability and simplicity are key, technical details, such as adequate but invisible plug points, embedded wireless connectivity and fully controllable lighting are so mundane as to not require mention in this essay. Coping with the delicacy and vulnerability of the now omnipresent projected light is something that all new galleries must cater for.

Artists require very little when it comes to spaces. A message for architects: try to assist in leaving some budget over from the extraordinary outlay at building stage for day-to-day programming, or there will be more ArtHouse replays[3] (so perhaps terrazzo in the toilets should not be prioritized this time). Make the spaces and surfaces robust, adaptable and repairable. Give artists a space that they can completely control and, at the end of the day, completely dominate. When artists leave the building they will leave it as they found it.

Good design will enable all these activities, poor design acts precisely in reverse.

[3]Arthouse (architect Shay Cleary/Group 91, 1996), a purpose-built and prominent centre for new media in Dublin's Temple Bar Area, closed due to lack of funding in 2003.

Investigations

Introduction by Gemma Tipton

[previous page:] Exterior, *The Irish Pavilion*, O'Donnell + Tuomey Architects, installed in the courtyard of the Irish Museum of Modern Art, 1991, photo John Searle, courtesy the architects

Adifficulty with using the ideas and practices of art criticism to discuss the architecture of arts spaces is that architecture has a definitive practical purpose, so looking at aesthetics and conceptual elements alone won't fully address the issues. On the other hand, architectural criticism has to be more than just a description of form, material and shape, because the aesthetics and conceptual elements of a space obviously play an instrumental role in how the art inside is appreciated and understood. Architecture shapes the spaces in which we live and work. It creates environments. It defines and contributes to atmosphere, ambience, mood and feeling. Architectural historian, Nikolaus Pevsner, called architecture "the most comprehensive of all visual arts," saying it "has a right to claim superiority over the others,"[1] and while one may choose to agree or disagree with him, architecture does play a powerful role in the ways in which a society and its culture operate. So, in addition to the physical, the formal, and the aesthetic; architectural spaces also need to be understood in sociological and philosophical terms. It seems a lot to ask. Perhaps a new critical vocabulary is needed? If that is the case, I would hope it would be one that avoids the pitfalls of jargon, which irritates as much as it occludes the processes of discussing, assessing, of making clear.

[1]Nikolaus Pevsner, *An Outline of European Architecture*, Pelican, Middlesex, 1963, p. 16.

Architectural criticism and analysis today often appears to be at the point which art criticism had reached about thirty years ago. Apart from a few exceptional examples it was not fully engaged (and engaging), being more concerned with its own practices and processes than with those it was intended to discuss. Beyond the art world, few were interested in the theories of art, or in 'why' and 'how' contemporary art works looked the way they did. In the intervening three decades, art criticism and discussion has matured and developed to the point where people are more likely to feel a sense of engagement with the art in major galleries and museums, as well as in our smaller spaces. Art criticism has evolved to a point where it doesn't so much seek to explain art as to offer a way in, a framework for deeper understanding and appreciation – with maybe a judgement or two added for good measure.

The discussion surrounding the Tate Gallery's acquisition of Carl Andre's minimalist work, the 'pile of bricks', also known as *Equivalent VIII*; is a good illustration of this development, and is relevant too as the piece in question has architectural resonances, as well as aesthetic interest. *Equivalent VIII* cost Tate £2,267.00 when it was purchased in 1972, and it was exhibited in 1974 and 1975 without attracting particular attention. In 1976, however, an article in the Sunday Times about recent additions to Tate's collection provoked mass outrage at what was deemed a waste of money. Not only were they expensive, the 'bricks' weren't even 'art'.[2]

[2]The *Sunday Times* article appeared on 15 February 1976. For more information on the controversy, see www.tate.org.uk/archivejourneys/reisehtml/mov_public.htm

Keith Waterhouse's comments in the *Daily Mirror* sum up the general feeling at the time: "Bricks are not works of art. Bricks are bricks. You can build walls with them or chuck them through jeweller's windows, but you cannot stack them two deep and call it sculpture."[3] Actually, there probably was just cause, if not for outrage, at least for expressions of disgruntlement. The work Tate had purchased was actually a fairly meaningless piece of art.

[3]Keith Waterhouse, *Daily Mirror*, 19 Feb 1976

The problem was not that *Equivalent VIII* consisted of one hundred and twenty fire bricks, or even that the one hundred and twenty fire bricks were not the original bricks from the work's first showing in 1966. The problem was that Tate's purchase had rendered the work irrelevant.

As a series, the eight *Equivalent* pieces, each made of an identical number of bricks, and therefore each having exactly the same mass and volume, demonstrated how identical materials could be arranged to produce entirely different shapes and senses of space. The series was a work which cleverly, and beautifully, addressed spatial concepts and ideas relevant to architecture, as well as to art. Purchased in isolation, however, *Equivalent VIII* had nothing to be equivalent to. Referencing nothing, it meant little. None of the outcry about the purchase of the piece considered this point. Tate had bought *Equivalent VIII* at a time when 'it's rubbish' was adjudged a valid criticism of art.

Thirty years on, Tate still occasionally courts controversy, especially with its Turner Prize selections, but now the outcry over Damien Hirst's formaldehyde animals, or Tracey Emin's installations tends to be more critically informed. Punters may still declare 'it's rubbish', but they will be prepared, and ready, to add a 'how' or a 'why' to their judgements. This level of engagement is (obviously) good for art, and plays a crucial part in an art world that is dynamic, lively and *relevant*.

So when will this happen for architecture?

Because of the functional role of architecture, it is even more important for architectural discussions to be inclusive and engaging. We need to be able to say 'this building is rubbish' (if we want to), but we also need to be able to address that crucial *why*? In order to focus on the practical aspects of these discussions, the essays in this chapter consider spaces for art both as elements of the arts infrastructure, and in terms of planning and strategy. In addition, two in-depth case studies assess two different forms of arts space. The Millennium Court Arts Centre in Portadown (architect Harry Porter) is a conversion of an existing building, located in a community context, yet with an ambitious programme of contemporary visual and verbal art. It includes digital and new media facilities. Meanwhile, the Lewis Glucksman Gallery (architect O'Donnell + Tuomey) is a new-build space with an experimental and innovative design. These spaces were chosen to reflect the diversity of how our spaces for art are conceived and created.

Returning to the question that runs throughout this book: *is there such a thing as the perfect space*? The answer is still: *probably not...* But knowing more about how and why museums and galleries come about, the elements which have led to the design decisions, the selection of architects, the spatial arrangements, the issues and the compromises, should bring discussions of architecture a step closer to our understanding more about architecture itself, to knowing *why* it is that we know what we like...

Glenn Howells Architects, exterior;
Market Place, Armagh, 2000, photo
courtesy The Market Place

Arthouses of the Pentapolis

by Damien Coyle

A great city is not to be confounded with a populous one

Aristotle, Politics, 4th Century B.C.

In 2002, Her Majesty, Queen Elizabeth II, conferred city status upon the towns of
Lisburn and Newry, bringing the number of cities in Northern Ireland to five. All cities
crave distinctiveness, recognition of their personality and uniqueness. Belfast is seen as
the capital, Derry as the independent second city-state and Armagh as the ecclesiastical centre of the island, steeped in history and tradition. Meanwhile, the two new cities struggle to
find that separateness, difference; that sense of identity. Lisburn suffers from its geographic
proximity to Belfast, and whilst Newry might have a sense of its own values and spirit, it sits
at the border on the entrance to no-man's land.

One of the processes used to create a sense of identity is through definition and re-promo-
tion of 'how' and 'what' you are at a cultural level. We have seen this process in Glasgow,
Liverpool, Dublin, Cork, and more recently in Gateshead with the opening of the Baltic.
This goal is achieved, in part, through the promotion of cultural programming and/or
through the physical cultural infrastructure, the architecture itself. The architecture can also
be used as a platform for creativity/creative expression. With building and design, however,
come problems. The more cynical among us need look no further than Seneca who said
'those were happy times before the architects and builders came along', or Frank Lloyd
Wright: 'the physician can bury his mistakes, but the architect can only advise his client to
plant vines'.

One of the first questions to ask is whether to opt for new-build or refurbishment? Another is cost, and following on from that, the next is how to fund, or who will pay? When the questions are answered, the process usually proceeds or moves back to the drawing board for something affordable, i.e. an 'affordable something' which often meets no one's needs or ambitions. Few seem to take the 'do nothing' option in the predictable land of the feasibility study. But there is always one certainty (like death and taxes) and that is that in all this building and development, the visual arts will not be well served.

The impact of the Arts Council of Northern Ireland's National Lottery programme in providing the financial store to drive forward the infrastructural needs of the arts cannot be underestimated. It is also important to note that whilst the Lottery Department had its own strategy for the distribution of Lottery funding, not all of the above towns/cities benefited to a comparable degree. Whilst Belfast, Derry, Armagh and Lisburn have profited from multi-million pound awards for large-scale infrastructural projects, Newry has not, and as a result is distinct in its lack of new-build dedicated arts infrastructure. A description of these cities, begins to highlight some of the issues that need to be addressed in the creation of a positive and productive infrastructure for the visual arts in Northern Ireland.

Lisburn Borough Council used to deliver its arts provision through the Harmony Hill Arts Centre, a faux Tudor country manor set in mature gardens on the outskirts of the town. Harmony Hill Arts Centre required access to public or private transport, due to its location, and there was limited access for disabled people. However, there was a dynamism and character in the building, and an interesting and diverse programme, given the limited space and physical resources available. Harmony Hill had a reputation for the quality of its visual arts programme, including its artist-in-residence scheme. Then the burghers of Lisburn decided they needed to create a new monument (to themselves, perhaps), and set about developing Lagan Valley Island. Lagan Valley Island is an enigma, part business and conference centre, part local authority offices and civic centre, part café/restaurant, and also home to the Island Arts Centre.

Architecturally the building reflects the garrison town history of Lisburn. One interpretation could see the building as a defensive bawn, bunkered down on its own island. One would anticipate, when entering through the main doorway into the large circular reception area, a welcoming festoon of contemporary art in a spacious central gallery. Instead the visitor is greeted by a large empty space. To the left is the generously-proportioned and naturally lit café/restaurant area, while straight ahead leads to the entrance of the theatre/ conference facility. To the right, a corridor with signposts towards artists-in-residence, music studio, workshop space, eventually leads to a reception area for the Island Arts Centre.

The tragedy here is that the Arts Centre is tidied away at the back of the complex. Though it also has its own entrance and its own reception, its being part of this bigger whole has also meant that what was seen as a defined service via Harmony Hill has lost its full sense of identity. Architecturally one could accept full integration, but this is compartmentalisation that only serves to isolate, celebrating exterior form over interior function. Additionally, one of the two exhibition areas suffers from being designed as a multi-functional space, where the needs of visual arts exhibitions do not seem to have been paramount. On a more positive note (unlike many other capital build projects), Lisburn did include an integrated arts scheme to incorporate newly commissioned artworks into the building from the beginning.

[from top:]Jacqueline Salloum, installation view, 2005, Void, photo Mark Willett; Amanda Coogan, performance still, Context Gallery, *Molly: Bloomsday,* 2004, courtesy Context Galleries

Derry/Londonderry, the maiden or stroke city, is administered by Derry City Council. Derry has had a particular penchant for arts facilities located in old school buildings (Orchard, Foyle, Playhouse and Verbal Arts). All were originally established by independent organisations with financial support provided by the Council. Derry City Council is also responsible on one hand for developing the Orchard as its own visual arts resource with an international visual arts reputation, and on the other for its demise. Money has instead been reinvested (along with the budget for the now-closed Foyle Arts centre) in a new state-of-the-art theatre. We should remember that it was the Orchard Gallery, and its then-curator Declan McGonagle, that placed Derry in the international arts scene back in the late seventies (if you don't include Dana, Phil Coulter and the Undertones). Its reputation at this time had been more linked to violence, unemployment, poverty and disadvantage; and the Orchard was one of the sparks that ignited the flame that brought about a climate change.

Temporibus Nostris, time is lost – and also flies, and the contribution that the Orchard had made to its cultural development seems to have been forgotten by Derry City Council. Despite the protests from local communities, they also built a 'monument' in the form of the single art form Millennium Theatre. The option (outlined in an ACNI strategy document), to upgrade St Columbus Hall, was ignored in favour of an expensive new-build. In this instance, I have no complaint here about the gallery being located in the coffee bar or in a corridor on the way to the toilets: there is no gallery.

Following the closure of the Orchard, the primary visual arts provision in Derry has been, up until recently, with the Context Galleries. The Context, and its then founder/curator Hugh Mulholland (now at the Ormeau Baths Gallery), built its reputation on the quality of its programme, not on the quality of the physical resources. The gallery is, in effect, a classroom, clad with partitioned walls to form the ubiquitous white cube. While having a high degree of autonomy, it is part of the overall Playhouse complex.[1] Whilst the programming reputation of the Context has been generally perceived to be of a high level, the physical resources are considered poor and inadequate. Years of underfunding have not been kind, but it has survived the Orchard. Void Art Centre, which opened in 2005 in the Old City Factory on Patrick Street, brings another visual arts venue to Derry. The space, a former shirt factory, was originally designed by Robert Young in 1861. Void houses gallery and studio spaces and was converted for use as an arts space by Michael Hegarty.

Armagh, an ecclesiastical city containing two cathedrals and (losing) one university, opted for the Theatre and Arts Centre model. The Market Place can be approached by two routes, one taking you to the main entrance where a Palladian stairway leads to a series of interlinked Loos-style cubes, with more than a soupçon of Van Der Rohe styling. The second approach is through the multi-storey car park, shared with the rabbit warren that is St Patrick's Trian and the cinema (the interlinking-cube effect by architects Glenn Howells is more obvious from this latter angle). Visually the building pays homage to simplicity and modernism; there is no arabesque, cartouche or running dog here. Again, as with many new multi-disciplinary arts facilities, the driver is the theatre. Armagh, famous for its ancient magic, managed to make a workshop space vanish from the original plans (it materialised as a storeroom instead). However, Armagh differs from many of these new resources in that it has made an effort to create a fitting visual art gallery, one that really is the white cube in all its glory. It shares a functional quality with the dull grey concrete space of the Douglas Hyde gallery, but thanks to a creative use of natural light and wall surfaces it has an inviting, contemplative atmosphere. I once spent a whole day in a gallery in New York, sitting in a white cube, where a Barnett Newman painting was hung on each of the four walls. Armagh has captured that sort of Zen-like meditative quality. What the Market Place gallery does share with the Island Arts Centre's visual arts space is that both are tucked around the corner from reception, seemingly out of harm's way. This would appear to be yet another sign of local government's embrace of theatre as the acceptable face of the arts, and the ambivalence toward, almost fear of, the visual arts. Remembering that, in Northern Ireland, local authorities have a statutory responsibility for arts and culture activities (under recreational provision) one wonders at what level, if at all, local authorities would embrace arts and culture were that not so.

The city of Newry, the administrative seat of Newry & Mourne District Council, is in many ways the poor cousin of the other cities in terms of its physical arts infrastructure. Perhaps they more wisely invest their money in programming before physical presence? Newry has an Arts Centre located in an old public building that sits adjacent to the canal. The Sean Hollywood Arts Centre possesses all the standard requirements for a regional/rural arts centre: gallery spaces, an auditorium, workshop space, café etc. There is also a darkroom. The main gallery is a respectable size and is suitable for the nature and scale of visual arts programming in the city. The gallery (and the centre) has no pretensions, yet it serves its function. Newry has other resources that are used for arts purposes, but the regeneration of the city has focused more on commercial elements rather than on the cultural. One of the other cultural resources is Altnaveigh House, a centre for those who wish to learn about and celebrate Protestant cultural tradition. This is a unique resource within Northern Ireland and welcomes people of all traditions. Again, this is located in an old building which has undergone a number of upgrades. Newry's reputation in the arts is based on music and theatre, particularly amateur dramatics. Coming from the 'No need for a physical resource' tradition of the arts I have a particular affinity with the Newry and Mourne approach.

[1] The Georgian period Playhouse has been seen on *Restoration*, a television programme in which historic buildings compete for the public vote, and ultimately cash, in order to complete refurbishment or restoration work.

Mike Hogg, installation at *Solid Space*, 2004, Ormeau Baths Gallery, photo courtesy Ormeau Baths Gallery

Visually, Newry is a hybrid of a border town, part northern with a southern twist, mixed with a blend of historic market town. It has a mix of ingredients: throw in one part through road, one part canal, one part dual carriageway, and add a gateway to the republican heartlands (north and south) of the border. It is not an architecturally attractive place, although it has buildings of historic/architectural merit, but there is a spirit and vitality which some of the other cities do not have. When Newry was elevated to city status one cynic was heard to comment, "See Naples and die, see Newry and Mourne".

We come finally to Belfast with its triumvirate of arts centres. There is the Crescent, a former school,[2] Culturlann which is housed in a former Church on the Falls Road and addresses arts and culture through the medium of the Irish language and the Old Museum arts Centre which was, not surprisingly, a former museum. All have had different identities over the years and have settled well into the functions of an arts centre. There had been discussion of a potential merger of two, to pave the way for a new-build arts facility. Surprisingly, this has not materialised.

Culturlann would have the visual arts lower down its agenda than the others. Old Museum has an acceptable, and almost church-like, gallery space. This exhibition area can be extended into a second ground floor space, dependent upon the exhibition. The main gallery is small, can be intimate, and has demonstrated scope for

[3]The Crescent has also been seen on a former series of *Restoration*; it didn't 'win'.

a diverse range of programming. The Crescent, like the Playhouse, has given its visual arts programming responsibilities to another. In this case it is the Fenderesky Gallery, housed in what would have been (at the time I worked in the Crescent) the best appointed portion of the complex. Running on two floors, Fenderesky Gallery is probably the best of the small-to-medium-scale visual arts galleries. Positioned on the right hand corner of the building, the large Victorian windows let in an abundance of natural light on the front and side façades. Programming has been criticised for its 'salon' approach, showing a limited range of artists. However, whilst not condoning the limitations of this approach, I have experienced some challenging and high quality shows at the Fenderesky, especially when Jamshid Mirfenderesky has curated themed, or group, exhibitions. The main issue for the Crescent is that it always seems to be on the verge of closure due to physical structural difficulties. There is a feeling of perpetual decay, or what medical professionals refer to as 'terminal drop'; the age at which the next stopping point is death. However, the Crescent now has a Lottery grant (for which they fought hard) and it is hoped that this will secure survival.

Belfast does, of course, have a dedicated contemporary visual arts facility in the Ormeau Baths Gallery (OBG). No prizes for guessing that its former function was as a municipal baths/swimming pool. The vote is split on whether OBG is a good gallery space or a poor one. I'm on the pro side. I believe OBG is a respectable facility for a city of the scale of

Belfast. There are four reasonably-sized spaces, each with a discrete, yet distinctive, character. The overall venue is flexible and adaptable. For a long period, the option of OBG moving to the proposed new Belfast City Arts Centre was discussed. OBG ultimately took the strategically correct (in my view) decision, and withdrew from the consortium. The machinations leading up to this decision, and the potential for negative fall out, provide enough substance for a separate article. On the curatorial front, OBG is far ahead of its rivals, with a quality and diversity of programming that encompasses the local, national and international. Director, Hugh Mulholland has taken over the cutting edge that was held by the Orchard back in the 80s, and has sharpened it some more.

Looking at these examples, I would conclude that the visual arts suffer when located within a new multi-purpose project. There would also appear to be more of a sense of dedicated space within older buildings, despite their physical limitations. In new-builds there can be a struggle for space, for identity and recognition, and in some instances, dignity. There is, in terms of the arts, a contradiction to the adage (in commercial property development) that it is cheaper to create new space than it is to buy and renovate old. New buildings can gravely suppress the sense of identity of a previously high-profile and energetic platform for creativity. Sometimes it is best to pay more for the recognition that the visual arts deserve. It may not always make the best business sense, but the arts is about much more than balancing the books.

Finally, while supporting the visual arts within existing buildings, I would add the caveat that sensitivity to the original design must be coupled with the recognition of the functional needs of a contemporary visual arts space, and the physical needs of its clients. Disabled access within existing buildings can be tricky, if not impossible. Yet I do believe that new is not always best, and that programming should be paramount. Form should follow function, but until we have the courage of that conviction amongst those whose job it is to carve the form, we are destined to have to work with the second-rate instead. Where are the people with the imagination to create visual art environments which live up to Brancusi's description of architecture as 'inhabited sculpture' or Goethe's reference to architecture as 'frozen music'?

The Crescent Arts Centre, Belfast; photo Séamus Loughran, courtesy Crescent Arts Centre

Cotton Court, The Cathedral Quarter, Belfast; conversion architects: Manouge, Courtesy Laganside/ McCadden design

Inside the Cultural Quarter

by Marianne O'Kane

Despite our familiarity with the term, cultural quarters are a surprisingly recent phenomenon. The natural development of cultural activity, concentrated in particular areas, occurred in London's Soho, the Left Bank in Paris, New York's SoHo (South of Houston St), and to a lesser extent in La Ribera in Barcelona. London, Paris and New York's success signalled the value of this type of regional creative and social activity in cities, and highlighted the potential of deliberately fostering such enterprise for urban renewal and revitalisation. With collective plans for urban regeneration comes the concomitant desire to infuse vitality into a given space. The most successful method is acknowledged to be by means of artistic and cultural investment.

The United States' 'historic district' can be seen as a forerunner of the planned cultural quarter and this is a sector that has been incorporated into a range of US cities. Renowned landscape planner Frederick Law Olmsted established the first US historic district in 1931 in Charleston, South Carolina. The concept was motivated principally by the desire to preserve historic heritage; the built environment was safeguarded for the urban public with networks of streets preserved and landscaped accordingly. In urban areas, the natural balance of history and modernity was to be effected in the ideal of the cultural quarter. This plan coincided with the Loosian belief that all culture depended on an element of continuity with the past and adequate retention of urban identity. In these instances of course, the 'culture' is one of preservation, and so the architecture is that of the past. The term 'cultural quarter' is also of American origin and it dates from the early eighties; describing districts in Lexington, Massachusetts and Pittsburgh, Pennsylvania. In development philosophy, Britain followed the States swiftly with 'culture' established as a byword in planning documents from the late eighties. Sheffield Cultural Industries Quarter was the first such development in the UK.

John Montgomery posits that "Cultural quarters should be expected to have a more active and discernible public realm than is generally found in an urban environment."[1] As a planning concept, the cultural quarter is designed to be largely self-sustainable; cultural elements function in tandem with private sector developments in the area. This means that the successful quarter's activity should cater for a variety of consumer activity, balanced between formal and informal, cultural and leisure; and should provide night-time activity and venues, to complement day-time providers. Within a given quarter there are generally integrated programmes representing specialist retail, culture, residential and hospitality industries. Landscaping with social movement as a prime factor is also an essential feature. There should be adequate meeting/gathering spaces to enable outdoor events and the areas are largely pedestrianised to facilitate a more socially and culturally intensive experience. Thus the ideal cultural quarter acts as an urban space for aesthetic awareness, relaxation, social interaction and general edification. It could be considered as the contemporary architectural equivalent to the city park – an urban escape.

[1] John Montgomery, *Cultural Quarters as Mechanisms for Urban Regeneration: A Review.* Leading Diversity: Planning Congress Adelaide, 2003, p. 10.

When establishing such a quarter one could argue that developers are creating a cultural ghetto, when instead they should attempt to effect a more comprehensive integration into the entire city space. Contemporary society, however, demands ease of access to culture and leisure facilities. Diversity of provision and the general absence of traffic in cultural quarters enable this. Sensitive, careful planning and sustained consultation are essential to any cultural development and it is crucial to resist the temptation to incorporate a quarter into any city demonstrating inadequate cultural provision. It must be the appropriate solution. The relative success of the fifteen-year evolution of planned cultural quarters lies in the novelty of the enterprise and limited examples, more or less suited to their urban context. Cultural quarters would be inappropriate in many cities and there are equally imaginative regenerative solutions yet to be employed. Even though cultural quarters are ideally self-sustaining, cultural organisations within a quarter will still require the same subsidies and supports that they did before the quarter came about. The area must also be well-served by public transport, and tourist access should be relatively easy. While the Guggenheim's role in regenerating Bilbao is a favourite example of culture's financial and tourist-pulling muscle, it shouldn't be forgotten that the city of Bilbao also invested heavily in a new airport, designed by Santiago Calatrava, and a new underground metro system, designed by Sir Norman Foster. The existence of an artistic and cultural heritage upon which to capitalise also helps.

It is noteworthy that a most frequently referred to model of a cultural quarter in Europe is Temple Bar in Dublin, considering that its inauguration in cultural regeneration terms was just over a decade ago in 1991. The area (of twenty-eight acres) is one of the oldest parts of Dublin, dating back to 1259. In the early eighties, due to low rates, the locality had already secured a diversity of arts and alternative organisations, but the area had been earmarked for demolition and redevelopment as a bus station. In 1989, Temple Bar Development Council, consisting of arts groups and businesses in the area began campaigning for cultural regeneration in the area. Group 91, (taking the name from the year of their initiation), a consortium of Dublin-based architects was responsible for the key renovations and new builds within the Temple Bar area. The most experimental and manifest examples of architecture in the quarter were for cultural use. There is no question in regeneration terms that Temple Bar has been a major success and yet culturally the achievement is less certain. One could argue that Temple Bar's cultural development should have continued unchecked, without official intervention. Natural progression attracted an extensive young audience and the area enjoyed relative prosperity. In this regard, regeneration and official cultural status was imposed on a somewhat dilapidated but otherwise thriving cultural sector.

A decade on, a number of the key cultural agencies and organisations have been forced out due to commercial competition and high rents. Perhaps in retrospect Temple Bar tenants might have preferred not to be redeveloped as a 'cultural quarter'. The disappearance of ArtHouse and DesignYard are testimony to this fact in visual art and craft terms. If Temple Bar was similar to Soho in the beginning, perhaps it would be more apposite to compare it to Covent Garden now, where the cultural organisations that are still operating have to do battle with the ever-growing pub-crawling crowds. A great many tourists love both Temple Bar and Covent Garden, so it should be noted that success can be defined on many different levels. In this vein, it is also worth noting that culture is dynamic and fluid; a thriving area now may become seedy or down-at-heel in ten years' time. Planned cultural quarters attempt to freeze this process, with the result that they also run the risk of becoming artificial, and even possessed of a 'theme-park' quality.

[2] Laganside Guide 2002-2003 – *Past Achievement/Future Opportunity*. BPC Magazines, Bucks., 2003.

[3] Laganside *Annual Report and Accounts 2002-2003*.

In Belfast, it is redundant city space that has been the subject of revitalisation, and the urban cityscape has benefitted. Established by government in 1989, Laganside Corporation received international recognition in 2002 from the Organisation for Economic Co-operation and Development (OECD), as "one of the best examples of urban regeneration in Europe"[2]. The organisation's commitment to arts and culture has been clearly stated since its inception. The most visible product of Laganside's arts strategy so far is the remarkable public art presence throughout the fabric of Belfast City. Since 1998, Laganside has been responsible for placing thirty artworks throughout its 200 hectare area.[3] In 1998, a vision had been formulated by Laganside to establish a cultural quarter in Belfast. Unlike Dublin, this new 'Cathedral Quarter' had not naturally acquired resident arts organisations before Laganside's intervention, and the development has enabled a number of the city's key arts providers to obtain adequate space and a central location in line with their individual requirements. Furthermore, in contrast to Temple Bar, Cathedral Quarter had been more or less 'dead' space, particularly after 6pm (the time when Shaftsbury Square becomes the unofficial city centre of Belfast) and one would hope that it will offer a counterbalance to cultural and entertainment provision in the University area. This quarter should play a crucial role in promotion, not only of its residents, but also of cultural organisations throughout the city as it provides a focus for activity, and can be a central information point for activities going on outside its own area. There is a broad network of artists' collectives and studio groups located in Belfast that the general population are unaware of, and it should not be the role of a cultural quarter to suck culture away from the rest of the city, and 'ghettoise' it within its own precincts.

The historical relevance of the chosen area is secure, as it is one of Belfast's oldest districts, and in terms of scale it marginally exceeds Temple Bar at thirty acres. Significantly, the College of Art is incorporated into the quarter's boundaries, and this echoes the proximity of the National College of Art and Design to Temple Bar, acknowledging the importance of provision of access to future practitioners and creative producers. The most substantial cultural provision in the quarter is under the Managed Workspace Scheme, where Laganside are accommodating a diverse range of established and emerging arts and craft organisations at affordable rates. These include Belfast Print Workshop, Vision Craft Collective and Belfast Exposed.

While the progress to date is significant, and includes Writer's Square, a major outdoor public space for social interaction and events, perhaps the most crucial development is yet to come. Laganside, in conjunction with the Arts Council of Northern Ireland and DCAL, is discussing plans for a major city centre arts centre in the Talbot Street development. The absence of such a focal point for the arts in Belfast has been acknowledged and lamented for decades. Coupled with the integral presence of the art college in Cathedral Quarter, such a centre would signal national and international cultural appeal for Belfast.

Europe's most recent international, and somewhat controversial, counterpart to Belfast and Dublin is Vienna. The stamp of history on the city of Vienna is unmistakable and its new Museum Quarter is one of the ten largest of its kind in the world. Architects Ortner and Ortner have quite literally poured stark modernity into the belly of eighteenth and nineteenth century history. Within the yard of the former Imperial Court Stables now stand two huge contrasting monolithic cubes. On one side is the Leopold Museum in white limestone and on the other stands the black basalt Museum of Modern Art (MuMOK[4]– the largest central European Museum for Modern Art). Here, the core is composed of modern high density visual art venues, while the old buildings in the vast complex house cultural organisations, cafes and some specialist retail outlets. Unlike Europe's other quarters, Vienna is an example of existing architectural infrastructure and public spaces redeveloped to satisfy cultural requirements. This could hardly be described as a natural synthesis of tradition and modernism or cultural respect for the past. This radical use of space uses culture's liberal rationale to subvert the limitations and boundaries of historical context.

[4] Museum für Moderne Kunst

The challenge in the creation of cultural quarters essentially resides in the fact that planners and architects are faced with the task of reconciling individual buildings and the overall architectural context, with the needs and requirements of 'cultural' providers. The emergence of cultural quarters as architectural playgrounds and showcases for innovation, while being a celebration of all that's exciting in architecture can have a negative effect on the functionality of these buildings as arts spaces. MuMOK in Vienna has already had an interior redesign, and the limitations of Temple Bar's now defunct ArtHouse (with its plate glass windows for viewing digital art; Shay Cleary) have been discussed elsewhere. It could be argued that Temple Bar's Gallery of Photography (O'Donnell + Tuomey) relates more to its context in Meeting House Square than it does to the needs of photographic and light-sensitive works that are to be exhibited inside. Bilbao's Guggenheim pulls in the crowds, but is certainly not ideal as an art space.

Communication and understanding on both sides should provide the key to this dilemma, and recognition has to given to the opposing needs of tourism (accessibility, immediacy, a 'wow' factor), and to the ongoing, sustainable development needs of cultural organisations (sympathetic spaces, decent revenue rather than just capital support, affordable rents, facilitation of cultural rather than entertainment profile). Due to the extensive organisation and capital involved, longevity is a crucial consideration, and therefore private sector investment in the quarter becomes the mainstay of its sustainability, and yet the excesses of private enterprise, in the guise for example of 'superpubs' has to be curbed. The future of cultural quarters is difficult to predict but when successful they become a crucial asset in raising a city's cultural profile.

Integration:
a multi-use space in an historic building

by Ciarán Mackel

Gallery 1, Milliennium Court Arts Centre, 2002, photo courtesy Milliennium Court Arts Centre

The image of Portadown has for many people been in a downward spiral for generations. Perhaps this started even before the current '66 – '96 conflict in Northern Ireland began; even before the death of Robert Hamill, and the notorious exploits of killer gangs and bombing campaigns. Why is this important? Because memories mark a place with as indelible a stamp of history as do the keystone and brickwork of the former market building in which the Millenium Court Arts Centre (MCAC) is housed.

Memories are attached to places and objects, to buildings, streets and landscapes, and a lively and relevant arts centre has to build from that repository. It has to afford a creative rediscovery so that memory is not lost. MCAC was intended by its Board; was designed by its architects (Harry Porter Architects, Portadown); and now seeks, operationally and programmatically, to challenge the remembered image and psyche of the place. The aim seems to be that rehabilitation and creativity will be complementary. Is there a resonance here with Tony Fretton's insistence, in his own work, that architecture includes the site with all its traces? Time will allow judgement on whether the Centre will stand as a contemporary cultural citadel or as an impotent attempt to impact on a wider process beyond its control. MCAC's tag-line is 'altering perceptions' and it has an unenviable task if it wishes to reach the aspirations of its energetic and enthusiastic manager, Megan Johnston, to be the 'Baltic' of Northern Ireland (no vernacular reverse pun intended) or to have an equal standing, in artistic terms, with Dublin, Glasgow, et al. The ambition is worthy and could make sense and prove a reality given Johnston's curriculum vitae – previously working in the the Weisman and Walker Art Centres, both in Minnesota; New York's Metropolitan Museum of Art, and at the Irish Art Centre in New York, before moving to Portadown.

MCAC occupies a total of 10,000 square feet primarily on the first floor of the converted redbrick building. It is a visual, verbal and multi-media arts centre with two galleries, an audio-visual / sound studio, video-editing suite, a verbal arts education room, a visual arts workshop, darkroom and an artist-in-residency suite. The ground floor still retains its original purpose of a market place, part of which incorporates retail units selling craft goods made by local crafts people. In their promotional material MCAC state that the aspect of the market is an important one 'in that the daily exchange between the market people and the public can continue but also be incorporated with, and work alongside, the cultural exchange of ideas of creativity with the Arts Centre'.

The insertion of the Arts Centre in the historic fabric is ably handled, though the use of bronze tinted glass in the ground floor retail units diminishes their potential to create an active and necessary relationship with the street and the people who use it. The decision adds to an anonymous, almost corporate, feel at street level. The central portico makes the entrance, and once through the main door everything seems too early in the sequence of interior spaces. The architecture wants to be about an active plinth containing all the public and support spaces, with the galleries held above under the long roof glazing, but it is compromised by the briefing requirement to include tiny, tiny retail rooms relating to a market hall which is too infrequently used and which does not seem to work – with the result that these same retail rooms are mostly vacant. The anticipated plinth is too empty; the shop is devoid of stock. Is it that stock is not affordable? And if it was, would the requirement for staffing necessitate a rethink of the reception area and the very real need for a first point of contact, given that the active spaces and the galleries are on the first floor? The architects have, unfortunately, relied on gesture to mark the public procession from the ground floor, the uses of a red wall and a purple wall are perhaps too obvious and 'fashionable' to contain the space of the principal gallery or to make a believable place.

Once in the Arts Centre proper, the compromises on the architectural or aesthetic intention are undoubtedly due to the conflicting financial restraints and to the requirement for multi-use. These have impacted negatively on the functionality of the spaces, but are these spaces ultimately satisfactory? Art on a first floor simply requires two things: one, proper lifts for access of large works, and two, controllable day lighting. Both are problematic here. During a visit (in 2004) to view the exhibition of Shane Cullen's *The Agreement*, the strong daylight cast unfortunate shadows across the sections of the Agreement relating to 'Policing' and 'Justice': a sign from above? Compromise and the multi-use requirement have produced a verbal arts space that is too low, too bright acoustically; it is a secondary art gallery that is just that – a secondary space. Why, too, are the offices located directly off the main gallery space? Their location reduces privacy in the working office spaces and requires a particular working strategy during opening events and launches. But what does constitute an 'ideal' space, if there is any such thing? German artist Georg Baselitz in his essay, 'Four Walls And Skylight Or Better No Picture On The Wall' probably identified the preferred standard for artists. "My decision is very clear, I believe the museum can only be understood as a protectory for a work of art, a place in which the viewing of artwork must be possible in a simple, complete, unhindered and unpretentious way (…) For this, space, walls, few doors, no side windows, light from above, no partitions, no baseboards, no base mouldings, no panelling, no shiny floors, and finally, no color, either."[1]

MCAC is though a place of huge potential. To quote Alvaro Siza's words as the ambition for MCAC: "to rediscover the magical strangeness, the peculiarity of obvious things."[2] Enthusiastic staff and an excellent programme of exhibitions, events and activities includ-

[1] *Museum Architektur, Texte und Projekte von Künstlern*, Walther König, Cologne, 2000.
[2] Alvaro Siza, *Architecture Writings*, Skira, Milan, 1997, from *Quaderns d'Arquitectura i Urbanisme*, no. 159, Oct.-Dec. 1983.

ing 'the exhibition of the woman with the dead things around her neck' (as a local resident remarked). This same Alice Maher portrait exhibition (2003) attracted a full page review in the Portadown Times – a first, probably, for that paper and a welcome sign of engagement, or at least a response to provocative portraiture. The mixed programme attempts to attract the local townspeople with book launches; music events; exhibitions; classes and work-shops; talks by visual artists and a varied community outreach programme in a series of events that permeate the building.

MCAC is run by Portadown 2000, an urban regeneration board which has no artists on its board but does have an Arts Advisory Committee made up of artists, collectors, communi-ty activists, teachers and business people. For a number of years Portadown 2000 has been a catalyst for change and improvement in the town. Its wide remit embraces the provision of town centre management, the development of the town centre and its environs, and the physical regeneration of Portadown. The Arts Centre, then, was the result of a partnership between the Regeneration Board and the local Borough Council.

In the late nineteenth and early twentieth century, Portadown was well established as a mar-ket town with a wide variety of markets and fairs being held virtually every day of the week. As Portadown grew in importance as a transportation hub (it still remains one of the few stops for the Belfast – Dublin express train), its market character developed into commer-cial retailing. In 1929, the Borough Council erected the purpose-built Municipal Central Markets (architect unknown) on the site of the Shambles at the corner of William Street and Market Street – the principal spine of the town. The location of the Central Market build-ing, immediately adjacent to a row of derelict houses, presented the opportunity for Portadown 2000 to not only renovate and develop the Markets building but also to regen-erate William Street. Flagship regeneration was the name of the game. Hope became the plan. Hope that the Millennium Court would be the stimulus to regenerate not only the building and the streets but also the community life of the town. It is an Arts-led regener-ation strategy, though, that does not seem to include a long term funding strategy other than a reliance on Borough Council funding with all the inherent longer term difficulties that may entail.

It is the agenda of improving the community life of the town and the need to appeal to potential shifting funding priorities that defines the multi-use nature of this Arts Centre. This is, of course, a common position for all Arts centres. As Vivien Burnside, among others, has written, such a "multi-use facility does at least offer a route for a broader constituency into the arena of contemporary visual art." And we desperately need that. Portadown, like most towns in Northern Ireland, if not throughout Ireland, has a poor visual culture, notwithstanding the efforts of many good people (notably Victor Sloan in the case of Portadown). This Arts centre has to serve many masters. It has to be a neutral venue acceptable in cross community terms; it has to be a vibrant tourist attraction; it has to provide facilities which did not exist at its beginnings; it has to be a focus for co-operation for the two main cultural traditions, and …oh yes, it has to do something with/for the visual arts. It has an almost impossible task. Is it perfect? No! Has it done the best possible job, given the circumstance and the huge agenda – to regenerate an area of town and solve the legacy of the troubles? …Well?

Conversation: James Kerr and Gemma Tipton on the making of an arts space

All images: Millennium Court Arts Centre, architect for the conversion: Harry Porter, 2002, courtesy Milliennium Court Arts Centre

Gemma Tipton: You were the first director of the company, Kaleidoscope, that was responsible for the development of the Millennium Court Arts Centre. At what point did you enter the building and design process?

James Kerr: As a background to the project, Kaleidoscope was a volunteer arts group in Portadown which had been formed with the idea of putting together a project that could access some of the Lottery money coming into Northern Ireland. They had seen what had been achieved for the arts in places like Derry and Armagh. One of the main artistic voices on the Kaleidoscope Board was Victor Sloan. Kaleidoscope teamed up with an organisation, Portadown 2000, a small urban-regeneration group that included members of the Borough Council. Between them both organisations were able to make credible bids to many different funding sources, for example over a million pounds was drawn down from the National Lottery (as administered by the Arts Council of Northern Ireland) for the Millennium Court.

And how was the building selected? Was a new-build ever considered? I think existing buildings can often be selected for conversion to arts spaces, particularly in a community context, because as well as making use of what's available, they also insert art into the established community, knitting it into the fabric of the environment.

From my recollection a new-build was not considered as the building more or less selected itself. It was an existing part of the Borough Council's portfolio of property, and was being used as a market, but was very run-down. Something needed to be done with it urgently; also the market value of the building was used as partnership funding for the Lottery bid, which was crucial. So initially it seemed to make practical financial sense. Problems arose, however, because the building project was conceived in two parts, the first being the renovation of the market building, and the second being a new-build for the market part to occupy, on the site of an adjacent terrace of derelict houses. This held up the project as there had to be a vesting process to gain ownership of them. On the positive side, Millennium Court is located in the centre of town, and you could argue that it is equidistant between a Protestant and a Catholic church. This was just coincidence, but it can make a difference in local perceptions. I joined the project at empty-shell stage; the new build hadn't commenced, but the building had already been selected.

How was the architect chosen?

Harry Porter, a local architect, was appointed to the project as he brought an understanding of the local area, and of the history of the building, to the design.

There are some interesting choices in the spaces at the Millennium Court. In the main space, particularly, it does look very much like an 'architect's conversion' in that there is a fascination with the existing fabric of the building and with retaining the natural light. Was the architectural spec drawn up in consultation with people like yourself and Victor Sloan?

In many respects it was a consultative process including the general public, and single-issue community groups. However, consultative processes are problematic with this type of project. There's a particular dynamic of influence and language in the architectural method which leads to misunderstandings and unrealistic expectations. Many of the design references for the space, and for the fittings and finishes were ultimately taken from the Lighthouse, Scotland's Centre for architecture and design in Glasgow.

In a regional gallery you end up having to serve many purposes, with the consequence that design compromises are made. An arts centre which stakes a claim for a local, as well as national remit will feel obliged to try to serve the broad-based local constituency by making it relevant to local needs. They will also want to put on work that is innovative and challenging enough to function in an international context. Meeting the needs of community groups, by holding, for example, a local group's Annual General Meeting in the evening, regardless of the current exhibition, is not always achievable.

Can you think of an example of where multi-use spaces have really worked? Can there be a way, without making too many compromises, of cross-fertilising your audiences? I think there have been lots of attempts, but I do think, ultimately, it's the visual arts that suffer most.

Usually, in a multi-use venue, the visual arts are given the least amount of space, and it's often left-over space – halls, stairways etc. It is clear that the design needs of performance spaces always come first. From my point of view, a multi-arts space works best when the drive is not to do with getting funding, but it's when money is limited and enthusiasm is high.

Like the old Project Arts Centre, for example?

Yes – the building may have been a bit tatty, but there was a tacit agreement between the public and the programming coordinators which was: *don't look at the fabric or fixtures and fittings of the building, concentrate on the art*. It may be regrettable, but the scruffiness of the building is often what creates the conditions for the exhibition of art that is challenging – because the focus and usage of the space is all on the art. It is undivided, and therefore the purpose of all those involved can be unified and coherent.

That's interesting in terms of the remit that an arts space is going to have to have now, for accessing and leveraging funding. In this way the arts policies of funders are shaping the kind of spaces that we have. Art is also now recognised as a tool for economic, social and urban regeneration. It is aimed at social inclusion, education, health – so those putting together funding bids often need to be much more 'knowing' in their approach. It's quite hard to do something now that's not self-consciously involved with that as a means of accessing funding. Do you think that puts an additional burden on the architecture, on the architect?

It does – it creates higher expectations. If the project is going to come from a funding-led perspective, then the stakeholders are going to want a certain type of building. Your political context is that it must reflect the aspirations of the people of the area – so then your programme has to reflect that. And that calls for a different kind of architecture, one that reflects the broad demographic of your potential audience. This brings us on to the thorny question of how you evaluate the success of a venue. If the measure of evaluation is numerical then it's purely a question of quantity. However, numbers are not enough to indicate success; the qualitative nature of the individual experience is much harder to define and is ultimately what we're always striving to address. Nevertheless, if you're in receipt of significant public funds for a capital project, quantity and frequency of audience/participant numbers will always be emphasised in business plans and economic appraisals. Of course inclusion should be an imperative, both in terms of depth and in terms of frequency of experience, but venues should fully understand what it means to have an inclusion policy, and the responsibilities that go with such a policy.
In terms of the design of the Millennium Court Arts Centre, what I do like is the size of that first gallery. In the Northern Irish geographical context: the fact that there is a space of that size in Portadown is a bold move. When the windows are blocked off, the second space works really well as a black box, and to have that in a small market town is to be commended. I also really like that there is a darkroom there, and a technology suite. That's something Kaleidoscope really pushed for at the design stage – advance local surveys indicated that this was an area of the arts that people would really engage with. A lot of people were interested in photography because of, for example, Victor Sloan's courses at UBIFHE (Upper Bann Institute of Further and Higher Education), so to give them access to a subsidized darkroom meant that we could start with art that was relevant to people's experiences and needs. The compromises Kaleidoscope was able to reach in the design process were in the secondary spaces, like the artist-in-residence space, rather than in the main area.

It is often the foyer and the main space where the architect feels: *here's where I can stamp my personality – here's where I can create a signature space…*

Yes, going up that staircase, that big sweep of the adjoining curved wall leading into Gallery 1 – that was clearly the main architectural statement. There were also minor statements such as the maintenance of the original market windows and skylights, as well as the unusual colour scheme.

On that question of art and architecture – architecture still forms the backdrop for the visitor experience. Do you think art needs to be challenged by its space, or accommodated by it? Or can it be both?

I think it can be both. In terms of accommodation and space, the space shouldn't be a hindrance to the reception of the work. It should do everything it can to support the work physically, in the same way that the staff should do everything to support the work conceptually and practically. The space must be accommodating (within budget constraints). If you clearly define the type of work and the type of artist you're going to work with, then you're obliged to accommodate those artists when you develop a programme. They may make demands beyond the existing setup – like changing, or inserting, a wall; painting the gallery black; blocking out the light. The space has to be able to accommodate all that.

In terms of the idea of challenge – many artists suggest that creativity can be stimulated by taking on difficult spaces, by the difficulties they present. What spaces do you think work particularly well?

If you take the example of the Context gallery, when it was in its old location, there were two pillars and three windows. So artists were coming in and responding to that architectural challenge, they had to take it on and deal with it – but after a while, there are only so many responses you can make to a challenging space, and it starts to define what you see… Internationally, I like the Whitney Museum. It's a space I have enjoyed visiting. It's like a labyrinth of spaces, you go in and it opens up, floor after floor, so you can have such a range of experiences. The spaces are relatively intimate, but the curatorial practice seems to be always to accommodate the work. I remember seeing the Kabakovs' hospital installation there – it was later shown in the Irish Museum of Modern Art – but at the Whitney, you walked through this small door into it, and it just amazed me. Seeing it in the environment of IMMA, it became art in an art space. In the Whitney you were walking into an actual hospital, all the more disconcerting then when you left the space and returned to the other galleries. What I think was so impressive was the manifest commitment of the Whitney to the artists and the artwork, and also of the artists to the work. Consequently you, as the visitor, felt obliged to put so much more into looking.

Do you think then that really committed curatorial practice can overcome architectural shortcomings? I have heard curators talking about sometimes going into a space and having first to get rid of the architecture.

That is a challenging statement to make. Understandably, with all galleries, there will always be some spatial shortcomings, you'll always be patching over. Maybe it'll be covering windows, blocking out light or whatever. In reality, however, this is just superficial, a curator is rarely in the position to get rid of the architecture. To do that you need to have a lot of autonomy – if the architecture is new, or is the property of the local authority, or the realised vision of the board, then it is unlikely that a curator will be given a free hand…

Additionally, the curator should respect the judgement of the architect. I do believe in principle that architects work to provide credible design solutions to the problems posed. Issues arise when you talk to an architect about the need for a space to be a white box or a black box, they perhaps fail to fully appreciate the point of the primacy of the art. So unless you're in control of the purse strings (in which case if you say you want a black box; then you get a black box) the architect will want to put the gallery space in an internal location of his/her choosing, with skylights. An architect will always talk about natural light, the movement of space and the spatial possibilities offered by modern building materials whereas most of the time, especially with contemporary art, a curator is wanting to confine the space, to close it down, to dim or block out the light – because it's all about accommodating the

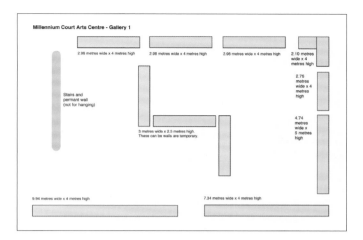

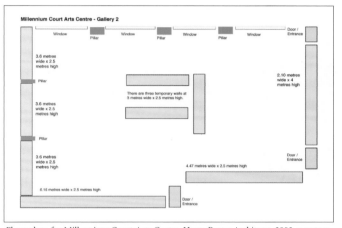

Floor plans for Millennium Court Arts Centre, Harry Porter Architects, 2002, courtesy Millennium Court Arts Centre.

needs of the artwork, and the integrity of the space will be a secondary consideration to that imperative. You'll find that that is an anathema to an architect. Architects deal with permanence, contemporary curators deal with transition.

My advice to anyone who is going to embark on a capital project is that you must find a way to be in control of the budget. You must be the person who is responsible for the decisions in terms of the space, and in terms of where the money is spent. Also you must have a very clear idea about what you want before you appoint your architect, because each architectural practice will bring a certain type of work to bear on the project. You also have to be very confident in your ideas because they will be challenged by the architect.

There are instances where that dynamic can be beneficial to the final design.

Yes, but the architect will have always had more experience and a better vocabulary in terms of defining space, and will be trained in presenting a spatial vision in advance of any construction. In many ways curators should not start second-guessing the architect, because the architect does have the necessary expertise. What you have to really be sure of is your curatorial policy, the type of work you'll be putting in, because the type of work should dictate, and be reflected in, the space. You have to go in with your eyes open: if it's going to be multi-arts and multi-functional then you have to be prepared to make the compromises.

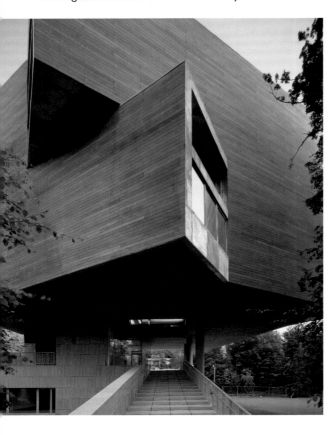

O'Donnell + Tuomey, Lewis
Glucksman Gallery, 2004, photo
Dennis Gilbert/VIEW

In Terms of Site

by Peter Murray

[1]While Limerick and Galway
have successfully adapted
spaces in existing buildings,
University College Dublin has
no art gallery. Trinity College
Dublin, not one of the constituent colleges of the
National University, commissioned the Douglas Hyde
Gallery (within the Ahrends
Burton Koralek arts building), in 1979.

[2]ArtHouse (1996) Group 91 /
Shay Cleary Architects.
DesignYard (1996) Felim
Dunne & Associates /
Robinson Keefe Devane
Architects.

The Lewis Glucksman Gallery, within the grounds of University College Cork, is set in a highly sensitive site. Until its construction (2003/04), the Lower Grounds of the University, a linear park stretching alongside the River Lee, had never before been built upon. Overlooking these Lower Grounds, the grey Neo-Gothic outlines of Sir Thomas Deane's 1849 quadrangle and Aula Maxima provide a romantic image of a university; dreaming spires rising over a sylvan setting of fields, trees and a riverside walk. The notion of placing a large new modernist building in this hallowed ground was strongly contested, but under college President Gerard Wrixon the project has been carried through success-fully, from fund-raising to completion. Cork is now the first of constituent colleges of the National Universities of Ireland to have its own purpose-built art gallery.[1]

Sheila O'Donnell and John Tuomey, the architects of the Glucksman Gallery, have already designed a number of buildings in Ireland for art and cultural activities. Their first essay was a red-painted structure, a temporary gallery made of galvanized iron and wood. Resembling something between a barn and a medieval siege machine, it housed paintings by Brian Maguire and greatly enlivened the courtyard of the Irish Museum of Modern Art during its inauguration year in 1991. While other cultural buildings in Temple Bar, such as the ArtHouse or the DesignYard[2], have floundered, O'Donnell + Tuomey's award-winning Gallery of Photography (1996) continues to function well, as does their nearby Irish Film Centre (1992). While this may be attributable to programming, the buildings are well-

designed and people clearly enjoy the experience of visiting them. Another project, the furniture-making college at Letterfrack in Co. Galway (2001), shows their ease with working with wood in a modernist idiom. Although described as modernist, or rationalist, their architecture has more complex roots, and thought goes into uncovering the history of buildings that they adapt, or into exploring the history and environment of sites where they are commissioned to build from scratch. The history of the Industrial School at Letterfrack, and the bleak experiences of many of the young people confined in such institutions, have invested the O'Donnell + Toumey building with a redemptive character. Its design expresses a generally-held wish in Connemara and throughout Ireland to look forward to a better future.

Unlike many of their architectural peers, who seek inspiration in Los Angeles or Milan, O'Donnell + Toumey have spent a great deal of time looking at the essential characteristics of older types of Irish buildings, including farm buildings, handball alleys and old castles. Their study of 16th century tower-houses has informed many of their late 20th century Modernist designs, in particular the way in which narrow, almost cramped, staircases open out suddenly into large spaces, passageways lead to garderobe-type rooms, and the sense of being in the building is highly experiential, in terms of textures, spaces and viewpoints. At the core of their design for the Glucksman Gallery is a simple, robust structure, a rectangular core that can be 'read' as a late-Medieval tower-house. Inside this core are staircases, a lift and other services. Made of reinforced concrete, with all forms and surfaces meeting at right angles, the central tower is clad externally in Irish limestone and is seven storeys in height. The narrow slabs of stone cladding are held in place using the Fisher system, hung with 6mm gaps on hidden metal rails. While the horizontal gaps are in a straight line, the vertical gaps are staggered, almost at random, evoking a form of musical notation. The opacity of the limestone is offset by translucent glass windows on either side.

Wrapped around this tower, about ten metres above the entrance level, is a steel and wood cantilevered structure that also extends outwards over the forecourt and entrance area for ten metres. This massive structure is supported by seven cylindrical concrete columns, all but one of which are contained within the plan of the smaller ground floor. The effect of the overhang, or cantilever, is dramatic. It provides shade and shelter for a large area of ground underneath. Its plain underside is enlivened through the addition of mica chips into the concrete mix: they sparkle as they reflect light from inside the building. If the core can be read as a tower-house, the cantilever, clad in unvarnished ship-lapped American oak (called Angelina di Campigna), echoes the wooden houses attached to stone castles in Medieval times. Contained within this structure are the three main exhibition galleries. Two are wrapped around the central core, while a third smaller gallery, at a mezzanine level, is contained within the core. This is referred to as the 'closed control' gallery, and is designed for exhibitions of particularly valuable or delicate artworks. A media room alongside, serves the needs of video and computer-based art. A clever touch is a narrow vertical slot high on the wall of the closed control gallery, through which videos and films can be projected onto the white wall opposite.

The gallery flooring is white oak, cut into narrow strips with a bandsaw, the strips then glued together in a random pattern, with the sawn edges uppermost. Underneath this wooden floor are concealed massive concrete beams supporting the cantilever. The double-height gallery walls curve gently as they wrap around the rectangular central core, giving the internal gallery spaces some interesting moments for those installing exhibitions. In addition, large rectangular windows on both main gallery levels jut outwards at an angle

[above:] O'Donnell + Tuomey, from top: interior, *The Irish pavilion* at IMMA, 1991, photo John Searle; Furniture College, Letterfrack,2003, photo Dennis Gilbert/VIEW; Irish Film Institute, Temple Bar, Dublin, 1996; [overleaf:] Lewis Glucksman Gallery, 2004, photo Dennis Gilbert/VIEW

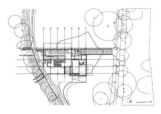

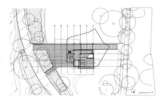

O'Donnell + Tuomey, from top: floor plans for Lewis Glucksman Gallery, ground, to second floor, 2004, courtesy the architects

from the lines of the timber-clad walls, framing breath-taking views of the old Aula Maxima, the steeples of William Burges' St. Finbarr's Cathedral, and the minaret-like St. Anne's Shandon. Above this are another two levels, the top-most being reserved for the plant room that services the building.

The simplicity of the Glucksman Gallery design, which echoes in some ways the brutal strength of the Whitney overhang, is tempered by the architects' introduction of a Rubik Cube concept to the building at several points. The elevation of the building as seen from the south, where the main ramp leads to the entrance, suggests two interlocked elements, while the plan of the upper main gallery with its two vista windows, reveals that it has been turned anti-clockwise through 20 degrees in relation to the floor space below it, as if seeking a better vantage point to view the surrounding hills and steeples of Cork city.

The Gallery has been designed with a high degree of sensitivity to its surroundings. In addition to its primary role as an art gallery, it serves as fulcrum, viewing point, a crossroads, a place for eating and meeting. Although a big building, it has been erected without disturbing nearby trees, the branches of a mature evergreen oak brushing against the timber cladding, twenty metres above ground level. Mooted by Wrixon as a building that would blend discreetly into its surroundings, the Glucksman Gallery is in reality something of a sleeping giant. The two gallery levels, nominally the second and third floors, are in fact at levels four and five. The first floor, with its forecourt, is actually level three. It contains the main entrance and a showcase area, where works of art are visible behind glass to passers-by. Below this are two levels containing restaurant, corporate dining area, kitchen, storage and deliveries. The first impression on seeing the Gallery is one of its substantial physical presence as a building. It is not discreet, but again echoing the stark simplicity of Medieval architecture, it asserts its presence in the landscape without undue showiness or frivolity. Much consideration has been given to allowing the building to settle into its surroundings, with the landscaped green areas of the Lower Grounds becoming vistas to be viewed through plate glass, and sites where open-air sculpture may be displayed. By way of compensation, the Gallery will attract more use by students, staff and visitors of the Lower Grounds and the riverside walk. Future plans aim to provide for a pedestrian footbridge over the branch of the River Lee, allowing access to the Gallery, and thence the main college buildings, from the University's swimming pool and running tracks at the Mardyke. However, in the final analysis, it is how the exhibition spaces perform that will define the success of this building, and while these may be literally eccentric, they do provide an exciting and interesting context for many forms of art, both traditional and contemporary.

Architecturally, the Glucksman Gallery represents a break from the incipient and rather dull tendency towards a Neo-Celtic Revival that has defined the main campus at UCC in recent years. Clustered around the Honan Chapel is a variety of new buildings, generally Modernist but clad in stone and sporting mock pinnacles and battlements. The success of O'Donnell + Toumey's design is that it avoids literal references to Medieval architecture, while retaining the spirit of the Norman tower-house. The Gallery provides badly-needed high-quality exhibition space for Cork, complementing the city centre municipal art gallery and providing a bridge between the orderliness of the university campus and the disorderly (but interesting) city.

Conversation: Fiona Kearney and John Tuomey, July 2004

Fiona Kearney: One of the challenges of creating this building was in addressing the attractive and historic riverside site of the University's lower grounds. It is a site with an important geographic location because it is situated just behind UCC's main gates. Yet this wooded area had become somewhat detached from the rest of campus life. I think one of the things that the Glucksman is going to achieve is a recuperation of that space back into the main University arena. Your building is a very considered response to these issues and the natural setting of the lower grounds.

John Tuomey: There are two aspects here. One is the process by which a building comes about, and the other is more internal to the discipline of architecture itself. In the case of process, that site had been earmarked for cultural use within the University since 1972. A previous masterplan indicated that the building should be low level, low profile and spreading over the ground of the site but we kind of reacted against that. For two reasons. One is that if you build horizontally across the site, you extinguish the very site that you have chosen to protect, so the sensitive approach isn't sensitive in that regard. And the other

All images: O'Donnell + Tuomey, Lewis Glucksman Gallery, 2004, all photos, Dennis Gilbert/VIEW is that you would be left with the issue of always looking down on a building from above. The only way to resolve that would be to bury the building in landscape and we felt that symbolically that was the wrong way to represent the project. To fold it into the ground would be a self-cancelling move. So we decided to do absolutely the opposite and build as high as possible in order to minimize the footprint on the site and protect more trees. We did this without an architectural design; it was simply an environmental idea that minimal footprint means minimal damage: lets have it that the top of the tree is the absolute datum and nothing will be higher than a tree.

On the other point about site: one of the things that is very important to us in our practice, in our sense of critical practice, is the relationship of architecture to site. This is to say a landscape is not necessarily a site, but if the landscape is the site, somehow or other the building should reveal the site rather than remove it. An example that really appeals to me are the piers that are all around Ireland from the 19th century – like the pier in Roundstone. People walk on those piers without thinking that they are buildings, they walk out, they go out on the water and come back, and there is no hierarchical difference between the form of the pier and the form of the land. In my mind that is what architecture should be like. It is not that architecture should vanish into nature, but architecture should have that sense of belonging to place. When you walk onto the podium of the Glucksman you are meant to feel that you are on ground; to feel that the ground is the limestone escarpment that the whole University is based on, and that this ground will take you down to the river as if there is no building. Then elevated above that ground is the celestial world of the gallery, and carved out of that ground is the café below. So before you start looking for the door or thinking about it as a building, it's meant to register in your inner mind as form which belongs to the place. You don't think this is a lovely site, pity there is a building in the middle of it; you walk on and you see the place with the building as your frame.

I wonder if one of the ways the building is achieving this is through the very careful use of materials. There is a sense in which the craft of every single person working on the building was valued throughout. I think one of the great pleasures for me in being involved and on site for the last year has been to see the sense of pride that people have in their work, and this has come from the way in which the use of materials and craft have been valued .

First on the materials: the materials are fundamental to the building. I talk about it in terms of form, because our primary task is the responsibility for form, but that is a kind of abstract concept because nothing exists except in the physical world, and you have to use material and use material with meaning. So in the building there is a line above which there is no stone and below which there is no timber. That is highly selective and goes right down to the tiniest detail: the handrails change once you hit the gallery level and you are on the timber floor, they change from metal to wood. But in the basement they are metal, and they are the same handrails that are outdoors. Once you are indoors in the foyer or down on your way to the café, conceptually you are still outdoors. You are still in the normal world of campus life and you are in the actual stuff of the University itself, the limestone of the University, the landscape of the University. What we are hoping is that the moment you come to the top of this massive stone stair and there is just one stone threshold to deliver you on to the wooden floor, that the acoustic changes, the light changes, the open space goes away and enclosure comes in and you have stepped up into a cloud, into a different environment. Use of material is crucial to creating that.

On the second part of the question: part of our training as architects, our college training and our professional training is to think of the building process as a contractual process, and to think of it as a hierarchical contractual process. Architects are trained and it is instilled in us not to talk to people on site. Every architect certainly of my generation, was given this attitude. And I completely reject that attitude. I rebel against that. Sheila and I talk to everyone on site, we compliment their work and we correct their work and we try to let them into the mystery and let them understand how their work is part of the larger picture. Our ambition, if it is possible, is to avoid all jargon and avoid all distance and to talk the same language to everyone we meet. They trust the trust I put in them, and if we have to change something, they know we are not changing it to be bloody-minded. I grew up on building sites. My father was a site engineer for John Paul building company. Maybe that schooldays experience is the thing that gives me the feeling of community that can exist on a building site.

I would like to come back to this idea of change and not changing things for the sake of it. Over the last couple of months of the process, we have made some changes to the building and I think the changes that we have made have been about trying to create the most flexible use of the space. One of the things that I admire about O'Donnell + Tuomey has been the willingness to see change as an opportunity, to discuss why we might need to alter a space. I'm thinking for instance of the very simple change we made on the upper floor where a bench became a desk. That was an important change for me because it meant respecting the scholarly reflective aspect of being a University gallery.

The thing about simplicity is that the building has to read utterly simply so that people will concentrate on the experience of the work, or even their own sense of a day out in the gallery, this the kind of space that galleries should provide in the mind. And perhaps some galleries don't do that because they surround you with clutter. On the other hand, if it were built simply as an empty white box, and if we then locked on that in our own minds as designers, that nothing touches the white box, then it would be a failure because it wouldn't be simple. It would be simple-minded. I think we worked hard, spending lots of time to make it look as if there is no effort in it at all. And the real content is how the complexities of new and rising requirements can be absorbed within the simplicity of a concept. And that is a test. It is probably a test of maturity, a test of the form, a test of the design. So when you say to me I need to change this, I have two reactions. One is 'oh fuck it, I don't want to change anything else ever again' and the other is 'oh good, another shake up' and there is a great feeling of what (and where) will this upset bring us. Usually if the atmosphere is right, and if the cooperation is right, it brings you to a better place.

I think the change I suggested, to get rid of a small office space to create a larger public area for the shop, is a fairly good example of that.

Yes, it improves the building.

So as well as creating a better retail and social environment, the introduction of light into that part of the building affects the experience of the space in a positive manner.

Also, from the podium there is only one peeled back bit of the timber that shows anything of the interior and that would have only shown an office. Now, standing on the podium, if you see someone in the shop, you can say 'that could be me' or 'there I am'. You can actually move in before you go in. Or from the shop, you can look down to the podium and say 'that is where I came from'. Now, unless you had intervened, that wouldn't have happened. People would never have had that look back, look out. I really enjoy that now. I also enjoy the creative interaction between us.

Galleries are public spaces of social interaction and encounter, but also places of internal personal experience. They are both communal and private. One of the reasons the white cube has been so dominant is that it is seen to offer the perfect contemplative arena for the work of art. I think the hegemony of the white box in the 20th century has meant that architects have been reluctant to challenge this space other than radically, for instance in the brash statement of the Bilbao Guggenheim which only allows a particular kind of art to speak. I'm going to suggest that the Glucksman is proposing a very different kind of architecture. There are two white cube type galleries, the closed control areas at the heart of the building, but it is the curve that defines the building. One of the most fascinating things for me will be to see how people respond to those curves. It seems to me that these long curved walls offer a new kind of viewing, a viewing which is moving you rather than stopping you, which is less confrontational and more a movement back and forth, more an open conversation between the works, offering a greater number of viewing points within the space.

If the space is an arena for difference, that would be an achievement. There is definitely a gentle rotation in the form of the building that is meant to encourage both movement and pause. Both a sense of being located and being in a reserved contemplative space. I think we are greatly helped by the site. I think a lot of galleries concentrate completely on removal from place. And we took a step in this gallery, which you might remember was the subject of huge debate all the way through, which is to keep contact with the outside world. We are screened by the trees, we have views to the river, it is not a very distracting outside world but we were determined that the building would not close itself from the outside world. I suppose the building lets you know that its primary containment is internal, but it is as if it just burst out a little bit of its boundaries to allow the outside world in. I think that is really important to the character of it. I also think it is really important in galleries that you are not locked in a capsule of abstraction. That white cube space which is meant to be the most neutral, is actually intimidating. I think it is possible, and I hope it is going to be the experience of the gallery, that you can have both contemplative space, and a sense of contact. The emphasis is on the artwork but the real world is in the side of your eye. And we have tried to treat the windows not as aligned vista points but as kind of leakages. You know that the real world is there, it is not your primary attention, it is kind of placing you as you move to the next part of the gallery. A lot of galleries have valves to release gallery fatigue, so that you walk into a room that has a bay window. Or in Tate Modern, you walk, for example, out of the gallery and into a glass capsule that overhangs the public space. We wanted not to have that separation. We wanted the two worlds in one world. I hope that succeeds. It means you can have daylight in the galleries, it means you can see trees out the window, see the world outside and still be in the reserved atmosphere of the gallery space. That is the aspiration for it.

There are a number of spaces beyond the dedicated gallery areas that offer opportunities to artists. Buildings are now made with the knowledge of the different ways in which artists work, taking account of the history of art and the development of site-specific and installation practice. There are several areas in the Glucksman that beckon to artists in this way. How concerned were you to think of the whole building as a gallery?

It is not that this is a building, part of which is reserved for display. You don't enter the display zone at a certain point. We have tried all through the design development of the project to remind ourselves that this is an art gallery through and through, top to bottom. We worked very hard to keep that sense of free-flow because we think it is possible to imagine installations at every point in the building, on the half landing, round the corner in the showcase, hanging from the ceiling, halfway up the stairs. You don't have to put your gallery-going hat on the moment you hit the wooden floor, you should be able to feel you are in the gallery all the time. From a technical point, it hasn't been easy to keep that sense of openness. But it is crucial to the character of the project. It is the conceptual corkscrew that allows a vertical building to work, like a tree that you keep clambering up. It will be interesting to see how artists respond to that.

In privileging that concept of flow, you echo the natural site and the river that runs by the gallery, but also the intellectual currency and free-flow of ideas in the University. Perhaps, this is what distinguishes a University gallery from any other kind of visual arts institution, that it generates a flow between art and other academic disciplines. It is almost as if you have set the ethos of the building in that open movement. All too often the University is seen as an ivory tower, a closed haven of scholarly thought, and one of the intentions of the Glucksman is to act as a portal between UCC and the wider community. So the gallery has to cater for a very diverse range of audiences. How do you envision that plurality of viewers when you are working?

If the building doesn't work in more than one way, it doesn't work. There are different ways through the building and I think those kinds of complexities are the outcome of more than one mind at work. I think they are the outcome of an exchange. One of the advantages I have is that I have a partner. Sheila and I talk everything through. We are soulmates while being quite different. We think differently. You were talking about difference between users so I guess I'm thinking that there is an advantage to difference at the beginning too.

If now at the end of the process I close my eyes and think: what do I want? I probably want this building to make people feel optimistic. Maybe that is a ridiculously ambitious thing to say, but we are not lost in a gloom. The world is very unattractive in the current preoccupation with materialism and consumerism, and architecture is not helping if all it is doing is mirroring. So in my view, a garden still restores the mind, a cloister still slows down your heartbeat – and architecture still has a human purpose.

Architectural Solutions

[previous page:] Micheal Heizer, *North, East, South, West*, 1967-2002; installation view at Dia: Beacon; designed by Robert Irwin, with OpenOffice architects, photo Tom Vinetz; courtesy Dia Art Foundation; gift of Lannan Foundation

Architectural Solutions

by Gemma Tipton

Between 2001 and 2004, *CIRCA* Art Magazine conducted an online poll to find what architectural solutions were considered to contribute to the optimum spaces for displaying art. Architects, curators, artists and arts professionals, as well as general gallery visitors responded, and the results showed that there are as many opinions about the architecture of art spaces as there are about the art they contain; and that it's possible for an art gallery to be considered simultaneously the best, and (joint) worst space in Ireland for showing contemporary art.

Asked what the best option for a contemporary art space would be: 32% said a conversion of an existing historic building, 54% opted for a purpose-built space, and 14% selected a modern extension of an existing art space. New-builds, such as the Market Place Armagh (architect Glenn Howells) do provide the opportunity for architects to explore and experiment with the idea of the 'perfect' space; but conversions can also present fascinating environments for art. Galleries such as the Ormeau Baths in Belfast (a former Swimming Pool, architects 22 over 7) may seem to limit the available space because of their existing template; but the dialogue between the historical architecture, and its present role, often enriches the experience of viewing art there. There is a similar sense in visiting a gallery like Fenderesky (located in the Victorian Crescent Arts Centre in Belfast, self-conversion); or the Millennium Court in Portadown (a former market building, conversion architect Harry Porter). Contemporary art is not made in isolation from history or tradition, and there can be much to be gained from the viewing experience reflecting that. Extensions are more problematic, as the transitions from one part of the building to another are difficult to handle architecturally. The National Gallery in Dublin is a good example of this, with awkward shifts between the original building, the 1986 OPW extension and Benson and Forsythe's Millennium Wing.

The second question on the survey considered the different elements of art spaces in more detail. The responses can be seen in Figure 1. Taking each of the fourteen

Figure 1.	good %	no diff. %	bad %
1. 'bold' statement architecture	55	29	16
controllable natural light	96	2	2
2. large atrium/foyer	51	42	8
3. large glass 'shop' windows	35	47	18
4. good storage area	85	15	0
5. impressive entrance	39	57	4
6. irregular 'free form' areas	48	43	9
7. gift/book/coffee shops	63	34	4
8. 'traditional' space (with own features)	29	62	9
9. a 'celebrity' architect	18	63	20
10. logical progression of rooms	80	16	4
11. neutral space	69	24	7
12. white cube space	46	39	15
13. 'difficult' areas that challenge the artist	36	38	27

points; the answers, and potential architectural solutions, are not always as clear-cut as they may seem.

So, is 'bold statement architecture' good or bad for an art gallery? 55% thought it was good, and 16% bad. But should art have to compete with the architecture which encloses it? When art becomes an excuse for architecture, collecting and exhibiting decisions can begin to be taken in terms of what will 'set the architecture off' well, and the museum which defines its identity around an architectural statement may well come to extend that identity to the art it exhibits.

Controllable natural light seems an easier issue to assess. 96% of respondents agreed it was good for a gallery, and it seems an unarguable prerequisite. And yet, Rem Koolhaas would disagree. According to the architect of the Las Vegas Guggenheim (2001), and the Kunsthal, Rotterdam (1987-92), "Contemporary art needs spaces equipped for the interaction of human beings and technological implements, people, and apparatus. Somehow, daylight is not conducive for this kind of interaction... Whereas painting and sculpture are best revealed in conditions of (simulated) daylight, new arts need a darker, more artificial accommodation... there is no escaping the inherent artificiality of the Museum..."[1]

So what about a large atrium or foyer? In *CIRCA* 90, Aidan Dunne discussed 'foyer syndrome' in his column. "Something seems to happen to an architect when they are enlisted to design a gallery space... Otherwise top-notch architects are overcome with the desire to... well, it's not entirely clear what it is they're trying to do."[2] 51% of CIRCA poll respondents thought the large atrium or foyer was a good thing, and only 8% that it was positively bad. The architects of today's art spaces are well aware that they are designing for more than

I.M.Pei, interior, East Building of the National Gallery of Art, Washington, D.C.,1978. The East Building's unique central space with its 16,000-square foot skylight, accented by the grand Calder mobile, is awe-inspiring. © Dennis Brack/Black Star, courtesy National Gallery of Art

[1] Rem Koolhaas, taken from his Architect's Statement in the Charette for the MoMA expansion project. Full version online at www.moma.org/expansion/charette/architects/koolhaas

[2] Aidan Dunne, *Visual Arts South*, CIRCA 90, Winter 1999, p. 13.

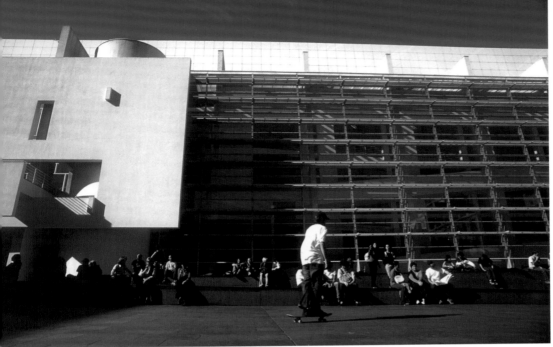

Richard Meier, Museu d'Art Contemporani de Barcelona (MACBA), © Javier Tles 2004, courtesy MACBA

[3] I.M. Pei, quoted by Poyin Auyoung in *Museum Space: Privatising Culture/Imaging Desire*, Øjeblikket, vol. 8, 1998, p. 113.

[4] Roundtable discussion, *P/A on Pei*, in Progressive Architecture, October 1978, p. 53, quoted in ibid, p. 117.

[5] Quoted by Ellen Posner, in *The museum as bazaar*, Atlantic, August 1988, p. 69.

[6] Including Aidan Dunne, CIRCA 97, Autumn 2001, p. 15; and Victoria Newhouse, *Towards a New Museum*, Monacelli Press, New York 1998, pp. 66-71.

just the viewing of art. That famed maker-of-entrances himself, I.M. Pei (East Building of the National Gallery of Art, Washington, D.C.,1978; and Grand Louvre project, 1989) described his thinking, saying that his "aim from the start in the East Building had been to design for a 'mob scene.' We needed to make the visit a pleasant one, so we built a circus."[3] But a review of the building when it opened suggested that this approach was not necessarily the right one: "The question of image is central to our comprehension of architecture: the fact that the gallery spaces of the East Building read as ancillary to the atrium space is thus significant."[4] My experience of the East Building would agree with this. After the scale of the atrium, the galleries are dark afterthoughts, and the art in them somehow diminished. Robert Venturi puts this idea another way: "…when you finally make it to the art, you may be either worn down by the banality of the maze you have traversed, or jaded by the drama of the spatial, symbolic, or chromatic fantasies… the art, when you reach it has become a kind of anticlimax – in fact dull, as you perceive it with your constricted pupils, jaded sensibilities, and loss of orientation."[5]

And yet, sympathetically handled, the foyer/atrium serves both as a social and catchment space, and also as an orientation court, to make the transition from street to art more complete. Architects Benson and Forsyth named the first space one encounters on entering their National Gallery of Ireland Millennium Wing extension (2002) a 'decompression chamber.' This idea has been explored with more drama and scale by Richard Meier in his MACBA in Barcelona (1995). The building has been criticised by some,[6] but with his bare entrance passageway and lobby, deliberately devoid of the usual gaudy cluster of shops and café/restaurant areas, Meier has at least induced visitors to leave the hot-earth tones and

ArtHouse, Shay Cleary / Group 91 Architects, 1996

clamour of Barcelona behind as they move through into the cool white spaces of his galleries.

And what about that favourite, particularly of the Temple Bar architects, the large glass 'shop-window' frontage? 35% thought it was good, and 18% bad. Glass has quickly become an architectural metaphor for transparency. It serves as a quick trick to demonstrate openness, saying "come on in, this art's for everybody…" and it's next to useless when it comes to showing art. Delicate works on paper are damaged by direct sunlight, which also reflects off glass for framed works. Digital art is impossible to view in such conditions, which makes it all the more difficult to believe that ArtHouse (Group 91/Shay Cleary, 1996) was really purpose-built as Ireland's Multi-Media Centre for the Arts. At ArtHouse, the expanse of inviting plate glass in the foyer left only a small rectangular space on the ground floor, and the rather forbidding basement, as areas suitable for showing digital art. Even Aileen MacKeogh, first Director of ArtHouse, was unable to give the building her unequivocal endorsement when it opened. Mentioning the "creative strains in the client/architect relationship," she went on to say, "Now, as an end-user of this arts centre, I ask myself did all the thoughtful research and consultation deliver a building that works. The honest answer is, I still do not know."[7]

[7]Aileen MacKeogh, quoted in *Temple Bar, The Power of an Idea*, ed. Patricia Quinn, Temple Bar Properties Ltd., Dublin 1996, p.156.

Meier's MACBA uses a different solution to attempt to have its architectural cake and eat it. Light plays in from the large glass-fronted façade, but is partially screened off from the galleries with brise-soleil partition walls. The effect in full sunlight is stunning, although more stunning as architecture than as an ideal space for looking at art. At the High Museum in Atlanta (1983), Meier ultimately had to replace the atrium's glazing with light-reducing glass, and also to cover the vertical windows with interior screens. While transparency and openness are high on the agenda of arts councils and policy makers, they are way down on the scale when it comes to actually looking at art.

The importance of having a good storage area seems obvious enough, and 85% agreed that it was a necessary part of the function of a contemporary art museum, with no one thinking it was a bad thing to have. And how could it be? The issue is more what makes a storage area good? Climatic controls are obviously important, and security is of paramount concern to museums with important and valuable collections. Indeed, from a security point of view, IMMA are cagey as to where exactly their unexhibited collection is kept. Both the Douglas Hyde and the Hugh Lane Galleries in Dublin have downgraded the importance of storage – the Douglas Hyde to create their award-winning Gallery 2 (architects: McCullough Mulvin, 2000-01), and the Hugh Lane to install the Francis Bacon Studio (architects: David Chipperfield and Mitchell Associates, 2000). Meanwhile spaces, such as the Gallery of Photography (O'Donnell +

Gallery 2, McCullough Mulvin Architects, 2001; at Douglas Hyde Gallery, Paul Koralek, Ahrends, Burton and Koralek Architects, 1978-79; photo and courtesy Christian Richters

Santiago Calatrava, interior, Milwaukee Art Museum, photo: Timothy Hursley, courtesy MAM

Tuomey, 1996) were designed and constructed with no storage space at all.

The Douglas Hyde is a gallery rather than museum, and its role is not that of a collector. However, the logistics of receiving touring exhibitions, and curating exhibitions to tour elsewhere, still call for adequate space for storage. The original store was very large (and when first constructed also contained racking for picture storage), and so the addition of Gallery 2 hasn't entirely compromised their space availability. Nonetheless installation access to the Douglas Hyde (architect: ABK, 1978) has always been problematic in a gallery notorious anyway for being a 'difficult space'. The store, which doubles as a loading entrance, is reached down a steep flight of external stairs and through two right-angled turns. As work is brought through into the gallery, a drop-height ceiling in the 'triangle' area means that while large canvases can be re-stretched inside the exhibition space, unnecessary limitations are placed on the size of the sculptural and otherwise rigid pieces that can be shown. The store and access to the Douglas Hyde should be a reminder that the unseen parts of an art space are as important as the seen.

In Las Vegas, Rem Koolhaas did away with these difficulties and limitations with a gesture on a scale to match the rest of Vegas. The Guggenheim Las Vegas (2001, now closed), located within the Venetian Hotel (which itself boasts a replica Grand Canal, complete with water and gondola rides inside, and on the second floor), included a 22.5 by 22.5 metre pivoting door, and a massive industrial bridge crane with a lifting capacity of 35 tons. Subtle it was not, but one was left with the impression (beloved of the new-breed Guggenheims) that there wasn't much art that wouldn't have fitted in here.

Access aside, the idea of the museum store still calls to mind the 'dormitory' and 'morgue' clichés of large collections, and while climate control and security cannot be neglected, there is something disturbing about taking a trip around a major museum's storage space. On a pre-opening tour of MoMA QNS in New York, the journey down through a series of deadening doors to the caged areas, where MoMA's massive collection is now located, was a disquieting experience. The cold, still air, and racks upon racks of MoMA's contribution to the canon of contemporary art made me think that perhaps, were I an artist, I would be less than glad for my work to be buried here.

Rem Koolhaas considered the issue in his presentation to MoMA for their extension and renovation project under the heading *Storage vs. Viewing*, "A museum is an ambiguous treasure house of collections: part is on view and accessible, an often larger part is hidden in storage, aggressively inaccessible… The museum is the only institution that systematically freezes its assets away. Within the [MoMA] extension, the notion of storage should be emancipated. New forms of automated storage, visible storage, and robotic retrieval eliminate arguments of difficult access, unwieldy logistics, and impossibility. Combined with the appeal for a more customized, individual museum experience, the rethinking of storage initiates a new way of conceptualizing the collection…"[8]

Koolhaas's ideas weren't adopted, perhaps due in part to the curators' desire to see their growing role of interpreting through presentation undiminished. *Matisse Picasso* wouldn't have been such a lucrative block-buster if people could create their own parallels within, and conclusions about, a museum's collection. Storage is a vital part of a museum's architecture, and yet until we see innovators such as Koolhaas being given the opportunity to experiment with their form and function, we can expect little more from these spaces than air conditioned racks of dead (or merely sleeping) works of art.

Back in the public gaze, 39% of poll respondents thought that an impressive entrance was a good thing for an art space to have. 57% said that it made no difference, and 4% that it was actively a bad thing. An impressive entrance is, of course, an external manifestation of the internal atrium/foyer pyrotechnics which have already been discussed in this essay. The investment in two Guggenheim museums in Las Vegas (the Guggenheim, and the Guggenheim Hermitage) renders any vestiges of doubt that art is not yet an entertainment, and as such in competition with other available entertainments, void. Having said that, the Guggenheim Las Vegas closed after just one year, and the space was turned into a theatre, so perhaps the terms of the competition need to be addressed a little more closely if art is to win in an environment like Vegas. The Vegas Guggenheim only had one show in the Koolhaas space – the very long-running *Art of the Motorcycle*. The Guggenheim Hermitage space is to remain open, and the Guggenheim itself has turned its attention instead to Rio, and also to Taiwan.

Santiago Calatrava, bridge and entrance, Milwaukee Art Museum, photo: Timothy Hursley, courtesy MAM

[8]Rem Koolhaas, taken from his Architect's Statement in the Charette for the MoMA expansion project. Full version online at www.moma.org/expansion/charette/architects/koolhaas

A spectacular entrance, while speaking to the outside world of the kind of experience that is available within, also sets the mood that will characterise the visit once you have moved beyond its doors. Santiago Calatrava's astonishing wing-like brise-soleil at the

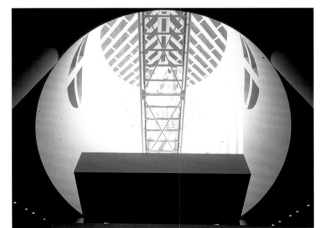

[left:] Mario Botta: SF MoMA, 1990-95, interior view, looking up at bridge, photo Richard Barnes, courtesy and © SanFrancisco Museum of Modern Art

[left:] Cook and Fournier, Kunsthaus, Graz, 2003, photo: Kunsthaus Graz / LMJ / Eduardo Martinez, May 2004; [right and far right:] Mario Botta: SF MoMA, 1990-95, interior view, atrium, photo Richard Barnes, courtesy and © San Francisco Museum of Modern Art; Frank Gehry: Guggenheim Museum Bilbao, 1997, interior view, photo Erika Ede, courtesy Guggenheim Museum Bilbao

[9]Stanislaus von Moos, 'A museum explosion', in Vittorio Lampugnani and Angeli Sachs (eds.), *Museums for a New Millennium*, Prestel, Munich 1999, p. 23.

Milwaukee Art Museum (1994-2000); I.M. Pei's crystalline pyramids at the Louvre (1989); the almost extraterrestrial shape of Cook and Fournier's Kunsthaus in Graz (2003); and the huge black-and-white striped oculus and entrance at the Museum of Modern Art in San Francisco (SF MoMA, architect, Mario Botta 1990-95) all advertise that something special is on view within, something exciting, something different. But when entrances in the museum-as-entertainment category strive to outdo each other, what is the logical (or illogical) conclusion? "The price of unlimited diversification in the marketplace of culture-as-an-industry is, first, accelerated disintegration, and then the total collapse of all rules of the game that makes 'culture' possible as a phenomenon that shares a common social goal. And the result? Finally, we find ourselves inside a museum unfit for use as such or else only fit to exhibit itself."[9] The question of how much of Calatrava's massive wing-span sun-screen, Botta's black-and-grey striped stage set, or Gehry's titanium arabesques you can leave behind in your mind when you enter a sparer space, or come face to face with a quieter work, inside is one that only the individual can answer, but sometimes it can be hard for a work to speak, when the conversation has degenerated into a shouting match.

[10]Damien Coyle, in conversation with the author, 2 August, 2004.

The idea of entrance and foyer also needs to be addressed in terms of access for visitors with special needs. Damien Coyle says that, as well as simple access requirements, there is a question of dignity at stake, "as a hearing impaired person, I also tend to look at venues with disabled access and resources in mind. *Adapt NI* has carried out some excellent venue assessments in this area, and I would note that while all spaces have lessons to learn, some come close to missing the point of equal respect for disabled patrons and participants altogether. One friend, a wheel-chair user, described the winding access ramps of one venue, as creating that sensation of being a lab rat in some disconcerting and elaborate endurance test."[10]

Away from questions of access to, and exhibition of art: how do gift, book and coffee shops fit into the contemporary art space? 35% approved of their presence, 19% thought that

they didn't make any difference, while 4% decided that they had a negative effect on the museum experience. According to Herzog and de Meuron (architects of Tate Modern, 1994-2000), "An art museum is a place for art and people: it is not Disneyworld; it is not a shopping mall; it is not a media center. It is a place where the world of art can express itself in the most direct and radical way – in spaces that find the approval not only of architects and critics but of artists and visitors, spaces that stimulate people to concentrate on the perception of art…"[11] But art does have a significant cultural value, and it is a value which is increasingly commodified and conferred on the goods available in gallery and museum gift, book and coffee shops, "…museums today are expanding into areas of social life such as shopping, dining and attending the performing arts, hosting receptions and parties. These commercial activities are aestheticized by the museum site as well as by museum packaging and logos, and promoted as pseudo-cultural products and events."[12]

The problem is that art does not necessarily have an unlimited and renewing reserve of cultural value to confer before the reciprocal nature of the exchange begins to have a negative impact. The Saatchi *Sensation* exhibition is a good example of this.[13] *Sensation* managed to cause an advertising man's dream of an eponymous sensation when it was shown in both London and New York. Interestingly it was different works which were calculated to provide the crowd-pulling outrage in each venue, but it was perhaps the gift shop which showed what the show was really up to. At the Brooklyn Museum (the venue for *Sensation* in New York), toilet rolls were sold wrapped around with yellow police crime-scene tape, while tin lunchboxes emblazoned with the legend *Toxic Biohazard* were available at similarly inflated prices. There were also rubber balls which screamed when you bounced them off the ground. Their connection to the exhibition was tenuous at best. These things were fun to see and buy, and there was no doubt as to the quality of much of the work in the exhibition, and yet the overriding memory was that of a marketing opportunity, and the experience of the gift shop uneasily usurped the experience of the show in my memory of the visit.

[11] Jacques Herzog and Pierre de Meuron, taken from their *Architect's statement* in the Charette for the MoMA expansion project. Full version online at www.moma.org/expansion/charette/architects/herzog_meuron/index.html

[12] Poyin Auyoung, in ed Sander, Sheikh and Østergaard,1998, *opcit*, p. 99.

[13] *Sensation: Young British Artists from the Saatchi Collection*, Royal Academy of Arts, London, Sept – Dec,1997; Brooklyn Museum of Art, New York, Oct 1999 – Jan 2000. Marcus Harvey's portrait of notorious child murderer Myra Hindley, *Myra*, caused a stir in London, but was largely ignored in New York, where the furore focused on Chris Ofili's painting *The Holy Virgin Mary*, an African Madonna which included elephant dung along with paint on the canvas. Ofili had won the Turner prize in the intervening year.

Of course art-viewing can be thirsty work, and tired feet need nice places to rest. A well-stocked bookshop is a useful adjunct to an exhibit, and people love to send postcards. People may have travelled considerable distances to visit a museum or gallery, so cafés and restaurants are an important component of the design. Yet increasingly the balance seems to have been disrupted. "I don't want to be educated; I want to be drowned in beauty…"[14] said Diana Vreeland who, in 1972, was appointed "Special Consultant" to the Metropolitan Museum of Art's Costume Institute in New York. But to paraphrase Vreeland's remark, we are being drowned in coffee and commerce, with education (and indeed contemplation) often coming a poor second. "An ace café with quite a nice museum attached,"[15] ran the V&A's memorable poster, and in the CIRCA poll, over 50% of respondents (including myself) said that they had visited a gallery or museum just for the gift shop or café, and skipped the art altogether. This in itself is not a problem, yet while we have investigated the cultural issue, the one for architecture is that increasingly the retail spaces are being given priority in briefings to architects by museum boards with an eye to ancillary sources of revenue. Arthur Rosenblatt, senior principal of RKK&G, Museum and Cultural Facilities Consultants (a New York-based office offering museum planning and design services worldwide) is aware of the key importance of the role of the client in briefing the architect. Quoting architectural historian Nicholas Pevsner, he notes that, "…the guardian of functional satisfaction is the client. His responsibility in briefing is as great as the architect's in designing."[16]

The Millennium Wing (architects: Benson and Forsyth, 2000-02) in Dublin's National Gallery sees the Clare Street entrance bringing you into an interior 'street' and past the large bookshop and café en route to the steep stairs which will bring the determined visitor up to the galleries. It was the commissioning panel who specified the gallery/other usage split, and here, as in New York's Met (original building: Weston, 1880, and Morris Hunt, 1894; extensions and renovations by Roche Dinkeloo, 1970-90), one's first impression is of retail, with exhibitions appearing as a corollary to that. The Metropolitan Museum has 12,500 square feet of sales space in its Manhattan site, with another 38 retail shops throughout the city, and worldwide[17].

All the issues discussed so far ought perhaps to be secondary (in an ideal world) to the central issue of what makes a good exhibition space. What makes the actual gallery spaces ideal for viewing art, as distinct from the other elements of the buildings which contain them?

Opinion in the poll was fairly balanced across the different alternatives of space. 'Free form' areas, 'traditional' spaces with their original features, white cube and neutral spaces, and spaces with logical room progressions were all considered (statistics above). In fact, each 'type' of gallery has examples which are so beautifully worked out and executed that, when inside, one thinks that maybe all galleries should be this way. And yet, how many are truly different, original or experimental, and how

[14]Diana Vreeland, quoted in Newhouse, 1998, *opcit*, p.190.

[15]"An ace café with quite a nice museum attached," advertising the Victoria and Albert Museum, London. The poster depicted an ivory sculpture of Venus and Cupid by Le Marchand being held in a hand. The text went on to read: "Where else do they give you £100,000,000 worth of objects d'art free with every egg salad?" Produced by Paul Arden and Jeff Stark for Saatchi and Saatchi Advertising Ltd., London, 1998.

[16]Arthur Rosenblatt in the forward to Justin Henderson (ed.), *Museum Architecture*, Rockport Publishers, Massachusetts, 2001, p. 9.

[17]Poyin Auyoung, in Sander, Sheikh and Østergaard (eds.), *op. cit.*, p. 112.

[left:] Frank Lloyd Wright, Guggenheim Museum, New York, 1956-59, interior view, photo David Heald, © The Solomon R. Guggenheim Foundation, New York; [right:] Richard Serra, *Torques Elipse II*, 1996; *Double Torqued Elipse*, 1997, Dia Art Foundation, gift of Louise and Leonard Riggio, 2000, installation view at Dia: Beacon, photo Richard Barnes, courtesy Dia Art Foundation

Walter De Maria, *The Equal Area Series*, 1976-77; installation view at Dia: Beacon; photo Nic Tenwiggenhorn; courtesy Dia Art Foundation

many are merely architectural cladding on the basic white space? Frank Lloyd Wright's Guggenheim New York (1956-59), Frank Gehry's Guggenheim Bilbao (1997), and Steven Holl's Kiasma in Helsinki (1998) all experiment with spaces beyond the 'white cube', yet all return at various points to the bare white space which is the basis of almost all contemporary museum design. Indeed, beyond the drama of Botta's black-and-grey foyer in San Francisco, and the façade of IMMA's conversion (conversion architect; Shay Cleary, 1991), even once inside the black basalt bulk of Vienna's MuMOK (architects: Ortner & Ortner 2001), what we are left with, as we come to the art spaces, are simple white rooms.

These rooms are, as this book has discussed, nothing approaching 'neutral', so what is the secret of that white space? What are its qualities? Simplicity is one key element. As juror for the competition to select the architects for Tate Modern, Michael Craig Martin noted that "the apparent simplicity of Minimalist works focuses attention without distraction on the straight-forward reality of the object, the relation of the object to the space in which it is seen, the relation of the viewer to this experience."[18] Thus, all services, such as wiring, plumbing, ducting, are hidden away, and flooring and finishes are kept to a minimal limit.

Yoshio Taniguchi, the architect of MoMA's 2004 extension project, recognises the primacy of the art spaces, and describes the process of creating these as "an interlocking dialogue of space, art, and architecture… The primary objective in the design of a museum is to create the ideal environment for the interaction of people and art. Galleries and public spaces are the core elements in a museum. A variety of gallery spaces appropriate to MoMA's collection of twentieth-century masterworks, as well as new galleries for the yet unknown works of contemporary art, is the first requirement."[19]

Taking up the idea of what should constitute that ideal environment, Steven Holl notes the importance of a quiet, intimate, meditative aspect: "The origin of museum as a room of the

[18]Michael Craig Martin, quoted by Raymund Ryan in *Building Tate Modern,* Tate Gallery Publishing, London 2000, p. 27.

[19]Yoshio Taniguchi, taken from his *Architect's statement* in the charette for the MoMA expansion project. Full version online at *www.moma.org/-expansion/charette/-architects/taniguchi/index.html*

muse, a place to think and consider deeply and at length, is an idea to contemplate as we are faced with a major transformation of the Museum of Modern Art."[20] It seems simple enough, yet how can it work so well in one gallery, Gallery 2 at the Douglas Hyde for example, and yet fail so sadly at the Project's art space in Temple Bar, Dublin (architect Shay Cleary, 2000). Niall McCullough describes the process as being about: "(a) having a working understanding of why the architecture should not come to dominate a space… (b) that architecture by definition exists in and around the art and will have form, and the challenge for architects is to find a narrow – but infinitely interesting – way between non-expression and over expression (my optimism is based on a belief that this can be done); and (c) that the basis for this lies – apart from the practicalities of site and structure – in mathematics, proportion, light – and circulation – how a room is entered/ exited etc. It is also clearly to do with the external expression of the building – what does it say about the content – and how that is balanced against its physical and cultural 'place'".[21]

Irish Museum of Modern Art (IMMA), courtyard view, courtesy IMMA

Circulation is a key issue, particularly as galleries and museums get larger and larger. Dia: Beacon and the Guggenheim Bilbao have more or less the same floor areas, yet a trip around the Bilbao gallery can be confusing, giving the visitor that *have I missed something*? anxiety so particular to museum visits. On the other hand, for all its vast size, Beacon is neither exhausting nor confusing. Routes through the exhibition space are left up to the visitor, but somehow engender none of that anxiety you find in other nonprescriptive spaces. This is achieved by an adherence to a simple set of rules, which are the result of Robert Irwin's master plan, then developed in collaboration with New York architects OpenOffice. "You enter on your own terms, not as a group – there isn't a bank of doors, you're an individual. Then, entering you are confronted with a choice, there are two sides of the de Maria piece, two choices of how to go through, so the experience of entering engages you as a thinking visitor, not as a passive one. This was something that was absolutely challenging to us as architects, and yet it's an amazing way to think of an entry sequence. Another is with such an enormous existing building, to not intersect the existing perimeter walls with any other material. And so you have islands of galleries in the centre. The central galleries receive indirect light from above and are designated for painting, and those on the perimeter which can receive western light on the left, and eastern on the right are designated as sculpture galleries."[22]

Dia: Beacon was the result of, as the architects put it, "a luxury of space, and a luxury of time."[23] It is also the closest thing to an ideal gallery in an ideal world that I have seen. Beyond that, in a world with less and less space and time, experiments in architectural spaces for art continue, with continuously interesting results. And for a final word: which space managed to top the *CIRCA* poll for simultaneously best space and worst space in Ireland? IMMA.

[20]Steven Holl, taken from his *Architect's statement* in the charette for the MoMA expansion project. Full version online at www.moma.org/ expansion/charette/- architects/holl/index.html

[21]Niall McCullough, McCullough Mulvin architects, interviewed by the author, RIAI, Dublin, 13 May 2003.

[22]OpenOffice, Art + Architecture Collaborative, interviewed by the Author, 16 June 2003

[23]*ibid*

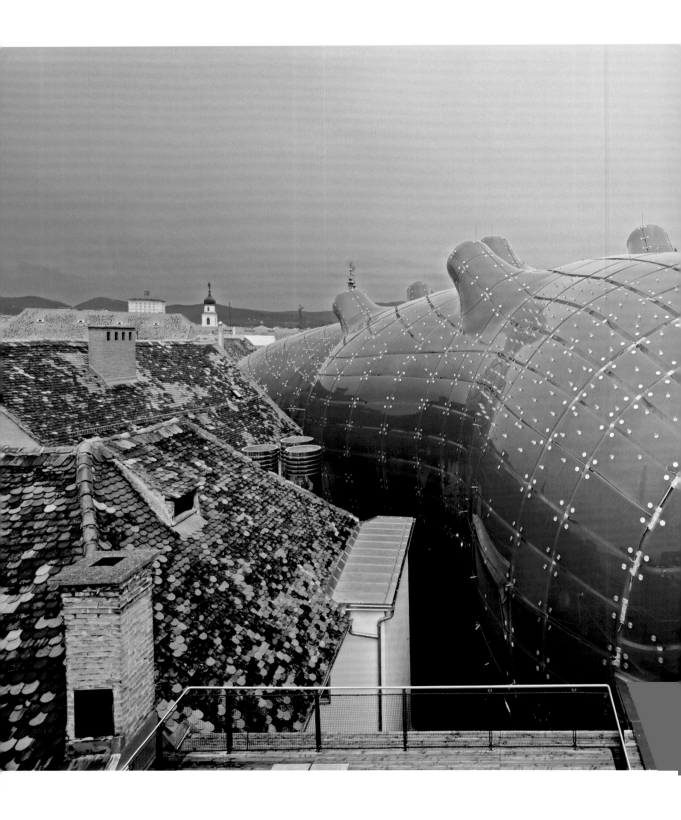

Inspirational Spaces?

Introduction by Gemma Tipton

[previous page:] Kunsthaus, Graz; Cook and Fournier, 2003, photo-credit Kunsthaus Graz / Zepp-Cam. 2004/Graz, Austria

[1] see my introduction to 'How Space Works', pp. 48-51.

D espite the gushing adjectives in many architectural reviews ('sculptural building', 'a work of art in itself…'), I do not believe that architecture is art, but I do think that sometimes it is in danger of wanting to become it. This is a process that is changing art. The shape and form of the container is influencing the shape and form of the contained. In some instances the art that is being made to fit and fill the massive spaces of our new art palaces, is, as it grows larger and larger, beginning to look like architecture. And then, of course, there is the architecture that is starting to look very much like art[1]. Alongside this is an insistence, from some quarters, that artists shouldn't complain about unconducive spaces, but instead work a bit harder to be worthy of (or stand up to) their new galleries and museums.[2] Art and architecture are in a conversation of sorts, but it is a strange and conflicting discussion at best.

[2] a position annecdotally attributed to Frank Lloyd Wright, countering criticism of the exhibition spaces in his Guggenheim Museum in New York.

So, against this background, what do we mean when we speak of inspirational spaces? Do we mean a space which inspires artists to create work directly in relationship to it? In that case, the Tate Turbine Hall would be inspirational, as would be the Guggenheim Museum in New York. Or do we mean a space which inspires other architects, or those commissioning buildings? In this instance, Frank Gehry and Daniel Libeskind have created utterly inspirational spaces. Architects can also be inspired by elements of buildings, or qualities of light, that artists might wish to edit from a space before installing their work. On the other hand there is the idea of a space where the art is given room (and time) to affect the viewer, to be inspirational itself. Alternatively, there are those spaces that put the visitor in the frame of mind to feel inspired, even before they have reached the artworks on display. Maybe the ideal would mix elements of all these, and yet, as the following essays, and the contributions to the *Vox Pop* at the end of this chapter explore, we seem to still be a long way from any clear conclusion. In this introduction, the discussion is focussed mainly on international examples, those 'famous' buildings (and famous architects) that have formed, and informed, what we now consider to be the 'ideal' for art spaces. The debates that have surrounded these 'signature' buildings are, however, equally germane to the debates that arise with any visual-arts space, whether of local, national or international size and significance.

[3] see my introduction, 'Where are the Museums', p. 12.

Art and architecture aren't entirely separate disciplines. The similarities shared by the two forms are discussed later in this section. There is still the fundamental issue, however, that gallery and museum architecture creates space; the space that is then inhabited by art. Space, as we have seen, is never neutral, it is always saturated with qualities.[3] These qualities were perhaps for the first time physically illustrated by Marcel Duchamp in his *Mile of String* at the *First Papers of Surrealism* show in 1942 in New York. The piece, which looped, wove and entangled the entire area of the gallery with a massive, messy spider's web of string, made it next-to-impossible to simply walk up to one of the (other) artworks. It also made one aware of the space itself, and so articulated the tension between the architecture and the artwork for dominance of that space; it made the unseen presences and qualities that the gallery brings, between the viewer and the work of art, physical. These presences and qualities, even as we negotiate them, change how we see the object we have come to view, so it is perhaps unsurprising that the dialogue between art and architecture can become oppositional at times.

According to Claes Oldenburg, "The difference between art and architecture is that architecture has windows and toilets,"[4], and while Oldenburg was undoubtedly being facetious, the remark does underscore the difficulty of pinpointing exactly how, and where, art and architecture differ. This difficulty allows a general blurring of boundaries between the two forms that has gained increasing currency over the past few years. This blurring allows the use of artistic terminology to be a lazy shorthand for the assessment of architecture, while also being employed as a final 'full stop' point in criticism. To call Frank Gehry's Bilbao Guggenheim Museum (1997) 'sculptural' begins to capture the crazy titanium shapes of the building. But the description is as incomplete as a description of a piece of sculpture as 'sculptural' would be, leaving the questions how, why, in what form, how do the shapes move, relate, work…? unaddressed. The description of a building as 'a work of art itself' is often used to shut down discussion of its relative functional merits and flaws, as 'art' becomes the unarguable descriptive form, subordinating all shortcomings to a higher aesthetic or creative purpose.

[4]Claes Oldenburg, speaking at the Chinati Foundation Art and Architecture Symposium, 25/26 April 1998, reported by Daphne Beal, p. 25, in Ed. Rob Weiner, *La Fundación Chinati*, vol 3, Fall 1988.

The motivations and processes of art and architecture are different. The cultural assumptions about the role of the artist and architect are different, and the reception and treatment of the finished works are the most different of all. Sometimes, the intellectual confusion between exactly what the differences between art and architecture are, leads to situations redolent with unintentional irony. In San Francisco, Mario Botta's SFMOMA (1995) is described by the museum's director, David A. Ross, as "a signal work in the Museum's collection – one that embodies all the attributes of great modern art."[5] SFMOMA dedicates a suite of galleries to its collection of architectural drawings, carefully conserved and displayed in frames as part of the museum's general exhibition programme. And yet, the Koret Visitor Education Center in that museum (2002) was designed by San Francisco firm Leddy Maytum Stacy Architects. The new centre occupies space on the second floor of the museum, and "its innovative plan echoes the aesthetic of the Museum established by Swiss architect Mario Botta in 1995, while addressing the specific demands of an educational facility."[6] So, at SFMOMA, architectural drawings are art, and the building itself is described as a work of art – yet it is a work of art which can be altered by a different firm of architects (artists?) when the need is perceived to arise.

[5]*San Francisco Museum of Modern Art*, ed. Janet Wilson, San Francisco, 2000, p.11

[6]http://www.sfmoma.org/press

To view the question from a different angle: if Yoshio Tanuguchi's Manhattan MoMA extension project (2004) came up with a room too big or too small for MoMA's Rauschenberg wall piece, would the museum employ a local artist to cut Rauschenburg's work down to size, or to paint on an extra bit to make it fit the new building? The specific absurdity of the proposition underlines the more general absurdity of claiming architecture as art, a claim which also holds architecture back from being judged intelligently on its own merits. Unsympathetic extensions and renovations have undermined the integrity of galleries for too long for anyone to believe that boards of directors and trustees truly value the principle of a museum (or gallery) itself as art. Attempting to view galleries as works of art also ties critics up in intellectual knots. In looking at the alterations and additions made to the 'father' of all 'sculptural' buildings, Frank Lloyd Wright's Guggenheim in New York (1956-59), Victoria Newhouse wants to have it both ways: "With the exception of Richard Meier's deferential Aye Simon Reading Room (1978), slipped into a leftover space off the main ramp, the various Guggenheim renovations have mutilated a great work of art, just as

[7]Victoria Newhouse, *Towards a New Museum*, Monacelli Press, New York 1998, p. 164

[8]Theodor Adorno, *Functionalism Today*,presented as a lecture in 1965, and translated by Jane Newman and John Smith in *Oppositions*, no 17, Summer 1979.

[9]Louis H. Sullivan, *The tall office building artistically considered*. Lippincott's Magazine, March 1896. Note too that Sullivan also talks about the architect's 'art'.

[10]Robert Irwin, interviewed by the author, 10 July 2003.

[11]Donald Judd, quoted in *The Museum as Muse, Artists Reflect*, Kynaston McShine, MoMA, New York, 1999, p. 230.

[12]Donald Judd, quoted by Charles Darwent in ed. Barbara Minton, *Writers on Artists*, DK Publishing, London 2001, p. 336.

surely as slashing the Mona Lisa, or chipping The Thinker, would."[7] Is the suggestion then that a 'deferential' Richard Meier slash to the Mona Lisa would be quite acceptable?

While Theodor Adorno described art's "definitive protest against the dominance of purpose over human life",[8] the form-follows-function adage of Louis Sullivan, made in 1896, demonstrates that the purpose of architecture is both definite and definitive. As an aside, it is interesting to see that Sullivan's actual text reads far more 'romantically' than its usage today might imply, and that in Sullivan's terms, 'functionalism' does not necessarily equal banal utilitarianism, "Whether it be the sweeping eagle in his flight or the open apple-blossom, the toiling work-horse, the blithe swan, the branching oak, the winding stream at its base, the drifting clouds, over all the coursing sun, form ever follows function, and this is the law. [...] It is the pervading law of all things organic and inorganic, of all things physical and metaphysical, of all things human and all things superhuman, of all true manifestations of the head, of the heart, of the soul, that life is recognizable in its expression, that form ever follows function. This is the law. – Shall we, then, daily violate this law in our art? Are we so decadent, so imbecile, so utterly weak of eyesight, that we cannot perceive this truth so simple, so very simple?"[9]

Artist Robert Irwin, who was asked to collaborate with architect Richard Meier by creating the gardens at Meier's Getty museum in Los Angeles, says the primary difference between the artist and the architect is one of responsibility.[10] The Irwin/Meier collaboration has become almost legendary for its acrimony, and the result is that Irwin has created a garden that turns its back on the museum complex beside it. Perhaps Irwin too had a responsibility to address Meier's architecture, but it is unarguable that architecture presupposes the idea of a user – and therefore a responsibility to that user, in a way which art does not.

The essays in this chapter follow different forms in meditating on the ideal of art and architecture. One of the problems with constructing an ideal is, of course, that we do not live in an ideal world. In the *Vox Pop*, artists, architects and curators consider their ideas of best spaces and worst spaces, and also what makes a space work for exhibiting art. A theme which occurs, here and throughout the book, is the idea of the 'difficult space'. Like the Guggenheims in Manhattan and Bilbao, the Ormeau Baths Gallery in Belfast, and the Douglas Hyde Gallery in Dublin have been described, in negative terms, by artists and curators as 'difficult spaces'. And yet, paradoxically, it would seem that artists are often inspired by difficult spaces, that they relish the challenges presented by them. The contradiction dissolves, however, when one realises that these artists and curators are not referring to the light-filled atriums of local authority offices; the angular areas (by the bar and on the way to the toilets) of some multi-use arts centres; or the architecturally 'challenging' spaces of those galleries which are most often described as 'sculptural'. The difficult spaces that inspire and challenge artists are more usually 'found' spaces, where the more obvious hand of the architect has been reduced by the passage of time, or by a change of use.

An extreme position within the discussion between art and architecture was, of course, occupied by Donald Judd. "Art," he said, "is only an excuse for the building housing it."[11] "Somewhere a portion of contemporary art has to exist as an example of what the art and its context were meant to be."[12] Judd, of course, created his own ideal at Chinati, where he had the time (and initially money) to consider the placement of his works, and those of his contemporaries. (Judd was backed in his purchase of the army base by the Dia Art Foundation, whose main source of cash was its co-founder Philippa de Menil. The de Menil fortune came from oil, and when oil stock fell in the early 1980s, and the funding dried up,

Judd sued his benefactors for full control of Fort D.A. Russell. He won. Re-christened Chinati in 1976, Judd used the site to realise his theories about the ideal ways to show art. When he died, the foundation was infamously left on the brink of bankruptcy, with between $240 and $400, depending on who's telling the story, to its name.) The Dan Flavin neon *Untitled* (1996) project, installed in six mess huts at Chinati, both manipulates and works with the architecture in the same way that Judd's installation of his own work does. Yet even at Chinati the spaces are only ideal for a certain kind of art; the huts devoted to John Wesley's paintings just don't seem to work with the art they contain, after all that sublimity of light and space they seem slight and wanting.

The problem is that Tate Modern, the Guggenheims, the Milwaukee Art Museum, even the wide, wild spaces at Chinati, have all taught us to expect the 'wow', the massive atrium, the mind-blowing foyer, the drama of approach and arrival. Statement architecture is increasingly used to make up for a lack of strength in a museum's collection: "I look at the building as an extremely important artistic statement... we'd have a building which would be at least as important as anything we'd have inside... I'm well aware that we are not likely to have a collection to rank with the world's most important, and I think that we make up for that to some degree by having a building that is truly distinguished."[13] In an environment where success is increasingly measured in terms of volume of visitors, this quote by Gudmund Vigtel, Director of Richard Meier's High Museum of Art in Atlanta, Georgia, makes marketing sense. But when a museum, like the Bilbao Guggenheim, is only ever discussed in terms of its architecture, and not its collection, things are out of balance.

Artist and architect Elizabeth Diller of Diller and Scofidio, while working on the Boston ICA building project, also noted that the balance has changed. "Museums are now more than just galleries, the gallery component is now only about 30%. Architecture is becoming more of a draw for museums, it is now the first part of the collection. Architecture has to deal with that development, we as artists and architects have to deal with that. We have to deal with the different speeds of visitors, and have the private, contemplative spaces as well as the social spaces."[14] And so, when the museums' endowments can't afford the crowd-pulling and pleasing Impressionists or Masters; or when the work on view doesn't quite stand up to our own ideas of inspirational; the foyer fulfils our expectations. It satisfies our requirement for wonder, a requirement which this new breed of art spaces has instilled. And when a new space fails to provide that, we think *is that it*? The value systems of contemporary art and architecture, which seem to rank innovation over everything else have themselves inspired these mad crazy spaces, spaces that may indeed be 'almost works of art in themselves'. These create, drive and inspire a desire that can make us hungry for everything but simply, functionally beautiful rooms.

In conclusion, perhaps an up-side to this turning of architecture into art is that, unlike some art, architecture is (at least) affordable. The $104 million paid in 2004 for Picasso's rose period *Boy with a Pipe*[15] would buy you:

- one Guggenheim Bilbao
- just less than nine Market Place Art Centres in Armagh
- seven and a half Lewis Glucksman Galleries in Cork
- two Dia Beacons (including all installation costs)
- three Millennium Wings for the National Gallery in Dublin
- or a Santiago Calatrava addition to the Milwaukee Art Museum (minus a small section of the tail).

[13]Gudmund Vigtel, Director of the High Museum of Art in Atlanta Georgia, quoted by Poyin Auyoung in *Museum Space: Privatising Culture/Imaging Desire*, *Øjeblikket*, vol. 8, 1998, p. 113.

[14]Elizabeth Diller, interviewed in her studio by the author, 5 July 2002.

[15]Picasso's *Boy with a Pipe* set an auction record, selling for $104 million on 5 May 2004 at Sotheby's in New York. The sale, to an unnamed buyer, included the auction price of $93 million plus Sotheby's commission of about $11 million. The pre-sale estimate was $70 million.

Molly and art spaces June 16th, 2004

by Noel Sheridan

Yes its all about spaces now but what was wrong with those wonderful Victorian spaces I want to know at least you knew where you were art palaces they were but of course that was what was wrong according to your man at MoMA whats his name Alfred Barr was it thats right democracy how are you what with his wall charts starting from Cézanne and all the little offshoots ending of course with the Americans just follow the rooms past the Brancusi into the Matisse and then the Pollocks Rothkos Newmans and the De Koonings imagine making love to him hed tear you to pieces but at least you knew where you were not like some of these conceptual merchants leaving you suspended like that so you have to finish it off yourself most of the time neutral white cubes they were supposed to be but Minimalism put a halt to that gallop looking around for the art O is that it and what about the fire extinguisher is that supposed to be art I blame the readymade the urinal typical of men no use to us but their spaces their buildings their erections their urinals will they ever catch themselves on although I must say I have a soft spot for Marcel Duchamp that piece in Philadelphia where you had to look through the key hole and there it all was holding a lamp in case you missed it a real gentleman but like the rest of them after the one thing an epiphany well thats one way of looking at it I suppose but vicious enough in its own way not like a kiss long and hot down to your soul almost paralyses you and where is that art Id like to know Giorgione and yes Rubens but of course now youre not supposed to like them politically incorrect my arse or their arses I suppose making objects of us but o rocks isnt that what its all about at the heel of the hunt and isnt that what makes us wonderful and powerful and what theyll never understand or be O yes lets see you try and make a victim of one of those Rubens women but it is their fault yes putting us into their rational spaces just lie on the couch there and wear this its for the colour or just sit on the grass in the nip and well keep our clothes on but you wouldnt want to see them anyway because isnt it only lust that lets us look at each other naked and thats true of art spaces trying to evoke desire and I suppose thats why the Victorian ones looked a little like high class bordellos I often thought that owning a Cezanne must be like having a wild animal in the house and they are zoos in a way so sad but then if we didnt have them wed never get to see the wonderful power of them and it must be something in us that were never enough for each other having to get all gussied up and I sometimes think its getting like that with art spaces although Id love to go to Bilbao to see whats his names building Gerrity is it

of course I put it all down to the 60s wanting to be free O yes the deep structural constraints of the white cube wasnt good enough for them so off to remote places earth art youd need an aeroplane to see half of it and of course then they had to bring us back the photos so we could imagine it or your man putting the tiles on the floor I liked that I felt like taking my shoes off and feeling them on the soles of my feet and that was alright with him but no everyone on their best behavior walking around the grid its funny isnt it that were the ones that want it up against the wall but not the Arabs those gorgeous men and their carpets on the floor walk all over them increases the value they say not because they get worn but because it loosens the stitching and lets it breathe but I always think of the little children going blind doing the work but then the formal qualities are supposed to blind you to that and thats what art spaces do but now Im starting to depress myself and I suppose the main point is that you have to give as much attention to the floors as to the walls not to mention the ceilings because artists are now obsessed with the container and I pity the poor buggers that have to make an art space for them because whatever they do will be wrong in some artists eyes and then the staff have to change everything move the walls and what have you that American that wanted the whole place painted black and he came back after a few days and said it was the wrong black and they had to do it all again but I suppose it makes it an industry and it gives employment and what with the collapse of the Church and people getting fed up being fed up with politics these are the cathedrals of today well the churches if its only a small space but hope for the future in this time of no-future

storage space is what they always seem to forget plenty of architectural detail and proper lux readings but no where to store the fucking work because its all about the look and they spend a fortune on the space and nothing on the staffing and upkeep and theres nothing sadder than an art space with nothing going on so once youve seen the 200 seat theatre and the carpet thats it except for the corridor and the foyer which is the gallery if it isnt some limbo afterthought that was supposed to be the gallery but they have to use it for storage and I think this giving them just enough money to choke on is typical because its all about property and restraint at the end of the day and whats this he called it O yes social engineering so tax payers can see where all their money went but there I go giving myself the glooms again and Ill get nothing done if I only keep upsetting myself about things like that and isnt it great that we have spaces at all where before there was nothing and Im sure we must be part of some larger plan the arts council has for us and the thing to do is just get on with it and be thankful to the sweet and divine that we have a space at all to do the dreaming nobody knows what you need for that broadband is it and plenty of electrical outlets but as sure as Christ whatever you put in will be obsolete next year and somebody will discover telepathy or something and artists will just lie in bed thinking

theyre all so different now installations performance multimedia how would you build for that shite specific if you ask me its the students I feel sorry for seeing it all and trying to do it themselves that year Viola was the big thing with half of them under water and the parents helping them install the work squaring up a pornographic image of some rossie and is that the way you want it yes thatll do fine dad O Im sure it will but isnt it wonderful now not like my time when if you showed an ankle you were the worst in the world O theres no shortage of talent and energy and there should be spaces for them for what do they want only to be that one in a million that will be immortal and dont worry therell be space for them then and maybe special days and this time we can say we cared and tried to help rather than send them off like shots off a shovel into exile but it will have to be them and it wont be easy in these times when there is no anchorage in the past and

Ive got to get out of myself because this would drive you up the walls more walls and I feel sorry for the artists too with nothing to cling to but themselves throwing shapes showing us all how difficult it is as if we didnt know but if anything good is to happen it will be from artists who will just have to keep on keeping on never mind the spaces and I could be their muse because I know things and theyll have to keep asking and yes I have the juice and I am the only source and space worth having and although at times it looks as if Im not looking Im here and Im asking them to ask me again and Ill draw them in to me into that special art space to hear their hearts asking me will I say yes and yes I will of course yes,

The ideal gallery subtracts from the artwork all cues that interfere with the fact that it is 'art'. The work is isolated from everything that would detract from its own evaluation of itself. This gives the space a presence possessed by other spaces where conventions are preserved through the repetition of a closed system of values. Some of the sanctity of the church, the formality of the courtroom, the mystique of the experimental laboratory joins with chic design to produce a unique chamber of esthetics.

Inside the White Cube, Brian O'Doherty
University of California Press, London 1999, p. 14.

A tour around the ideal space for exhibiting art

by Eamon O'Kane

The museum is situated on the edge of a lake in a spacious, old park with a view across the water. It houses a collection of modern art by international artists. It is not merely an experience in modern and contemporary art, but a reflection of the interplay between art, architecture and landscape. The park serves as an ideal setting for displaying the museum's collection of modern sculptures. Similarly the museum buildings offer a fascinating background for the permanent collection of twentieth century art. Both the buildings and the collection are owned by the museum and it has been built in eight stages between 1958 and 1998. The total area covered by these buildings is 22,500 square metres, of which 17,500 square metres are used for exhibition purposes. The museum is entered through the original building which faces an industrial part of the city. This first section of the museum is above ground and the visitors can proceed upstairs into the upper galleries or underground into the lower galleries which form a subterranean structure that snakes throughout the complex, breaking the surface at certain points to facilitate access to the sculpture park. A Georgian style manor house has also been preserved within the grounds of the park and this contains an eccentric collection of arts and craft displayed in a domestic setting where important works of art can be viewed alongside craft and design.

Originally, the museum was to be housed in a new building on a site south of the train station. However, implementing the plans of the architect would have exceeded the allotted budget by far. After long and heated debate, the idea of a new construction was abandoned. Instead, a historic monument was chosen - the vast edifice of a former munitions factory, was to become the home of the extended museum. The architects undertook planning, reconstruction and renovation, converting a structure of dominating, static monumentality into a building ideally suited to presenting advanced technologies and artistic experiments. (In the early phases of its founding and construction, the museum's offices were scattered across the entire city.) The permanent collection is displayed in a logical progression of rooms. The museum has an impressive entrance with large glass window frontage which because of the museum's position on a hill above the city is visible from many locations. On entering the space there is a large atrium where the foyer is housed, this tall, light space gives a huge impact whilst providing the necessary access to all floors.

Another part of the museum is housed next door in a former wool-spinning mill that has been transformed by the architects into a space where contemporary art can be seen at its best. The vast, light main area of the enormous old factory and the intimate 'wool-storage rooms' constitute a beautiful environment for the many works of art. The collection includes important works from younger as well as older artists. In addition to a fairly permanent display of work from the collection, three large and several smaller exhibitions are organized annually. Visitors enter this part of the museum through the original entrance-way. Via an expanded lobby, they have direct access to the renovated exhibition areas of the old museum, the new library, and a new foyer leading to the new museum. Using a grand staircase or the lift, visitors descend to a connecting foyer in the basement. Both the new exhibition wing as well as the new building section with facilities for the public's use can be reached from here. The interior is a balanced variety of vast high-ceilinged spaces versus smaller and more intimate places. Despite its monumental character, the new building maintains the human dimensions so characteristic of the former building. Massive installations or sizable exhibitions as well as smaller intimate projects – such as showings of prints and drawings – can all be presented thanks to the variety of the exhibition areas. This part of the museum also has a whole range of facilities which include an auditorium and an education centre, which will accommodate a wide spectrum of public events. The library, in its striking new home, ranks among the leading scholarly centres for the visual arts in the world.

from *Studio in the Woods* Series, 2004, Eamon O'Kane

The main exhibition gallery faces you at the far end of the building. The space can be freely partitioned by using twenty suspended panels. It is an ideal space for exhibiting works of art such as paintings, photographs, or sculptures. The gallery has controllable natural light and can be blacked out to enable video works to be projected. This exhibition gallery also has an internet location which amalgamates a physical and virtual environment, relating contemporary visual arts with the information technology revolution. The museum has established an education program that emphasizes the creative process and its positive effect on problem-solving in daily life and other academic areas. The museum aggressively educates and encourages viewers – regardless of prior experience – to examine the relevance of art and creativity in their own lives. Its confirmed belief is that contact with experimental work allows viewers to explore and to more directly access their own experience than is generally possible in a traditional museum setting. By collecting permanent installations, it

from *Studio in the Woods* Series, 2004, Eamon O'Kane

has also established a frame of reference for seeing and understanding contemporary works. In the process, the museum's expansion is energizing its neighbourhood on the city's north side. It identifies properties, dispersed throughout the community, that do not contribute to the economic, social or cultural benefit of the area. It then acquires and rehabilitates selected buildings as exhibition sites, artist housing and rental properties both to improve the neighbourhood and to support its artistic program.

The museum is also a research and development lab for artists, it commissions new site-specific works, presents them to the widest possible audience, and maintains selected individual installations in a growing and distinctive permanent collection. Its work combines production and research, exhibitions and events, coordination and documentation. The museum's physical and organizational environments have grown out of and in response to a central focus on the process of creativity. Professional artists, at varying stages in their careers, experiment with ideas and materials within an integrated residency and exhibition program. In spaces that function equally well as private working studios and as public exhibition spaces, each artist receives an uncommon level of curatorial support. The museum combines white cube neutral spaces with other areas that challenge the exhibiting artists. Twenty-five artists can be housed within the various buildings and are provided with accommodation, subsistence and a materials allowance to carry out their work. In addition their studios are usually housed in or near to the spaces that they will exhibit in at the end of their residency which enable them to spend invaluable time getting to know the space or constructing complicated site specific work that would not otherwise have been possible.

This overview highlights how the museum is attempting to create the ideal environment to exhibit, produce and archive contemporary art. In the future it will continue to respond to the rapid developments in information technology and today's changing social structures and will establish itself as the most important museum and art institution in the world.

This is a fictional construct, based on the descriptions of five key art institutions.

from *Studio in the Woods* Series, 2004, Eamon O'Kane

Studio in the Woods Series

In this body of work, a series of large-scale oil paintings on canvas and drawings on paper, Eamon O'Kane meditates on the idea of the ideal artist's studio. The works are depictions of buildings by some of the world's foremost Modernist architects, Frank Lloyd Wright, Lacaton + Vassal, Alvar Aalto and Elam & Bray as well as imagined building constructs usually set in isolated forests. There are no signs of human presence in the works apart from the warm light emanating from the windows in the night-time scenarios and so these are places in which the artist can work seemingly without disturbance. However, although they appear to be ideal spaces for artistic contemplation, O'Kane is aware of the dangers of working in a location removed from society. These studios promise aesthetic pleasure, but may turn out to eat up the artist, physically and mentally.

...the Parthenon is the supreme example of an object which is basically functional and still made up from universal harmonies

Le Corbusier and the Tragic View of Architecture, *Charles Jencks*
Penguin, Middlesex, 1987 p. 66

Architecture: Possessing Art

by Jimi Shields

It is easier to state what architecture is not, rather than what architecture is (for that I would refer to Vitruvius' *Ten Books on Architecture*); suffice to say that a great many architects do not in fact practice architecture; they are instead primarily concerned with the occupation of being 'service providers', shirking their responsibility to society as a whole, while ably assisting their clients' needs for accommodation. That there is a difference between construction and architecture must be understood. "The creation of Architecture must involve more than the production of commodities, however elegantly formed… and must recover ways to re-connect with 'everyman' by interpreting, giving expression to, and often guiding their fundamental aspirations."[1]

Architecture occurs at a certain level within the mind of the architect and their under-standing of it. The true architect will preview the dialogue between building and user; they will rehearse the scene many times alone in their studio whilst simultaneously editing and sequencing until the blueprints to a narrative have been produced and formulated. There is an intention to impart meaning. Of course, much of the value depends on the architect's ability, but a certain amount also depends on the ability of the user to interpret. Architecture can and does possess many of those qualities that we ascribe to art. Consider the striking parallels between Frank Lloyd Wright's interpretation of "…the very image of man's desire to be at one with nature"[2] or God, at Falling Water[3], and Michelangelo's own depiction of that same desire on the ceiling of the Sistine Chapel. These ideas are well accepted and taught within the architecture community, but not often recognised by the artists who are forced to take a critical view of architecture when exhibiting their work with-in its walls.

Though the photograph can represent it, it can never fully capture architecture. The five senses must combine to give us the sense of bodily position and movement through space. Thus arises the issue of spatial composition, "the masterly, correct and magnificent play of masses brought together in light[4]". As with all creative endeavours or actions pursuing the realisation of an idea, the transition from the limitless boundaries of the mind to the phys-ical world guarantees at least a small amount of compromise. As Tadao Ando puts it, "per-haps it does not matter how pretty the details are, or how beautiful the finish is, what is important is the clarity of one's logic – that is, the clarity of the logic behind a composi-tion…the quality that one recognises through reason, not perception"[5]. This is not to undermine the importance of the crafts men and women whose hands help to realise the thoughts, ideas and concepts of the architect, but rather states that their poetry exists on yet

[1] Tom Heneghan, *Tadao Ando: The Colours of Light*, Phaidon Press Ltd., London, 1996, p. 31.

[2] Edgar Kaufmann Jr. quoted by Robert McCarter, *Falling Water*, from the *Architecture in Detail* series, Phaidon Press Ltd., London, 1994, p. 34.

[3] Falling Water is situated at Bear Run, Pennsylvania, USA. Designed by Frank Lloyd Wright, it was built in 1935 for Edgar Kaufmann as a weekend retreat.

[4] Le Corbusier quoted by Charles Jencks,1987, *op cit.* p. 65.

[5] Tadao Ando, 'From the Periphery of Architecture' in *Japan Architect*, Jan. 1991, 1, p. 19.

Frank Lloyd Wright, Fallingwater, exterior detail; photograph of Fallingwater courtesy of the Western Pennsylvania Conservancy. Fallingwater is located in Mill Run, Pennsylvania

another level; the knowledge that all forms of expression are ultimately framed by the limitations imposed by the human condition.

(Is a Girl a Boy?)

Hence we return to the notion of the 'neutral' space, a place void of expression, or statement, in which to exhibit art. Such a place is not, in the strictest sense, possible. Absolute neutrality of space in fact implies something wholly extraterrestrial, and in terms of an art-viewing destination it is, after all, a planet, not a black hole, which we seek to create. So we have the enticing problem of the art space, the compulsory interface of the two worlds of art and architecture. These worlds which are equally worthy; who are different, yet who also share so many characteristics are still to be found sitting awkwardly beside each other, like the girl and boy on their first day of school, wondering whether (or how) to talk to one another.

"The creation of architecture must be a criticism of the problems of today. It must resist existing conditions. It is only when one faces up to today's problems that one can really begin to deal with architecture."[6] In dealing with the art space we must deal with the architecture of that space. The venue must be given shape, a shape that is appropriate, functional, communicative and quietly inspiring. The art community must accept that it is also an impossibility to extract the 'place' from the edifice. It would be ill advised to demand a venue devoid of 'place', devoid of 'Architecture', but therein lies the true ethical dilemma: how do we as artists, art custodians, and architects define and attain the correct balance of art and place? In order to be worthy of the name 'Architecture', the building must move us. The museum must, in and of itself, possess the spirit of inspiration, the upheaval of the soul common to all great works of art. Just as sacred architecture often symbolises the spiritual path and its goal, (a place apart), so too must museum architecture aim to show an awareness of, and to some extent guide, the events contained within.

[6]Tadao Ando, quoted in Heneghan, 1996 *op cit*. p. 29.

The Good, the Bad and the Ugly

What works for art, and is there such a thing as the ideal space?

Norman Foster, Sainsbury Centre for Visual Arts, photo Pete Huggins, courtesy SCVA

Designed by Norman Foster in 1978 the Sainsbury Centre of Visual Art at the University of East Anglia is an amazing deluxe hangar of a building. What I really like are the comfy areas dotted about the display area for the eclectic Robert and Lisa Sainsbury collection. I recall low tubular glass and stainless steel tables, loaded with art magazines, matching seating and giant potted palms. This, the quality of the architecture and the proximity of the UEA's classic 1970s brutalist university campus creates and environment really conducive to reposeful thinking and art appreciation.

Jason Oakley, Publications Manager, The Sculptors' Society of Ireland

The kind of space an artwork needs is entirely dependent upon the nature of the artwork. The best space is one that allows the work to reach its full potential and that allows the work to address its audience immediately and directly. I think it's not possible to design a best space for all artworks. What will happen is that the clever work will always challenge these conceptions of space and extend our awareness of what is possible. A more productive way of approaching the issue of accommodating artworks is to accept that there can be as many spaces as there are practices and to be open to that. Then the key to choosing the right space for the right artwork lies in recognising the characteristics of the work and what it requires in order to communicate to its audience.

Eoghan McTigue is an artist living in Berlin

The worst art space is easy to choose, possibly because there has been so much hype about the Guggenheim Museum in Bilbao. Certainly it is an extraordinary urban punctuation mark, but the actual display of art seems to be very much a second thought. Architects rarely have any problems finding their way around buildings, but I found the Bilbao a particular challenge.

The best place I have seen for art is the Beyeler Foundation in Basel, maybe as an architect I am seduced by the beautiful form of the building, but somehow the architect has managed to combine a strong architectural form, linked to the outside, daylight and a variety of spaces. How many galleries could show at the one time, a major Rothko exhibition in one part and Paul Klee drawings in another?

John Graby, Director, RIAI

As someone who works as an installer in an art gallery I have a different view of how a space should work to when I am working as an artist on my own work. Most galleries designed by architects inevitably are on the second floor without an elevator and have windows that don't open to allow big works of art to be lifted through. You usually can bet the doors are too small by perhaps two inches to get crates through, the list is endless. Neutral spaces are the best for installing but when I come to making my own work it's totally different – I love difficult spaces. Spaces which demand consideration. I suppose it has to do with the challenge but I suspect it has more to do with trying to use and understand something that seems to be becoming increasingly remote – spaces with their own unique character.

Brendan Earley is an artist based in Dublin

The galleries that I have visited that seem least suitably equipped to fit their function are ones where either the ego of the architect(s), or a misconception about what is needed in a gallery, got in the way of good architecture. Some of the things to look for in a good purpose-built gallery include (i) a sense of spaciousness without being a vacuum; (ii) ease of access for artworks; (iii) the use of natural light; (iv) the option of secondary, or private, viewing space; (v) generous, professional storage facilities.

Whatever about their storage facilities, Tate, St. Ives; Guggenheim, New York; and Ormeau Baths Gallery, Belfast are difficult spaces that do not always allow easy or optimum viewing of art. In the case of the Tate, St. Ives and, to a lesser extent, the Guggenheim, New York, the architects were too focused on creating emblematic and symbolic architecture, and so thwarted the prime function of their buildings.

Jerome O Drisceoil, Director, Green on Red Gallery, Dublin

In my personal experience the need for space is something that has driven the work, having resorted to occupying spaces that were wholly unsuitable for it, solely for the purpose of making itself visible and having my choices limited for me. Who can say that any space their work has occupied has been an ideal. And where do I store all this work when it is not occupying a visible space? Another suitable space? I wonder if I ever considered my studio suitable, with its pigeons, ready to shit on your work quicker than the meanest curator, the leaking roof or its final propensity to mysteriously burst into flames destroying just less than everything I (and others) had made. It seems inevitable that my current spatial refuge is the hard drive, no more waterproof than my old studio but mercifully free of pigeons. Still, forty gigabytes doesn't seem large enough but there will always be room (space?) for improvement.

Allan Hughes is an artist based in Belfast

Contemporary art is so varied in its form that is difficult to be definitive as to the kind of space it needs in a general way. For example, works by James Coleman or Luc Tuymans would look their best in different situations. The space has to have architectural quality to start with. Even eccentric buildings like the Guggenheim in New York do sometimes work, and it does because in spite of everything it is good architecture. My favourite space is the Beyeler Foundation in Basel, by Renzo Piano, which besides the building has the most spectacular collection to go with it. Sometimes old buildings provide very interesting spaces like the Reina Sofia Museum in Madrid, IMMA in Dublin or the Castello de Rivoli in Turin. However, the best spaces are possibly some of the New York galleries. I am thinking of Cheim & Read, Paula Cooper or Matthew Marks that have been designed having contemporary art practice in mind.

Enrique Juncosa, Director of the Irish Museum of Modern Art

It doesn't really bother me to see artwork in spaces that are a bit raw or quirky. It's more depressing to walk into a cool, pristine space to find uninspiring work. Phrases like 'silk purse' and 'sow's ear' come to mind. Fundamentally it's just dressing. Obviously all artists want their work to be displayed appropriately but this doesn't necessarily mean the white cube scenario as innovative exhibitions like *Via* have recently proved. What art needs (here) is more shows beyond the realms of the institutionalised gallery. Artists passionate about their practice can take risks on their own terms, out of their own pockets if necessary. It's just not realistic to sit around waiting for arts council hand-outs to make something happen.

Alison Pilkington is an artist and runs the Workroom studios and gallery

Louisiana Museum of Modern Art at Humlaebak near Copenhagen: there is something very intimate about this Museum. It is one of those places that is particularly impressive for the fluidity of the space and for the interaction it allows with the landscape outside. It is more domestic than monumental in scale and white cube space exists alongside other rooms where, for example, the backdrop for a range of Giacometti works is a water garden, seen through floor-to-ceiling windows. When you are led seamlessly into the part of the sculpture garden nestled between the buildings and the sea you realize how well the accretions of the design work.

Dr Suzanne Lyle, Arts Development Officer, Visual Arts and Collections, at the Arts Council of Northern Ireland

Louisiana, exterior the Graphics Wing, the Greenhouse, photo Jens Frederiksen, courtesy Louisiana Museum of Modern Art

It has to be said: sometimes I hate gallery spaces. With their clinically white walls and sealed windows, the gallery can become an artificial white cube devoid of feeling and experience. It's like going to a solemn, unfriendly church, intimidating and slightly uncomfortable.

What art needs is a space, people and work that will engage with audiences and enhance their creative experience. It needs a bold environmental approach to gallery space in order to re-define the conventional notions of the white cube. This inversion introduces new audiences, tempting them into new ways of seeing, creating and perceiving. We need to break out of our post-modernist ideas of the white cube, and get away from the ideological whitewash of gallery spaces.

In a world where the city has become paramount in the arts, we may find that unconventional spaces, in alternative towns, with inverted notions of space and attitudes, may provide a variety of new ways to see, new ways to feel, and new ways to reach audiences interested in the arts.

A white cube church is fine – just make mine Southern Baptist.

Megan Johnston is the Manager at Millennium Court Arts Centre, Portadown

The best space for an artist to exhibit their hopes, dreams and perceived realities is up on the third floor of a block of semi derelict apartments awaiting demolition, up the bleach cleaned stairs, past the washing lines and through a double bolted steel door into a council flat, overlooking the city as it develops from an unloved space to a crane hungry battleground of commerce, speculation and corporate investor desire which eat the old buildings with no salad, and the scrape the skyline with lazy forks of redbrick and cream that will soon become as unloved as their predecessors.

Brian Duggan, **Mark Cullen**, Pallas

The best art space is the one you can not remember exactly because the art took all of your attention. The worst is the opposite of that.

Noel Sheridan is an artist who has directed spaces for art: Experimental Art Foundation Adelaide South Australia; Perth Institute of Contemporary Arts Western Australia and the National College of Art and Design Dublin

Block of flats containing Pallas, photo courtesy Pallas

I don't think the qualities of an art space in which a work is placed are that important. If the artwork is good or bad, the space will only influence the experience – and the technicality of its installation – not change it drastically. The success of an exhibition is more dependent on the dialogue the artist and the curator manage to create between the work and a place. Unless the arrogance of a space really doesn't allow a work to exist (like the Benson & Forsyth new museum of Scotland – not technically an art space), there is always a game to play between the context and a piece of work.

Charles Blanc & Tristan Surtees, Sans façon

Artists have consistently re-imagined conventional spaces; hospitals, phone booths, airports. Dorothy Cross memorably recast the public toilets opposite Trinity College, and artists transformed a Ballymun house in *Superbia* (2003). In the V&A's recent summer show the ordinary garden shed became an art space. If Cornelia Parker's *Cold dark matter* blasted apart the garden shed and suspended the debris in the gallery, Tracey Emin and others have rebuilt and reconfigured this icon of suburbia through sound, image and lighting – suggesting that there are no limits to what an art space might be.

Stephanie McBride is Chairman of the Board of the Gallery of Photography, Dublin

My favourite art spaces are not just physical locations, but rather times and circumstances. They can come about or be happened upon when travelling, or be under your nose in your hometown. In my first year at art college, wandering the then-undeveloped Temple Bar I was fascinated to come across a series of site specific art projects, including a sculpturally arranged stack of sliced white bread disintegrating and developing mould in an old shop window. Equally memorable was *Excellent Dynamite*, one of the first shows held at Pallas Studios. There was a great buzz at the opening about the space, the diverse range of artworks, and the idea that it came about through the efforts of a couple of young guns just getting out there and doing it. I wasn't long out of college so it was a pretty motivational event that made it feel exciting to be an artist in Dublin. I've had similarly self-affirmative experiences when visiting foreign cities, deriving feelings of comfort and belonging in local art museums and contemporary galleries.

Cora Cummins, artist

What Art Needs: a playground. There is need for a space, any kind of space; publication, office, bedroom, hotel room, garden, shed, artist-run space, gallery, internet, flower bed, etc. The most important thing is that this space is inspired, unconventional, unafraid of taking risks, humorous, adventurous, good parties, informal, provocative, spontaneous. This space should create possibilities for the unpredictable. Open itself to individual projects. Be a venue for work in progress projects rather than fixed exhibitions. Be more interested in doing, than presenting art. Today's art needs a space that is not necessarily an art space. We need a space for conversations to develop.

Katie Holten represented Ireland in the Venice Biennale 2003. She is currently living in New York working on independent research with a Fulbright Scholarship

The Fenderesky Gallery: the mass exodus which followed the victory of the Ayatollahs in Iran was that country's loss and the world's gain. In the darkest days of the Irish conflict, a small gallery was opened in Belfast by the Iranian émigré Jamshid Mirfenderesky. Uncompromising in its commitment to contemporary Irish art, the eponymous Gallery, now in the Crescent Arts Centre, survived (worse than bombs and bullets) the indifference of a provincial bourgeoisie. Now approaching its fourth decade, the gallery can claim to have nurtured the talent of many of those who now grace the Aosdána benches. Irish art owes a lot to the Ayatollahs.

Jim Smyth, art critic and cultural commentator living in Belfast

I love tiny spaces like the Return in the Goethe Institute in Dublin and the Douglas Hyde's miniature Gallery 2, which houses the Paradise series. I am regularly charmed and surprised by what can be achieved in these unassuming, diminutive spaces.

It's fascinating how a space can profoundly change a work. The sound installation, *Witness* by Susan Hillier, was originally installed in a dilapidated Baptist chapel on Golborne Road in London. The work was atmospheric and compelling, the space adding overtones of religiosity and eeriness. Installed six months later as part of the group show *Intelligence* at Tate Britain, the

Perfect Space, Garrett Phelan, 2004
Garrett Phelan is an artist based in Dublin

[right:] Exterior, Tate Modern,
conversion Herzog de Meuron,
photo courtesy Tate Photography

work became somewhat sanitised. It felt as if the meaning of the work had been culled by the order and institutionalization of the space.

Worst spaces for art are often Art Fairs, by their nature a mixum-gatherum of work and galleries. As the fair draws to a close there's a strange, combined atmosphere of excitement, fear, desperation and lethargy. They are a necessary evil, but, exiting those claustrophobic spaces I am often filled with a cynicism about art that I rarely feel at other times.

Joy Gerrard is an artist and lecturer based in Dublin and London

I have to admit to being underwhelmed by my first visit to Tate Modern. The hype didn't match my experience. I put this down to my big-city art-gallery conditioning: the need for the familiar neoclassical façades and lavish interiors that are the common experience of museum goers. This was naked, raw and a touch brutal.

Many subsequent visits have left me, nonetheless, overwhelmed by the stunning commissioned works for the Turbine Hall, presenting big art experiences which other galleries simply can't. The division between space on an ostentatious scale and the more traditional white-box arrangement of the galleries offers a unique and totally contemporary experience, making Tate Modern one of the most compelling art spaces in these islands.

Nóirín Mc Kinney, Director of Arts Development with the
Arts Council of Northern Ireland

A gallery is a place that supports and champions the various work of artists, past and present; and the primary direction of the gallery should be towards the public, and the experience of looking and contemplating. However it is now really important to consider the function of art in society. It is my belief that art should be at the heart of the community, and that current practice in art making should be engaging with its audience. As an artist, a sense of 'context' has become the most valuable aspect of showing my work. It adds to the experience of looking at art and avoids the problems inherent in the traditional gallery system. The 'gallery' for me has become a very broad term, and I now enjoy the temporary and permanent 'galleries' that I create with other professionals in the built environment. There are of course occasional difficulties, but the creative challenge and collaborative possibilities are well worth the effort. Unfortunately the funding structures we have at present are as antiquated as the gallery tradition. If art is to fulfil its potential and become a powerful force in our lives then it should not always be removed and placed in a white box, even if it is occasionally pleasant to spend an hour or so there on ones own.

Rita Duffy is an artist who lives and works in Belfast

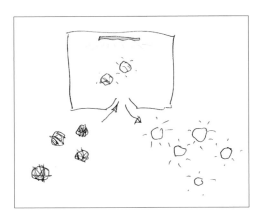

My ideal space: I would like to see spaces for art located on busy thoroughfares in town centres. Each space would be some variation on the white cube; quiet, contemplative. It would hold one artwork at a time - be it two- or three-dimensional, or even a performance. With any luck, people would leave the space in a better state than they came in; see diagram.

Peter FitzGerald is an artist, and is Editor of
CIRCA Art Magazine

In general, collectors want to view artwork in the white cube, where the objects are treated with respect, their auras remain intact and the line gets toed. The increasingly daunting expansion of that white cube – more like a white cavern really at this point (thinking Chelsea, New York) – has had a nice kind of backlash from artists and curators who are on the lookout for alternatives. It's been refreshing to see how Dublin has responded with installations in off sites, and museums taking a more progressive approach within the constraints of their architecture. Remember, caverns are yawning for a reason.

Allyson Spellacy is a Dublin-born artist living and working in New York. She is the co-director of Parker's Box Gallery in the Williamsburg section of Brooklyn

Donald Judd: *untitled*, 1976, installation view at Dia: Beacon; gift of the Brown Foundation; photo Bill Jacobson; courtesy Dia Art Foundation; Dia: Beacon conversion designed by Robert Irwin, with OpenOffice architects

The best space I've been in is the Dia Art Foundation at Beacon, NY. Prior to that my best space would have been Dia in Chelsea, NYC. The integrity with which Dia selects and exhibits work is quite extraordinary. At Beacon the art can breathe and live and allow a sense of magic. That work is given such respect is wonderful. It is a tough space and not all the work is enhanced by being there, but it is allowed to be itself. It is a great example of the simpler the space, the greater the opportunities.

Oliver Dowling

There is an elegant yet non-ostentatious Georgian building in Belfast that, in some ways, offers both the best and the worst space to art lovers and practitioners. The Old Museum Arts Centre houses an intimate theatre and two exhibition spaces, the best of which is adjacent to a pleasant coffee bar area. This modestly-scaled gallery boasts an arched entrance, high ceilings and skylights; all of which combine to give an airy sense of space, despite the fact that it can accommodate, perhaps, only eight medium sized wall works. OMAC's greatest problem is access for the disabled: with no ramps or lift facilities for wheelchairs, the centre can never truly be the community cultural focal point which it strives to be.

Gavin Weston is an artist, writer and lecturer

Pure aspiration and ambition should dictate the brief for the next generation of spaces and buildings for the arts here. Ireland's had enough restorations, refurbishments and changes of use! We've done the 'para-arts agenda' as well, and Ireland has gained many arts and cultural buildings that were developed under non-arts and non-cultural funding programmes whether for tourism, economic or social development. It's time now for buildings gratia artis! So, for an example of bald-headed aspiration and ambition check out The Sage Gateshead by Norman Foster, home to Folkworks and the Northern Sinfonia.

Dermot McLaughlin is Chief Executive of Temple Bar Properties Limited and a traditional musician

Architecture, cinema and public events (meetings, deaths of the famous, the fall of walls and towers, wars) are the art forms of our age, taken as signifiers of grand narrative. Architecture speaks of structure, cinema of vision, events of belief. To interrogate each is to ask: what is it as a particular of space and time?
Structure is a metaphor for processes of human interaction. These processes operate on a scale from relative autonomy to relative institutionalisation. Their purpose is to effect transformation.
The creative project of the industrial age has been to develop (or at least plan) spaces that bridge human interaction and structure – spaces in which human endeavour can be experienced as whole. In so doing it proposes the erasure and surpassing of cultural relationships as purely metaphorical.
We inhabit the ruins of this project.

om lekha

Flaxart studios was located on the top floor of a disused linen mill in North Belfast, on the Crumlin Road one of Belfast's former main industrial thoroughfares, affording a view of the post industrial landscape nestled against the mountains. The Crumlin Road bore witness in its time to thousands of mill workers, and more recently to interface clashes. I had a studio space there for 12 years until the premises was gutted by fire in June 2003. The studio provided both a physical location and urban context for planning and producing work. Flaxart's city centre studio now affords a fine view of the M2 joining the M3 and the Larne railway line.

Aisling O'Beirn is an artist based in Belfast who is interested in how 'place' articulates political context

Now demolished, the original Catalyst Arts, based in an old shirt factory in Belfast, was both the best and worst of art spaces. Best, because it was the platform for an unprecedented series of great projects, parties, events and debates. Worst, because it was cold, damp and dark, with life-threatening electrics and rancid plumbing. Neither of which had much to do with architecture. Artists, I think, are particularly sensitive to what Dennis Hollier has identified as the oppressiveness of architectural 'idealism' (in *Against Architecture*, his study of Georges Bataille). With its terminology of cornerstones, foundations, structures, facades, architecture's metaphorical power is guaranteed by language and orders daily life in a way that is inherently hierarchical. As Bataille wryly states, "Architecture is the expression of the very soul of societies, just as human physiognomy is the expression of the individual's souls. It is, however, particularly to the physiognomies of official personages (prelate, magistrates, admirals) that this comparison pertains." Catalyst Arts' heartening recent decision to opt out of the Laganside Corporation-sponsored 'cultural quarter' in Belfast underlines how irrelevant spanking new purposely-designed art spaces can look in the face of a local industrial context that is real, however architecturally challenging.

Mark Orange is an artist from Belfast, curently based in New York

I've always been attracted to spaces that offer freedom and challenge to the artists and curators who use them. Invariably they were not designed for the purpose they now serve, often found in older buildings, frequently away from where one would expect a gallery to be, and perpetually precarious in terms of their decoration and solvency. Yet they continually present eclectic, dynamic and idiosyncratic programmes; fuelled by a characteristic passion and vision of one or two dedicated individuals, and puzzlingly achieve a greater reputation abroad than at home. The Golden Thread Gallery on the Crumlin Road in Belfast is one such space.

Chris Bailey, Director, Northern Ireland Museums Council

I think all spaces hold challenges for artists and curators and I don't have any favourites because they all change with the experience of seeing the art. However I am still very fond of the Orchard Gallery in Derry (RIP) because of what I saw in it. I only noticed how crap the space was when there ceased to be any thought given to what was exhibited there – then I saw it for what it was, a cramped dark basement under a parish hall. Who would have

Interior, Golden Thread Gallery, photo courtesy Golden Thread

thought it could have attracted some of the most prominent international artists of the time! I like difficult spaces, I can remember the experience of seeing Anselm Kiefer's lead airplane at the Douglas Hyde when I appreciated just how amazing that space could be, and all they did was lift the carpet revelling a place as raw as the work. It's not the space that's important it's the work.

Hugh Mulholland,
Director, Ormeau Baths
Gallery, Belfast

The upstairs gallery at the Crawford Municipal Art Gallery, part of the Erick van

Egeraat extension (actually an infill), has real presence, even though it is also a fire escape route, and access route for disabled persons. It is a gloriously big space with brilliant natural light and an interesting, tapering shape, ideal for large installations. The controversial stepped floor levels are now being eliminated, allowing you to wander freely in the wide-open, high-ceilinged space, enjoying the huge, organically-shaped window that acts as a frame or backdrop for larger pieces, and the surprise internal view of the project room below.

Alannah Hopkin is a writer and journalist, and a member of AICA (Ireland); she is also a CIRCA contributing editor

The PS1 Gallery in New York, an affiliate of MoMA, is a school building, renovated by architect Frederick Fisheran. One of my favourites… Formal space seems almost non-existent, and boundaries between public and private within are blurred. It is a series of rooms, corridors and courtyards; a place where college and gallery cohabitate; artists fuelling gallery, gallery inspiring artists and visitors. The use of otherwise unutilised space for installations and evocative suggestions of contemporary creativity; wallpaper in toilets - a large repeated print of a urinal, the stairs that brought you back to where you started, services rooms in the basement open to the public. And that's before the installations. Huge spaces, not pristine or precious, truly usable

Upper gallery, Eric Van Egeraat extension to Crawford Municipal Gallery Cork, installation view, Airgeadoir exhibition, designed by Wilson Architecture, photo courtesy, Janice O Connell, F22 Photography

spaces by the artist. The whole building emits a strange sense of reminiscence or familiarity. A comfort. An ideal foundation for both the artist to work in and the observer to observe.

Barbara Griffin, is an architect working for Wilson Architecture, Cork

I always prefer to see art when I least expect to. Christo's removal of art from the predictable white box into the outdoors has brought many more people in touch with art – people who'd not normally visit an art gallery. In this respect my perfect place for art is the seaside walk between Bondi and Tamarama Beaches in Sydney, where the yearly Sculpture by the Sea takes place. Here, from morning until night you can stumble across sculpture and artworks nestled into the rocks, floating in rock pools, and perched on cliff tops. Judging by the thousands who visit every day and the smiles on faces, it's as close to spatial perfection as the best architect in the world could hope.

Liz Aders is International Editorial Adviser with *CIRCA* Art Magazine

The Museo Nacional de Bellas Artes in Havana, Cuba, is a refreshingly political building. The contemporary art housed within emphaises and supports the State's governing ideology in a completely overt manner. Pristine white walls frame paintings which point to the inevitability and subsequent celebration of the Revolution, while capitalism is put to work for Cuba in the shop and the ticket office with prices which unashamedly transfer wealth from the First to the Second World. Here, art tourists pay for the effects of the embargo, while being made aware of the absence of time's arrow in the societies to which they will return, poorer and richer in unequal measure.

Brian Harten is Arts Officer with Louth County Council. Previously, he was Director of the Basement Gallery in Dundalk

I spent a year in Barcelona studying for a Masters in Fine Art. Initially I was quite taken with their Museum of Contemporary Art (MACBA), especially the long walkways, filled with light, which took up most of the front area of the building. However, on subsequent visits it became more obvious that these walkways, dramatic though they were, were merely access routes, and the exhibition rooms which were the main focus of the museum were poorly lit and comparatively small. The extent to which the architectural design of the building failed to contribute to its ostensible function as an exhibition space was disappointing. This is a not-uncommon occurrence with regard to the design considerations of museums/ galleries, and we don't have to look too far from home to see it happening with showpiece new wings in our own art spaces.

Cian Donnelly is an artist and writer based in Belfast

Architecture infuses the creative process with a fundamental priority of functionalism. The 'art', of architecture has an underlying purpose, whether it is physical or psychological; this sets it apart or adds another layer of meaning and raison d'etre. The architectural process differs from other arts in that it is a group or team affair. Many disciplines, and the client, all participate in this. The spaces within which architects perform must facilitate this interaction, whether by means of electronic communication of information/ideas, or providing the physical space to accommodate the meeting of many opinions and disciplines. This team-based ethic has directly informed the spaces which our own team has assimilated over the years. From basement beginnings with one large 'last supper'-type table to work around, to a Georgian second floor, with the same non-insular ideals. Soon we move to our new studios in the Coombe. The model is simple: we work as a team, over-hear each other's conversations, pass each others drawings on the wall, sit in on each others meetings, interacting constantly. All of this is facilitated within one simple large space. An environment within which to create environments.

Fiona Killeen, Senior Architect at Cooney Architects, Dublin

Form isn't enough: on a recent visit to the Basque Country, I realised that as a curator it is possible to laud a building like the Bilbao Guggenheim purely as an artwork, utilising the form of architecture. Never before has a building reached immediate iconic status, so much so that one could not imagine the City of Bilbao, without this wonderful edifice, its unusual choice of materials, curvature and siteing on the river. The only difficulty with the great building is that it does not need artwork inside, it is enough in itself! Meanwhile an hour's

Richard Meier, Museu d'Art Contemporani de Barcelona (MACBA), © Javier Tles 2004, courtesy MACBA

drive away there is the much more modest but well designed modern Artium Museum in Vitoria Gasteiz, where I had the pleasure of seeing a wonderful exhibition entitled the Laocoon Devoured, Political Violence and Art. Given the Basque country's difficult history, and the international breath and authority of the selection, I found it the most interesting exhibition I have seen in a long time and I did not even notice the Architecture…

Mike Fitzpatrick, Director/Curator of Limerick City Gallery of Art and also an artist

My favourite art exhibition space is Mies van der Rohe's Neue Nationalgalerie (New National Gallery) in Berlin. Mies van der Rohe, who had practised architecture in Germany and Berlin until 1937 when he emigrated to the United States, returned for this special commission (1962-8). He envisaged the space, in an almost classical way, as a shrine to art and created a modernist glass and steel temple: a flat steel roof over a glass hall on slender columns. Outside are sculptures by Henry Moore and Alexander Calder. The gallery is entered via a podium (housing essential visitor services) while the actual exhibition space is reached by descending the stairs. On various visits, the gallery never appears to be the same, as a flexible partition system can be rearranged to suit the shows. At gallery level,

Interior, Catalyst Arts; photo courtesy Catalyst Arts

there is also visual connection with a garden. The Neue Nationalgalerie houses an impressive collection of late 19th and 20th century art. While by no means a radical new space, the simplicity of 'form meets function' creates a timeless, artless space in which to appreciate modern art. During my last visit, the simple white planes were given over to Andy Warhol's pop art. The gallery responded well to the changing scale of Warhol's work and allowed for both intimate viewing and dramatic impact.

Sandra O'Connell, Editor, *Architecture Ireland*

Limerick City Gallery of Art's initial collection has been on display at the Carnegie Free Library from 1949, with exhibition areas since developed that inhabit the entirety of the building and into a new wing. This ongoing relationship between art and architectural edifice has brought artists towards parts of the building not necessarily intended as exhibition spaces. The front façade and a storage basement have facilitated artistic interventions by Mike Fitzpatrick, Andrew Kearney and Ouch!Electro. In many ways the engagement of such alternative spaces is part of a natural progression, as art continues to colonise the site and building.

Sean Lynch is an artist based in Belfast

Catalyst Arts' wrangle with Laganside Corporation in 2002-3, during design consultation for the managed workspaces in the Cotton Court development, speaks volumes about the dangers of prioritising space over independence and autonomy when relocating an organ-

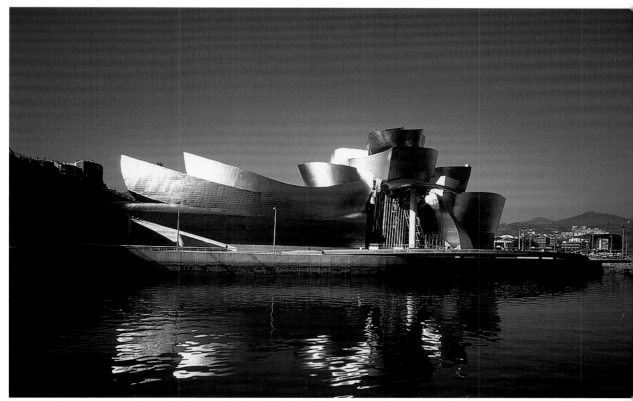

Exterior, Guggenheim Bilbao, Frank Gehry, photo Erika Ede, © Guggenheim Bilbao

isation which holds diverse cultural events. The considerable debate by Catalyst's committee and members at that time was about the sustainability of moving into a corporate-developed building while negotiating considerable interference into its events and work practices. The subsequent decision to end the arrangement in Catalyst's case was for the organisation, and to me as a committee member, a cautious reminder that a purpose-built space should not take precedence over the integrity of an organisation.

Chérie Driver is a former director of Catalyst Arts and is currently a candidate for a PhD at the University of Ulster

Best space for me, unhesitatingly, is the Guggenheim in Bilbao. I've been three times now just to see it and every time I want to throw my arms around its sensual curves, sculpted, as they are, out of titanium, limestone and glass. The first time I saw it, I was driving into the city from the airport – which, incidentally, is undoubtedly the best designed airport I've ever landed in – and I burst out laughing at its sheer audacity, rising majestically and improbably above traffic that seemed to scuttle across its girth, whilst simultaneously dwarfing the mountains against whose outline it is silhouetted. If Goethe's evocation of architecture as frozen music stands, then Frank Gehry's Guggenheim is positively symphonic.

Roisín McDonough, Chief Executive of the Arts Council of Northern Ireland

Conclusion

Art: Beyond the Gallery Space

by Brian Kennedy

When I first started to think about what type of spaces I have worked in I realized that very few of them were originally built as contemporary galleries. Some places had been converted from a previous use to a place for showing contemporary art. Others had originally been designed to show art when artists still made small to medium sized paintings and sculpture that sat on plinths. Practice has changed and even these places could not be considered as places designed for contemporary art.

Then there are all the alternative spaces. Deconsecrated churches, listed buildings, anything in fact that cannot be knocked down, but is difficult to develop, often end up being converted to house art. Then there are the buildings that get taken over for short periods of time, perhaps just for one-off exhibitions. These types of buildings have given me the chance to work in such diverse venues as a funeral parlour, disused factories, an ancient salt store and basements Sometimes these spaces offer exciting possibilities.

Where else would I have been able to combine marks on a wall left there by a long lost fresco if I had not been working in a deconsecrated twelfth century church in Italy? Closer to home, the rambling building that is the Old Museum Art Centre allowed me to meander through it with different but interrelated works. In the Ormeau Baths Gallery I chose to work in galleries 2 and 3, which are where the original baths were. While I have enjoyed playing with various spaces, I think it is important not to let the space dictate the work. The work should coexist in a harmonious way with the space but retain its own integrity. Then there are the spaces that are beyond architecture altogether. Fields, mountains, rivers, the shoreline – these have all become sites for the staging of projects.

Places where art is shown can also have a social and political background. Religious buildings, a disused American naval base, old peoples' homes all have their baggage. Perhaps the most poignant for me was showing in an 'underground' gallery in Crackow. It was while the communists were still in power. The building was on the edge of town and there was a general feeling of suppression that must have made its presence felt in the work. At that time the city had few streetlights so even putting up the posters and traveling to the show was a dark experience. It felt like the old joke was true and that the police really did go round in threes; one to ask the questions, the second to write down the answers and the third was there to keep an eye on these two dangerous 'intellectuals'.

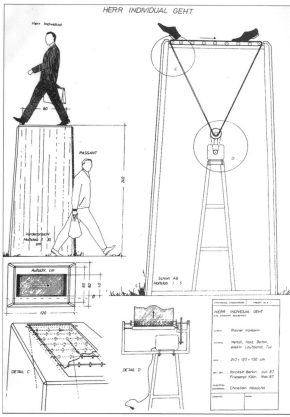

Christian Hasucha, *Mister Individual Walking*, part of *City Fabric*, Dublin, 2001, photo and drawing: Christian Hasucha.

An electric conveying belt is integrated into the top of a 2.4 m high concrete-plinth. Walking on this belt is a normal looking man. He walks 2 hours in the morning and 2 hours in the afternoon without rest. The man appears every day over a period of two weeks. The performance is neither announced nor labelled. Realized in Berlin, Cologne, Frankfurt/Main, Pécs (Hungary), Dublin; Actor in Dublin, 2001: Marcel Hager.

Strangely, it was when I returned to work in Crackow that I had the opportunity to work in a gallery that had been made specifically to show art. After the fall of communism, the artist's union in Crackow regained their building that had been designed specifically as a gallery. The gallery was a large plain white space. The windows were at the top of high walls and did not interfere with the wall space. The ceiling was slightly sunken, as it neared the walls and windows it angled up at about 45 degrees so that light coming in from the windows bounced off it into the space below. It was a fine space to show work in, but after my earlier experience in Crackow it felt clinical. I also felt that the way the audience looked at the work had changed. Before they were keen to engage and be part of something that came from outside the system. Now they coldly walked around looking at art. The way of viewing had become more abstract, less passionate.

Another new 'build from scratch' space I was involved in was the new civic building in Lisburn. I was the RSA sponsored artist on the design team. The "RSA Art for Architecture is a catalyst for collaborative ventures between artists and architects, landscape architects or engineers,"(according to their blurb; the scheme has been discontinued). The bottom floor of the new civic building was to be an art centre. However, even starting a new building from scratch did not mean a blank sheet. The floors above the art centre where the civic offices were had an effect on the overall floor plan. Engineers and architects were concerned about costs. Probably where the greatest compromises were made was where rooms had to be dual purpose. Could a room be used as a conference room as well as a gallery? Could it be divided up and sometimes used as both. So even starting with a new building there were compromises.

Having worked as a curator as well as an artist I have tried to show work in a way that uses to its advantage place and location. For *Inner Art*, which I co-curated with Tony Sheehan, we used the fact that inner city Dublin had its own culture and way of looking at what affected it directly. We were careful in selecting artists who could deal with issues important to the inner city; like drug abuse, poverty and the vitality of the people. We used sites that the target audience would feel comfortable with. The inside of a confessional in the local church, a small side chapel in another church, the local TD's surgery, a safe house for local children, anywhere in fact that did not look like a gallery as that would have seemed alien to the art, the audience and to what the artists were trying to achieve.

As well as dealing with so called non-art audiences and non-gallery spaces I have worked with different organizations that would not normally be associated with the art world. For *City Fabric*, which was again based in Dublin, various organizations gave their support. Trinity allowed a work to be shown on their campus. The Guards used one of their surveillance cameras to video another work. The city council brought electricity to an outdoor site, Christ Church Cathedral's bell ringers rang out a work. The open-topped tour buses unasked, even made one work a point of interest along their route causing traffic chaos while they stopped so that the people on the bus could photograph the work.

Contemporary painting would have had a very limited audience in the inner city, while an abstract corporate sculpture would have been unlikely to have tour buses stopping. Where a building that is to house art is situated and the type of audience expected should have an effect on that building. The old patronizing view that art, like an apple a day, is good for you has gone. Simply creating a gallery and filling it with art without thinking of context is a hangover from a time when the poor and underprivileged were given libraries and museums. This attitude might have had its merits in the nineteenth century, but no more.

[opposite: Brian Kennedy, *Aotearoa / New Zealand,*a project for CIRCA, 2004, part of an ongoing series by the artist; photo courtesy the artist. [below:] Sean Lynch; *alteration to the now defunct Scottish Presbyterian Church, Sean MacDermott Street, Dublin*, temporary installation, for *City Fabric*, 2001, metal structure attached to portico of building; photo courtesy the artist.

An art venue today must be sympathetic to the art, artist and audience. It is the place where the interaction between the art, artist and viewer takes place. Most importantly it should welcome its specific audience. I once did a twelve-hour performance with Alastair MacLennan and Brian Connolly that involved blowing up five thousand black balloons in Temple Bar Gallery. The audience was locked outside. As the work progressed they grew in number and started demanding to get in. When the doors were finally opened they rushed in. People who had walked past the gallery without ever thinking of entering now rushed in. One father told me that he had taken his family to museums but never before had the courage to enter a galley. He also said that he would bring them back when there was some 'real' art there. At least the barrier between street and gallery had been broken.

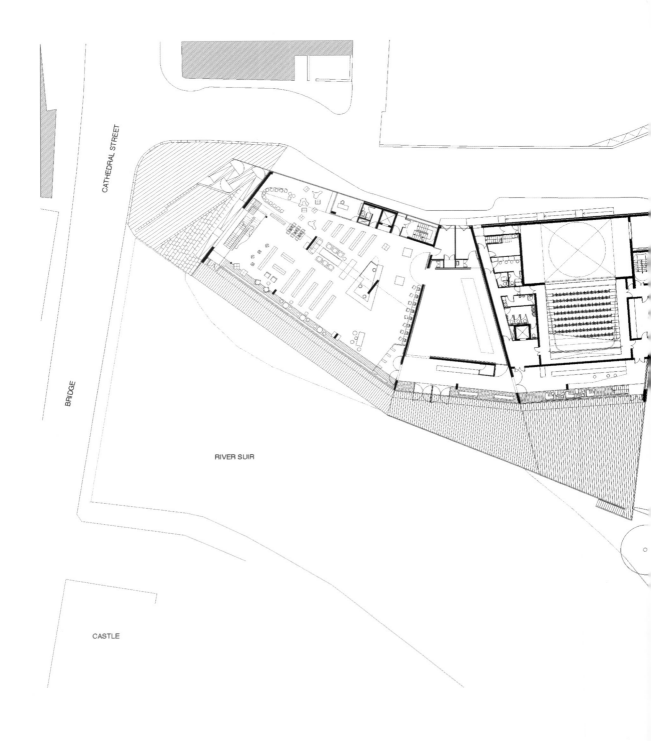

CATHEDRAL STREET

BRIDGE

RIVER SUIR

CASTLE

Directory:

Spaces for Contemporary Art in Ireland

[previous page:] Ground plan for
Thurles Arts and Civic Centre,
McCullough Mulvin Architects,
courtesy the architects

The ideas, essays and discussions raised in the first section of the book show that when it comes to spaces for contemporary art there are no clear rules, no one 'right way' of doing things. There is no single 'best' style of architecture, just as there is no single 'best' style of art. Against that background, this directory aims to provide an overview of spaces for contemporary art. Ideas and discussions raised in the first section of the book are illustrated architecturally here. There is, of course, a great deal of exhibiting and arts practice that takes place off-site, in ad-hoc spaces and in temporary venues. Yet the architectural infrastructure, the buildings in which art is made and shown, provides the physical landscape and context for the visual arts in any region or country.

So, of what does the physical landscape of the visual arts in Ireland consist? Arts spaces exist as the homes of institutions, commercial galleries, public exhibition venues, experimental spaces and local authority exhibition areas. There is no doubt that a great number of arts spaces in Ireland resonate with history. Names such as *The Linenhall* point to one of the major industrial traditions of the north, and yet Ireland lacks the history of heavy industry which has provided the massive industrial buildings ripe for conversion as museums and galleries, like Gateshead's Baltic. Instead, the colonial past has provided spaces like the former military infirmary that is the Irish Museum of Modern Art. There is also the legacy of the social agenda of the Victorians, which built the public swimming baths, now the Ormeau Baths Gallery in Belfast. Other conversions, renovations and extension projects include a prison (the Basement Gallery, Dundalk), a hay loft (the Green on Red, Dublin), and schools (the Verbal Arts Centre in Derry and the Model in Sligo). Then there are the town halls, the market places, and more recently shops and spaces located within blocks of flats (Pallas in Dublin).

We have been slower to build from scratch. In Northern Ireland, the capital programme of the National Lottery is changing that, resulting in an altered architectural landscape for the arts. This is discussed by Paul Harron (p. 26). And yet, as Harron notes, we have been slow to embrace the idea of the destination museum, of architecture as the major draw in the museum or gallery. Whether that is a good or a bad thing has been debated throughout these pages. Nonetheless, the idea of the architecture of art galleries as 'an art in itself' has been steadily gaining currency, and we are seeing more and more spaces creating (or indulging in?) those impressive atriums and fascinating façades.

Directory entries are the result of research and questionnaires, which were sent to over 300 arts spaces, and represent a collation of the available information. Where possible, the architectural history of the building is listed. The *Directory* cannot (and does not) aim for completeness. Given the complexity, the energy and the vibrancy of the contemporary arts in Ireland at the beginning of this millennium, it is unlikely that such a thing would be possible in a printed publication. Basic criteria for inclusion are that there is a dedicated space for exhibiting a changing programme of contemporary visual art, and that artists may apply to exhibit, although these criteria are flexible. Future editions of this directory will correct omissions and reflect changes in the arts landscape.

Entries have been selected to demonstrate the breadth and variety of exhibition spaces here. Directory listings are arranged geographically (by county), and alphabetically, and they are fully indexed at the back of the book. Each geographical section also begins with a comprehensive listing of spaces with contact details, bold headings indicate where the arts space also has a full-page entry. All infomation was correct at time of going to print, but check individual gallery and museum websites for full updated details, visiting arrangements and additional information.

Co Antrim

Arches Art Gallery
2 Holywood Road
Belfast BT4 1NT
Contact person: Ms Cowan
Tel: +44 (0) 28 9045 9031   Fax: +44 (0) 28 9045 4513

Art Act
32 Castle Street
Lisburn BT27 4XE
Contact person: Anthea McWilliams
Tel: +44 (0) 28 9266 3179
E-mail: artactlisburn@aol.com

Art Gallery
34 Lisburn Street
Hillsborough BT26 6AB
Contact person: Bill Morrisson
Tel: +44 (0) 28 9268 9896 Fax: +44 (0) 28 9268 8433
E-mail: info@whiteimage.com www.whiteimage.com

Art Tank
58 Lisburn Road
Belfast BT9 6AF
Contact person: Adam Jaffa
Tel: +44 (0) 28 9032 6795   Fax: +44 (0) 28 9022 1232
E-mail: adam@gdconline.co.uk

Ballymena Museum
3 Wellington Court
Ballymena BT43 6EG
Contact person: Jayne Olphert
Tel: +44 (0) 28 2564 2166 Fax: +44 (0) 28 2563 8582
E-mail: ballymena.museum@ballymena.gov.uk
www.ballymena.gov.uk

Belfast Exposed (p. 154)
The Exchange Place
23 Donegall Street
Belfast BT1 2FF
Contact person: Karen Downey, Pauline Hadaway
Tel: +44 (0) 28 9023 0965   Fax: +44 (0) 28 9031 4343
E-mail: info@belfastexposed.org www.belfastexposed.com

Belfast Print Workshop (p. 155)
Cotton Court
30 – 42 Waring Street
Belfast BT1 2ED
Contact person: Paula Gallagher, Struan Hamilton
Tel: +44 (0) 28 9023 1323 Fax: +44 (0) 28 9023 0323
E-mail: info@belfastprintworkshop.co.uk
www.belfastprintworkshop.org.uk

Bell Gallery (p. 156)
13 Adelaide Park
Belfast BT9 6FX
Contact person: Nelson Bell, Pauline McLarnon
Tel: +44 (0) 28 9066 2998
E-mail: bellgallery@btinternet.com www.bellgallery.com

Tom Caldwell Gallery (p. 157)
429 Lisburn Road
Belfast BT9 7EY
Contact person: Chris Caldwell
Tel: +44 (0) 28 9066 1890 Fax: +44 (0) 28 9068 1890
E-mail: info@tomcaldwellgallery.com
www.tomcaldwellgallery.com

Castle Upton Gallery
Templepatrick
Antrim BT39 OAH
Contact person: Danny Kinahan
Tel: +44 (0) 28 9443 3470
E-mail: info@castleuptongallery.com
www.castleuptongallery.com

Catalyst Arts (p.158)
5 College Court
Belfast BT1 6BS
Contact person: the committee
Tel: +44 (0) 28 9031 3303 Fax: +44 (0) 28 9031 2737
E-mail: info@catalystarts.org www.catalystarts.org

Cavehill Gallery (p. 159)
18 Old Cavehill Road
Belfast BT15 5GT
Contact person: Catherine and Joseph McWilliams
Tel: +44 (0) 28 9077 6784
E-mail: art@cavehillgallery.com

Church Lane Gallery
11 – 13 Church Lane
Belfast BT14QN
Contact person: Christopher Gilmore
Tel: +44 (0) 28 9032 4647

Clotworthy Arts Centre (p. 160)
Antrim Castle Gardens
Randalstown Road
Antrim BT41 4LH
Contact person: Cathy McNally
Tel: +44 (0) 28 9448 1338 Fax: +44 (0) 28 9448 1344
E-mail: clotworthyarts@antrim.gov.uk
www.antrim.gov.uk

Coloured Rain
886 Antrim Road
Templepatrick BT39 0AH
Contact person: Martin Donnelly
Tel: +44 (0) 28 9443 9494
E-mail: info@colouredrain.com   www.colouredrain.com

Gerard Dillon Gallery / Cultúrlann McAdam Ó Fiaich
216 Bóthar na bhFál
Béal Feirste BT12 6AH
Teagmhála: Máire Nic Fhionntaigh
Eolas: +44 (0) 28 9096 4180
www.culturlann.ie

Eakin Gallery
237 Lisburn Road
Belfast BT9 7EN
Contact person: Brian Eakin
Tel: +44 (0) 29 9066 8522
E-mail: eakin@paintings.freeserve.co.uk
www.eakingallery.co.uk

Engine Room
414 Newtonards Road
Belfast BT4 1HH
Contact person: Clifford Brooks
Tel /Fax: +44 (0) 2890 45 5184

Fenderesky Gallery (p. 161)
2 University Road
Belfast BT7 1NH
Contact person: Jamshid Mirfenderesky
Tel: +44 (0) 28 9023 5245 Fax: +44 (0) 2890 24 6748
www.crescentarts.org

Golden Thread Gallery (p. 162)
Brookfield Mill, 333 Crumlin Road
Belfast BT14 7EA
Contact person: Peter Richards
Tel: +44(0) 28 9035 2333
E-mail: info@gtgallery.fsnet.co.uk
www.gtgallery.fsnet.co.uk

Gormley's Fine Art
670 Ravenhill Road
Belfast BT6 0BZ
Contact person: Oliver Gormley
Tel: +44 (0) 28 9066 3313
E-mail: oliver@gormleys.ie
www.gormleys.ie

Higgin Gallery
Malone House
Barnetts Desmesne
Belfast BT9 5PE
Contact person: Jonathan Megaw
Tel: +44 (0) 28 9068 1246
E-mail: mhreception@malonehouse.co.uk
www.malonehouse.co.uk

Hughes Gallery
257 Lisburn Road
Belfast BT9 7EN
Contact person: Michael Hughes
Tel: +44 (0) 28 9066 2772
E-mail: michael@irishartgroup.com
www.irishartgroup.com

Island Arts Centre (p. 163)
Lagan Valley Island
Lisburn BT27 4RL
Contact person: Siobhan McCormick
Tel: +44 (0) 28 9250 9509 Fax: +44 (0) 28 9250 9510
E-mail: arts.information@iac.Lisburn.gov.uk
www.lisburn.gov.uk

Irish Art Group
100a Glenshesk Road
Armoy
Ballymoney BT53 8RZ
Contact person: Darach Hughes
Tel: +44 (0) 28 2075 1898
E-mail: info@irishartgroup.com   www.irishartgroup.com

Johnathan Swift Gallery
3 Kilroot Park
Carrickfergus BT38 7PR
Contact person: Peter Brennan
Tel: +44 (0) 28 9335 1448
E-mail: peter@johnathanswiftgallery.com
www.johnathanswiftgallery.com

Linen Hall Library: The Vertical Gallery (p. 164)
17 Donegall Square North
Belfast BT1 5GB
Tel: +44 (0) 28 9032 1707 Fax: +44 (0) 28 9043 8586
Contact person: Carolyn Mathers
E-mail: info@linenhall.com   www.linenhall.com

Mullan Gallery
239 Lisburn Road
Belfast BT9 7EN
Contact person: Robin Mullan
Tel: +44 (0) 28 9020 2434
E-mail: robin@mullangallery.com www.mullangallery.com

Naughton Gallery at Queens (p. 165)
Lanyon Building
Queen's University Belfast
BT7 1NN
Contact person: Shan McAnena
Tel: +44 (0) 28 9027 3580 Fax: +44 (0) 28 9027 3401
E-mail: art@qub.ac.uk

Ormonde Gallery
195 Upper Lisburn Road
Finaghy
Belfast BT10 0LL
Contact person: Colin Stewart
Tel: +44 (0) 28 9030 1613

Ogham Gallery (p. 166)
497 Antrim Road
Belfast BT15 3BP
Contact person: Eimear Maguire
Tel: +44 (0)28 9077 2580
E-mail: oghamgallery@hotmail.com

Old Museum Arts Centre (p. 167)
7 College Square North
Belfast BT1 6AR
Contact person: Anne McReynolds
Tel: +44 (0) 28 9023 5053 Fax: +44 (0) 28 9032 2912
E-mail: info@oldmuseum.co.uk
www.oldmuseumartscentre.org

Ormeau Baths Gallery (p. 168)
18A Ormeau Avenue
Belfast BT2 8HS
Contact person: Hugh Mulholland
Tel: +44 (0) 28 9032 1402 Fax: +44 (0) 28 9031 2232
E-mail: admin@obgonline.net www.obgonline.net

Queen Street Studios (p. 169)
37 – 39 Queen Street
Belfast BT1 6EA
Contact person Ursula Burke
Tel: +44 (0) 28 9024 3145 Fax: +44 (0) 28 9033 0910
E-mail: qsstudios@btconnect.com

Safehouse Arts Space Gallery
25 Lower Donegal Street
Belfast BT1 2FF
Contact person: Danny Burke
Tel: + 44 (0) 28 9031 9950
E-mail: arts@safehousearts.org   www.safehousearts.org

Space Gallery (p. 170)
5 – 7 Conway Street
Belfast BT13 2DE
Contact person: Moya Hinds
Tel: +44 (0) 28 9024 9323   Fax: +44 (0) 28 9032 4309
E-mail: info@conwaymill.org www.conwaymill.org

Stables Gallery
27 Ballywindland House
Ballymoney BT53 6QT
Contact person: Stuart Moore
Tel: +44 (0) 28 2766 5919
E-mail: stuart.moore@btinternet.com
www.stablesgallery.co.uk

Taylor Gallery
471 Lisburn Road
Belfast BT9 7EZ
Contact person: John Taylor, Stephen Donnelly
Tel: +44 (0) 28 9068 7687
E-mail: taylorgallery@btinternet.com

The Tile Refinery Gallery (p. 171)
11 – 19 Blythe Street
Belfast BT12 5HU
Contact person: Director: David Scott
Tel: +44 (0) 28 9023 2136
E-mail: david@davidscott-tiles.co.uk

Townhouse Gallery
125 Great Victoria Street
Belfast BT2 7AH
Contact person: George Hunter
Tel: +44 (0) 28 9031 1798
E-mail: townhousegallery@fsbdial.co.uk

Village Gallery
4 Bendooragh Road
Ballymoney BT53 7ND
Contact person: Trevor Owens, David Murray
Tel: +44 (0) 28 2766 5528
E-mail: info@thevillagegallery.co.uk
www.thevillagegallery.co.uk

Ulster Museum (p. 172)
Botanic Gardens
Stranmillis
Belfast BT9 5A
Contact person: S. B. Kennedy
Tel: +44 (0) 28 9038 3000
www.ulstermuseum.org.uk

Belfast Waterfront Hall (p. 173)
2 Lanyon Place
Belfast BT1 3WH
Contact person: Adam Turkington
Tel: +44 (0) 28 9033 4400 Fax: +44 (0) 28 9024 9862
E-mail: turkingtona@waterfront.co.uk
www.waterfront.co.uk

Belfast Exposed

The Exchange Place
23 Donegall Street
Belfast BT1 2FF

Tel: +44 (0) 28 9023 0965
Fax: +44 (0) 28 9031 4343
E-mail: info@belfastexposed.org
www.belfastexposed.com

Conversion of an existing building

Contact person / Director: Karen Downey, Exhibitions Programmer;
Pauline Hadaway, Director

Architects for the conversion: Consarc

Specifications: The gallery is on the ground floor. The walls consist of painted MDF panels suspended 30 cm above ground level, panel height 2.44 m. They are lit by Zumtobel wall washers. Suitable for small and large-format photographs.

Access details: The building had a disability access audit in 2003. It is fully statutory compliant.

Exhibitions policy / 'ethos' of gallery: Exhibition of contemporary photography. Darkroom and digital training resource. Digital archive browsing facility.

What should interested artists do? Belfast Exposed Photography is interested in commissioning and showing contemporary photography that is socially and politically engaged. Work can be sent as prints or on CDROM with a statement about the work and a CV. A stamped addressed envelope should be sent if work is to be returned. A nominal fee for loan of work is generally paid. The photographer/s will be invited to be present at the opening of the exhibition and if desirable give a talk about their work. All publicity, transportation and insurance are covered by Belfast Exposed Photography. Work is made available for sale through the gallery.

Management structure: Company limited by guarantee, with charitable status; managed by a Board of Directors.

Established in 1983, Belfast Exposed is Northern Ireland's only dedicated photography gallery. It houses a gallery for the exhibition of contemporary photography; digital archive browsing facilities; a B&W photographic darkroom and an 8-person Apple Mac digital-suite. The production of socially and politically engaged work and dialogue is the driving force behind all aspects of the Belfast Exposed project. A policy of project origination and publication, exhibitions, screenings and talks, as well as provision of photographic facilities and training, all fuel this process. Belfast Exposed's building was renovated for use as an arts space in 2002.

Number of rooms / galleries; area in square metres: Gallery: 156 square metres (20 x 7 m); administration area: approximately 80 square metres; archive storage area and conference room: approximately 18 square metres; darkroom, digital suite, workroom and studio: 135 square metres; Total: 389 square metres.

Belfast Print Workshop

Cotton Court
30 – 42 Waring Street
Belfast BT1 2ED

Tel: +44 (0) 28 9023 1323
E-mail: info@belfastprintworkshop.co.uk
www.belfastprintworkshop.org.uk

Renovation of an industrial building

Contact person / Director: Paula Gallagher, Director;
 Struan Hamilton, Manager

Architects for the renovation: Manouge Architects

Renovated in 2002/3, the gallery is on the
top floor of a former bonded warehouse,
now run as a managed arts space. There
are four other groups in the building, as
well as another gallery and wine bar.
Belfast Print Workshop has been in
operation for 25 years.

**Number of rooms / galleries; area in
square metres**: Two open plan rooms, 350
square metres.

Access details: There is a lift in the building and disabled toilet facilities.

Exhibitions policy / 'ethos' of gallery:
Exhibitions are mainly based with workshop members, and all exhibitions are primarily concerned with printmaking.

What should interested artists do?
Exhibitions are mainly open to members.
Contact the director for more information.
The gallery takes 25% commission.

Management structure: Run by a Board.

Bell Gallery

13 Adelaide Park
Belfast BT9 6FX

Tel: +44 (0) 28 9066 2998
E-mail: bellgallery@btinternet.com
www.bellgallery.com

Refurbishment of an existing building

Contact person / Director: Nelson Bell, Pauline McLarnon

Original architect: William Fennell
Architects for the conversion: Self-conversion

The Bell Gallery is housed in a red brick villa, the original architect being William Fennell in 1899, with later work in 1905 by JJ Phillips. The gallery was opened in 1964, and prior to this use, the building housed medical consulting rooms and a residence.

Number of rooms / galleries: The Bell Gallery comprises two rooms and a hallway.

Specifications: Traditional wall finishes, hanging rods and carpeted floors, also suitable for the display of small sculptures.

Access details: No disabled access.

Exhibitions policy / 'ethos' of gallery: The Bell Gallery specialises in traditional Irish arts. When there is no specific exhibition scheduled, the gallery stock of paintings and sculpture is on display, and for sale.

What should interested artists do? Artists may submit work by e-mail, with a CV and cover letter. The Gallery takes commission on sales, and percentages are negotiable. Some services and advertising are included in the gallery's commission, extra expenses may be shared with the exhibitor.

Management structure: Private.

Tom Caldwell Gallery

429 Lisburn Road
Belfast BT9 7EY

Tel: +44 (0) 28 9066 1890
Fax: +44 (0) 28 9068 1890
E-mail: info@tomcaldwellgallery.com
www.tomcaldwellgallery.com

Renovation of an existing building

Contact person / Director: Chris Caldwell

Architects for the conversion: Self-conversion

After 60 years in Belfast's Bradbury Place in the Shaftesbury Square area of the city, The Caldwell Gallery moved in 2004 to the Lisburn Road. Built some time in the 1960s or 70s as an electrical retailing outlet, the building was recently renovated by the gallery as an arts space. The gallery is on two floors (first and second) both served by a lift. The space, which displays the art in conjunction with the very best of Italian design furniture, is one of the largest commercial gallery spaces in Ireland – 300 square metres in total. On two floors, it provides space for one-person shows while still able to exhibit work by other gallery artists. Occasionally a one-person show takes over the two floors.

Number of rooms / galleries; area in square metres: The second floor gallery (used for solo shows) has about 33 linear m of hanging space (painted white walls) Approximate height is 2.5 m. The first floor gallery has about 40 linear m of hanging space, again about 2.5 m high.

Specifications: Second floor gallery: lighting is low voltage on a highly versatile unit. Hanging by hook (walls repaired after each show). First floor gallery: same hanging method but lit with par 38 bulbs. Both spaces are suitable for large works. Although not a major part of the portfolio, the space is also suitable for sculpture.

Access details: Access to gallery by lift.

Exhibitions policy / 'ethos' of gallery: The gallery specialises in predominantly Irish living art but does also work with other contemporary artists from elsewhere. The aim is to work with and represent a manageable stable of artists so that each is able to have a regular one-person exhibition every other year. Two major group exhibitions each year: one in the summer and one at Christmas.

What should interested artists do? Artists who might be interested in showing with the gallery should send a CD or slides initially but it is important to see the original work too. Appointments should be made with Chris Caldwell. Artists supply their work to exhibition standard (framed); the gallery covers all exhibition costs of invitation, mailing and reception. When a brochure is produced the cost of this is shared between the gallery and the artist.

Management structure: Private.

Catalyst Arts

5 College Court
Belfast BT1 6BS

Tel: +44 (0) 28 9031 3303
Fax: +44 (0) 28 9031 2737
E-mail: info@catalystarts.org
www.catalystarts.org

Conversion of an industrial space

Contact person / Director: The committee (changes every two years)

Conversion: In consultation with committee members

Catalyst Arts has been operating since 1993, and in its current location since Autumn 2003. In a four storey building in Belfast's city centre, Catalyst occupies the second floor space, with open-plan gallery space, office and storage space, and an outdoor roof garden, (available for showing art work). The building is a converted industrial space now used by commercial and voluntary organisations. The essential quality of Catalyst Arts' space is in how it operates. Catalyst is independent, grass-roots and multidisciplinary, therefore control of how the space is used is paramount.

Number of rooms / galleries; area in square metres: Reading area: 12.5 square metres; gallery: 200 square metres; office / archive area: 50 square metres; store: 12.5 square metres; toilet / bathroom: 2 square metres; outdoor roof garden: 45 square metres.

Specifications: The gallery has a concrete floor, wall space is approximately two thirds fabricated walls and a third original brick. Exclusive of the available 'hanging' wall space, about a quarter of the entire gallery wall space has banks of windows providing good natural light. The space can be adapted to show all kinds of work.

Access details: No disabled access.

Exhibitions policy / 'ethos' of gallery:
Catalyst Arts shows contemporary art in all media by artists at all levels of career

recognition. The rolling-committee structure ensures that the way shows are curated is continually changing. Catalyst attempts to facilitate work in media that otherwise would not be shown in Belfast, particularly with public interventions and installation works. Catalyst also serves as a venue for activities outside of the visual arts. This includes film screenings, contemporary dance, book launches, talks, music events, parties and meetings for political and other organisations. Catalyst publicises and organises openings for shows and events, providing for design and printing and distribution of all promotional material. All events are documented on the Catalyst website and catalogues or publications are occasionally produced for shows. Arrangements for fees paid to artists vary with individual shows and events.

What should interested artists do? Slides and CV are both acceptable. A clearly and concisely written proposal of work and description of work practice is essential. Applicants should pay attention to forthcoming open submission exhibitions. Contact Catalyst for details of curatorial themes for forthcoming shows to enable targeted applications. Catalyst is a non-commercial space.

Management structure: Catalyst Arts is run by a committee of artists on a voluntary basis. Each committee member works in Catalyst for a two year period. Catalyst is ultimately a membership-led organisation, which is open to anyone on an annually renewable basis. Decisions that change the constitution or the fundamental nature of how Catalyst is run are taken by members at its annual AGM or specially convened EGMs.

Cavehill Gallery

18 Old Cavehill Road
Belfast BT15 5GT

Tel: +44 (0) 28 9077 6784
E-mail: art@cavehillgallery.com

Conversion of an existing building

Contact person / Director: Catherine and Joseph McWilliams

Architects for the conversion: Self-conversion

Cavehill Gallery is a private gallery occupying the front ground floor rooms and hall of an Edwardian double-fronted house. The original building dates from 1900, while the gallery has been in operation since 1986.

Number of rooms / galleries; area in square metres: Two rooms, and hall: 100 square metres (approximately).

Specifications: Walls: paper over brick. Floor: grey carpet (gallery 1), dark green carpet (gallery 2) dark red patterned carpet (hall). Hanging: nails in wall, picture rails. Light: good natural, ceiling mounted spots. Storage: none. Loading doors 2.11 m. Room for 2 / 3 large works on canvas 5 x 6 m and some free standing sculpture.

Access details: Disabled accesss is limited, there are two steps into the building. Doorways are wide enough for wheelchairs. Parking in front of gallery.

Exhibitions policy / 'ethos' of gallery: Cavehill holds three to four exhibitions annually. These consist of one or two large group shows, two solo or two-to-four person shows. Work is generally of a figurative nature, although there are exceptions. Cavehill shows living Irish artists who may be established, but under-exposed, and younger emerging artists. The gallery exhibits mainly painting, some sculpture, and occasionally ceramics and textiles.

What should interested artists do? The exhibition programme is booked out for two to three years, and Cavehill generally prefers to invite artists, rather than have them send slides. The gallery does not pay a fee. Gallery provides opening reception, invitations, price lists and press coverage.

Management structure: Private gallery, run by a partnership.

Clotworthy Arts Centre

Antrim Castle Gardens
Randalstown Road
Antrim BT41 4LH

Tel: +44 (0) 28 9448 1338
Fax: +44 (0) 28 9448 1344
E-mail: clotworthyarts@antrim.gov.uk
www.antrim.gov.uk

Renovation of an historic building

Contact person / Director: Cathy McNally

Architects: unknown

Clotworthy Arts Centre is the flagship arts venue of the district of Antrim. It was built last century as a stable block for the now demolished Antrim Castle. The building itself is in Tudor style but has undergone complete refurbishment. The Centre is set in Antrim Castle Gardens, which are unique to Northern Ireland. The Centre was refurbished in 1993.

Number of rooms / galleries; area in square metres: The arts centre encloses an open-air courtyard. The main facility of the centre is a 96-seat studio theatre. The Centre is equipped with two gallery spaces, (one dedicated to photography). There are several conference rooms of different sizes that can be hired for events. Main Gallery: total hanging space 25 square metres; smaller upper gallery (photography). A smaller Theatre/Reception Gallery is used for informative and heritage displays.

Specifications: Work exhibited can include painting, photography, craft, sculpture and jewellery. A TV and video

are available for video installations, however the spaces are not particularly suited to wall-projected video work.

Access details: The venue is equipped with a text telephone facility, accessible toilet and dedicated lift and dedicated parking. Lecture Room and Main Reception are equipped with a loop system, for those with hearing impairments. The programme is available in Braille, large type and cassette on request.

Exhibitions policy / 'ethos' of gallery: Main Gallery: contemporary art by local, national and international artists; smaller Upper Gallery: photography.

What should interested artists do? The centre holds approximately 24 – 36 exhibitions per year, which change on a monthly basis. Programming is 6 months in advance. Artists interested in exhibiting should forward a CV and examples of recent work (photographs, slides, CD ROM or e-mailed images are acceptable) to Cathy McNally for consideration by a programming panel. Clotworthy Arts Centre does not pay or charge an exhibition fee. The venue provides invitations and an opening night reception with wine and can also arrange transportation to and from the gallery depending on each exhibition. A technician works on site to hang the exhibitions in liaison with the artist. Clotworthy Arts Centre undertakes all marketing and publicity for each exhibition. A 20% commission fee is charged on any work sold. The amount of work sold varies from exhibition to exhibition.

Management structure: Managed and owned by Antrim Borough Council.

Subscribe to CIRCA Art Magazine
Special Discount Offer to Readers of
Space: Architecture for Art

Published quarterly, CIRCA Art Magazine is Ireland's leading journal of contemporary visual culture

Subscribe with this card, and receive a discounted rate on a two-year subscription*

Special Two-Year Discounted Subscription Rates:

	Individuals:		Institutions:	
Rep. of Ireland	~~€38.10~~	€35.00	~~€82.50~~	€75.00
UK	~~£25.00stg~~	£22.50stg	~~£55.00stg~~	£50.00stg
Europe	~~€53.25~~	€50.00	~~€104.80~~	€92.00
World	~~€81.65 / US$79.50~~	€77.50 / US$75.00	~~€137.00 / US$79.50~~	€123.00 / US$110.00

*Offer applies on two-year subscriptions on this card only, until 31st December 2005

One Year Rates

	Individuals:	Institutions:
Rep. of Ireland	€20.30	€44.45
UK	£14.00stg	£29.00stg
Europe	€29.45	€56.45
World	€45.55 / US$45.50	€72.50 / US$71.50

Please circle the rate that applies to you, fill in your details below, and start receiving CIRCA

Payment by cheque, postal order, VISA, Mastercard, Laser. We also have back copies available; please ask or see online at www.recirca.com/backissues.

name: ....

address: ....

....

....

....

visa/mastercard/laser: .... exp. ....

Send completed card to

Subscriptions
CIRCA
43 / 44 Temple Bar
Dublin 2
Ireland

Tel/Fax: +353 (0) 1 679 7388
E-mail: subscribe@recirca.com

☐ please send me a complimentary issue (*institutions only*)

☐ please invoice me for one year / two years (*institutions only*)

please start my subscription with issue _____
(only complete if you do not wish to start with the current issue)

www.recirca.com

Subscribe to CIRCA Art Magazine
Subscribe to CIRCA Art Magazine
Subscribe to CIRCA Art Magazine
Subscribe to CIRCA Art Magazine
Subscribe to CIRCA Art Magazine
Subscribe to CIRCA Art Magazine
Subscribe to CIRCA Art Magazine
Subscribe to CIRCA Art Magazine
Subscribe to CIRCA Art Magazine
Subscribe to CIRCA Art Magazine
Subscribe to CIRCA Art Magazine
Subscribe to CIRCA Art Magazine
Subscribe to CIRCA Art Magazine
Subscribe to CIRCA Art Magazine
Subscribe to CIRCA Art Magazine
Subscribe to CIRCA Art Magazine
Subscribe to CIRCA Art Magazine
Subscribe to CIRCA Art Magazine
Subscribe to CIRCA Art Magazine
Subscribe to CIRCA Art Magazine
Subscribe to CIRCA Art Magazine
Subscribe to CIRCA Art Magazine
Subscribe to CIRCA Art Magazine
Subscribe to CIRCA Art Magazine
Subscribe to CIRCA Art Magazine

Fenderesky Gallery

2 University Road
Belfast BT7 1NH

Tel: +44 (0) 28 9023 5245
Fax: +44 (0) 28 9024 6748

Conversion of an existing building

Contact person / Director: Jamshid Mirfenderesky

Architects for the conversion: Self-conversion

The Fenderesky Gallery is located within the Crescent Arts Centre in Belfast. The Crescent is an old building which was renovated for use as an arts space in the 1980s. In operation since 1984, the Fenderesky Gallery has an established reputation, and has been in this location since 1995.

Number of rooms / galleries; area in square metres: Three gallery spaces. Gallery 1: running wall space 30.85 m, two pillars, grey linoleum floor; ceiling height 4 m; door height 2.25 m. Gallery 2: running wall space 21.32 m, wooden floor; ceiling height 3.34 m; door height 2.25 m.

Specifications: White walls. Spotlights and natural light from a bay window in each gallery.

Access details: Access to Gallery 1 on the ground floor.

Exhibitions policy / 'ethos' of gallery: To show contemporary Irish art.

What should interested artists do? Artists should submit a CV and around 15 slides or large photographs of new works for consideration; or proposals for installation or video works. Applications for exhibitions are considered by the gallery's exhibition committee, and applications should reach the gallery no later than the end of June or December for consideration. The gallery neither pays nor charges an exhibition fee, gallery commission is 40% on work sold, and the gallery provides invitations, publicity and reception.

Management structure: Run by a Board; supported by the Arts Council of Northern Ireland.

Golden Thread Gallery

Brookfield Mill
333 Crumlin Road
Belfast BT14 7EA

Tel: +44(0) 28 9035 2333
E-mail: info@gtgallery.fsnet.co.uk
www.gtgallery.fsnet.co.uk

Conversion of industrial space

Contact person / Director: Peter Richards

Architects for the conversion: Self-conversion

The Golden Thread Gallery is located within an old linen mill complex on the Crumlin Road. In operation since 1998, the gallery has a fairly rough-and-ready feel, retaining a sense of its industrial past.

Number of rooms / galleries; area in square metres: One rectangular exhibition space of approximately 200 square metres.

Specifications: The gallery has no natural light and is very suitable for media / projection works. It is generally painted white, though this does change in relation to the particular project/exhibition. Approx. half the walls are block and the other half plastered. Height of walls is approximately 3 m. The gallery does suit large scale works.

Access details: Disabled access.

Exhibitions policy / 'ethos' of gallery: The Golden Thread Gallery is primarily a neutral venue for the presentation and education of contemporary visual art and asso-

ciated activities, located on an interface in North Belfast. It was reconstituted in 2001, with the aim to provide an environment where in particular the residents of and visitors to Belfast regardless of political, religious, ethnic or sexual persuasion can experience, engage with, participate in and evaluate a programme of high quality contemporary visual art. The gallery is committed to maintaining a platform for local and international contemporary visual artists, particularly those engaged with themes relevant to residents of Belfast and the contemporary urban condition. The gallery strives to promote Belfast, Northern Ireland as an important centre for the production and evaluation of contemporary visual art through partnership and participation in the development of local, national and international networks.

What should interested artists do? The Gallery maintains a curated programme and does not accept unsolicited proposals, with the exception of specific projects / exhibitions that are advertised. The Gallery does pay exhibition fees to artists, and works with exhibiting artists to assist with the realisation of the project / exhibition. Note each project / exhibition has different requirements / needs, which are discussed and agreed with the artists. The Gallery also covers costs of invitations, the reception, high quality documentation and so on. Selling of work is not a primary concern, however the Gallery does and has sold a number of works. The Gallery takes 25% commission on sales, in line with other publicly funded galleries in Belfast.

Management structure: Not-for-profit company limited by guarantee, acknowledged as having charitable status by the Inland Revenue.

Island Arts Centre

Lagan Valley Island
Lisburn BT27 4RL

Tel: +44 (0) 28 9250 9509
Fax: +44 (0) 28 9250 9510
E-mail: arts.information@iac.Lisburn.gov.uk
www.lisburn.gov.uk

Purpose-built multi-use space

Contact person / Director: Siobhan McCormick, Arts Manager;
Christina Hurson, Arts Programming Coordinator

Architect: Consarc Design Group

Nestled at the banks of the River Lagan at Lagan Valley Island, Island Arts Centre is Lisburn City Council's new arts base for Lisburn City's cultural and creative scene. Designed to showcase artistic excellence and innovation, Island Arts Centre is an impressive purpose-built contemporary arts venue, placing Northern Ireland firmly on the international art stage. Bursting at the seams with creativity, Island Arts Centre runs a programme of diverse classes and workshops including visual and verbal arts, community arts, performing arts and a full education programme that actively encourages people of all abilities to explore and preserve our arts heritage. The centre opened in 2001.

Number of rooms / galleries; area in square metres: Gallery 1: 104 square metres, total wall run: 36 m, 2 – 113 square metres; Gallery 11: 113 square metres, total wall run: 33 m; Artists' studios; Artist-in-residence studio; Dark Room (7.2 square metres); Multi-media suite (15.98 square metres); Pottery Studio (40 square metres); Sculpture Trail & Gardens.

Specifications: Ground-level gallery spaces. Facilities: Hanging system and spotlights. Gallery II is available for hire for exhibitions (subject to availability).

Access details: Physical access is unrestricted at Lagan Valley Island. Induction loop system and textphone facility.

Exhibitions policy / 'ethos' of gallery: A balance is sought between solo shows by established artists, to artists at the beginning of their careers, to group shows by arts societies etc, and also between the types of media exhibited. Occasionally high profile touring exhibitions will be hosted, however the majority of shows are originated by the Island Arts Centre. Both galleries are professionally managed with hanging / technical work carried out by centre staff. Exhibitions are generally programmed two years in advance. The programme is supported by complementary events such as illustrated talks, workshops and demonstrations, which are aimed at a wide range of visitors.

What should interested artists do? Send CV and slides, CD ROM or e-mail with images attached to Arts Programming Coordinator. Generally a preview will take place. Island Arts Centre will provide invitations and postage up to a maximum of 200 addresses (not including IAC's mail list) and refreshments. Work sells in the space, depending on the exhibition, and the gallery commission is 25% plus VAT. A fee is paid on commissioned exhibitions only (usually once a year). Gallery 2 is available to hire on a weekly basis. No commission is deducted from sale of works. An artist will not normally be re-invited to exhibit within a two-year time frame (group exhibitions excluded).

Management structure: Local Government.

Linen Hall Library: The Vertical Gallery

17 Donegall Square North
Belfast BT1 5GB

Tel: +44 (0) 28 9032 1707
Fax: +44 (0) 28 9043 8586
info@linenhall.com
www.linenhall.com

Conversion of an historic building

Contact person / Director: Carolyn Mathers

Original Architect: Lanyon
Architects for the conversion: Hall Black Douglas (Vertical Gallery)

The world famous Linen Hall Library is a unique institution. Established in 1788, it is Belfast's oldest Library and the last subscribing Library in Ireland. A Heritage Lottery extension in 2000 provided the Library with 50% more space including a gallery, performance area and full disabled access. Visitors to the Library rose by 30,000 last year, proof that increasing numbers are appreciating that it is the only institution devoted purely to cultural purposes in the heart of Belfast. Today the Linen Hall offers a full programme of events – from monthly exhibitions and music to theatre and lectures. Visitors are always welcome to visit the Linen Hall – to browse the collections, take in an exhibition or just relax in the licensed coffee shop.

Specifications: Concrete walls with wire hanging system. Suitable for slide installations, video installations, large works on canvas and free-standing sculpture. Access: there are no restrictions to vehicle access to the premises and there is a goods lift to gallery. Security: extensive CCTV surveillance with TV screens and monitors which are digitally recorded. Alarm and security system at exit. Environmental conditions: temperature and relative humidity is monitored on a regular basis.

Access details: Full disabled access including Induction Loop facility.

Exhibitions policy / 'ethos' of gallery: Policy covers all art forms but must be Northern Irish premieres.

What should interested artists do? Apply either by e-mail or in writing with CV and images. Fees negotiable. Private press previews, invitations and extensive media coverage can be provided by the Linen Hall. Also inclusion in Events Guide (which is distributed widely throughout Northern Ireland) and Linen Hall Newsletter.

Management structure: Registered charity run by a Board of Governors.

Number of rooms / galleries: Vertical Gallery (can accommodate up to 40 A2 images); Northern Room (can accommodate up to 20 A2 images) Maximum size of object: 3 m x 4 m.

Naughton Gallery at Queens

Lanyon Building
Queen's University Belfast
BT7 1NN

Tel: +44 (0) 28 9027 3580
Fax: +44 (0) 28 9027 3401
E-mail: art@qub.ac.uk

Conversion of an historic space

Contact person / Director: Shan McAnena

Original Architect: Sir Charles Lanyon
Architects for the conversion: Dawson Stelfox and Bronagh Lynch, Consarc Conservation, Belfast

The Naughton Gallery is on the first floor overlooking the quadrangle at Queen's University. Situated in the Tudor revival Lanyon Building, named after its designer, Sir Charles Lanyon, it was built in the 1840s, and the space was originally the Technical Drawing Department. The Gallery was converted in 2001.

Number of rooms / galleries; area in square metres: Two rooms: total 110 square metres.

Specifications: The gallery is in a listed-building and the space is L-shaped. The walls are lined with plasterboard and are painted with a stone-coloured finish. The annex has a dark green carpet and the main gallery space has a woodblock floor. Access is by staircase or domestic lift. The ceilings are 4m high and doors are 2 x 3 m. The space is lit by adjustable filtered spots on suspended track system. The environment is controlled to museum standards (temperature, UV and relative humidity). The space has been used for artworks and installations of many kinds – free standing and wall mounted sculpture, built environments, large canvases – and can be blacked out for video installation if necessary.

Access details: Access by lift in the Visitors' Centre and Great Hall. Wheelchair available.

Exhibitions policy / 'ethos' of gallery: The gallery has a rolling programme of exhibitions, historic and contemporary, with the emphasis on artists whose work responds to or reflects the University's own areas of endeavour.

What should interested artists do? Artists should submit images and a CV to the Curator of Art. The Gallery negotiates terms with individual artists and curators. Whilst this is not primarily a commercial space, some shows contain work for sale – the gallery takes a commission of 30% plus VAT on works sold.

Management structure: The Naughton Gallery is a department of Queen's University and is managed by the Queen's Art Board. It is also has full registered museum status.

Ogham Gallery

497 Antrim Road
Belfast BT15 3BP

Tel: +44 (0)28 9077 2580
E-mail: oghamgallery@hotmail.com

Re-use of existing space

Contact person / Director: Eimear Maguire

Architects for the conversion: Self-conversion

Ogham Gallery is located in a four story, terraced, Victorian building. Many of the building's original features have been retained. Prior to use as a gallery, the space has been an architect's office.

Number of rooms / galleries; area in square metres: Basement: 4 square metres; Gallery One: 5.5 x 4.5 square metres; Gallery Two: 4 x 4 square metres; also studios and storage. Total of nine rooms.

Specifications: The original wooden floor has been restored in the gallery space. Paintings are usually hung from original picture rail using small chains. Two storage areas are available for work. There are suitable spaces for slide / video installations, works on canvas and freestanding sculpture. Hanging varies according to size of work.

Access details: No disabled access.

Exhibitions policy / 'ethos' of gallery: The Ogham Gallery provides a space for emerging artists to exhibit work. The Gallery has mainly exhibited traditional painting and sculpture, however, work is underway to provide spaces for contemporary art as well.

What should interested artists do? Artists should send CV and CD ROM / e-mail and CV attached. The gallery provides an opening reception. It does not charge a fee, and gallery commission is 30%.

Management structure: Private.

Old Museum Arts Centre

7 College Square North
Belfast BT1 6AR

Tel: +44 (0) 28 9023 5053
Fax: +44 (0) 28 9032 2912
E-mail: info@oldmuseum.co.uk
www.oldmuseumartscentre.org

Conversion of an historic building

Contact person / Director: Anne McReynolds, Gillian Mitchell

Architects for the conversion: Self-conversion

OMAC is a city centre venue housed in a Grade 1 listed building in Belfast, and is widely recognised as a leading contemporary arts centre in Northern Ireland. It has a black box studio space, and visual art gallery. Built in 1830, originally, as the name suggests, the arts centre was a museum, until 1910. The building was then used by various organisations as office space and for storage. It then fell into a state of disrepair, until work began in the late 1980s to restore it to a usable space. OMAC has been in operation for 14 years.

Number of rooms / galleries; area in square metres: Two exhibition spaces. Main space: 5.5 x 6.2 m; Secondary space: 7.6 x 5.4 m.

Specifications: Walls are finished in matt white emulsion. Hanging is via nails or screws depending on the artists' requirements. Each room has a lighting track to highlight the work, and the main space has excellent natural light. Each room has open floor space suitable for secure free standing exhibits. There is access to power points. Access to building is up front steps, and there is a height restriction of 2.12 m and width restriction of 88 cm. No storage space.

Access details: No disabled access.

Exhibitions policy / 'ethos' of gallery: The Old Museum Arts Centre presents work by new and emerging artists from the UK, Ireland and beyond. The programming policy places particular focus on lens based media and installations of a site specific nature. Exhibiting artists will have undergone a process of formal training and will be able to demonstrate the technical ability to realise their artistic ambitions. OMAC is a contemporary non-commercial gallery

with a reputation for showcasing experimental and abstract work.

What should interested artists do? Send examples of work in any format along with a CV and dates of when they would like to exhibit. The space is programmed about 8 months in advance. Fees are not normally paid to artists. OMAC does not charge an entrance fee. 30% commission is taken, and sales are very much dependant on the nature of the work. More traditional work and photography both sell well. Artists will be included in the OMAC brochure, which has a distribution of 12,000. Invitations for launch are printed, and an opening night is hosted for artists.

Management structure: Run by a Board.

Ormeau Baths Gallery

18A Ormeau Avenue
Belfast BT2 8HS

Tel: +44 (0) 28 9032 1402
Fax: +44 (0) 28 9031 2232
E-mail: admin@obgonline.net
www.obgonline.net

Refurbishment of an historic building

Contact person / Director: Hugh Mulholland

Architects for the conversion: 22 over 7

Ormeau Baths Gallery is located within a former red-bricked Victorian bath house, dating from 1888; its conversion to an art gallery was completed in 1995. The gallery has been open for eight years.

Number of rooms / galleries; area in square metres: OBG has five gallery spaces; Gallery One is 71 square metres, Gallery Two is 60 square metres, Gallery Three is 115 square metres, Gallery Four is 138 square metres and Gallery Five is 143 square metres.

Specifications: The walls in all galleries are rendered concrete. Flooring on the ground floor galleries is wood; first floor galleries are concrete. Works are hung using mirror plates and fixed directly to the walls. OBG has a suspended lighting track with daylight tubes as well as points for spotlights. There is also natural light from a glass atrium in Galleries One and Four. OBG is suitable for all forms of presentation.

Access details: The gallery has disabled access via Aspey Street, to the left of the main entrance. Once inside all floors are completely accessible. OBG also has disabled toilet facilities.

Exhibitions policy / 'ethos' of gallery: Ormeau Baths Gallery delivers exhibitions of quality by nationally and internationally recognised artists, working across a broad range of contemporary visual art practice. The gallery originates all its exhibitions, most of which are commissioned specifically for OBG. OBG also operates a Guest Curator Programme which facilitates a project by an external artist / curator. Details of previous exhibitions can be viewed on the website: www.obgonline.net. OBG takes a commission of 30% on work sold. Due to the nature of the programming OBG do not generally have commercial exhibitions. However when work is presented which is suitable for sale, it does make sales.

What should interested artists do? Artists wishing to submit work for exhibition can do so in whatever form best represents their practice (ie, slides plus CV; CD ROM plus CV; e-mail with images and CV attached). The gallery does offer an exhibition fee to artists it commissions projects from, which is in the region of £1,000. OBG does not charge exhibition fees. The services available to exhibiting artists are: the gallery will be responsible for all the costs incurred in relation to the installation of the artists project, hire of equipment, construction of spaces etc. OBG also covers the cost of the opening and invitations and in some cases produces a catalogue.

Management structure: Ormeau Baths Gallery is a company limited by guarantee and is a recognised charity run by a Board of Trustees.

Queen Street Studios

37-39 Queen Street
Belfast BT1 6EA

Tel: +44 (0) 28 9024 3145
Fax: +44 (0) 28 9033 0910
E-mail: qsstudios@btconnect.com
queenstreetstudios@hotmail.com

Conversion of an existing building

Contact person / Director: Ursula Burke, adminstrator

Architects for the conversion: Self-conversion

Queen Street Studios is a gallery space within an artist-run studio group, occupying part of the third and the whole fourth floor of a building in Belfast city centre. The building itself dates from 1890, and Queen Street Studios has been in operation since 1984.

Number of rooms / galleries; area in square metres: Twenty-three studio spaces; digital studio; one gallery (1.27 x 2.74 square metres).

Specifications: Mulitfunctional sapce.

Access details: No disabled access.

Exhibitions policy / 'ethos' of gallery: Open submission policy showing contemporary art.

What should interested artists do? Send CV, proposal and visual material. The gallery pays an exhibition fee of £250, and takes 10% comission on work sold.

Services to artists include: opening, reception, postcards, invitations.

Management structure: Run by volunteer Board of artists.

Space Gallery

Conway Mill
5 – 7, Conway Street
Belfast BT13 2DE

Tel: +44 (0) 28 9024 9323
Fax: +44 (0) 28 9032 4309
E-mail: info@conwaymill.org
www.conwaymill.org

Conversion of an industrial building

Contact person / Director: Moya Hinds, Development Coordinator

Architects for the conversion: Self-conversion

Conway Mill is a Belfast flax-spinning mill complex. Established in 1842 and enlarged in 1900, it consists of two main mill blocks with engine and boiler rooms and four outbuildings. The Space Gallery is on the Top (third) floor of the Old Mill and leads to ten studio units housing artists and craft workers. There are a total of 23 individuals involved in the creative industries working throughout the complex. The Space Gallery was the original reeling room in the Old Mill, which then became the engineers floor. The Space gallery has been in operation for three years.

Conway Mill is negotiating a £4.2 million funding package for the refurbishment of the entire complex. It is hoped to have one floor (approximately 790 square metres) as a Gallery Space within two years, depending on the success of the funding applications.

Number of rooms / galleries; area in square metres: The Space Gallery is approximately 162 square metres. The Space Gallery is the main dedicated gallery area, however there are several other areas which can be (and have been) used to exhibit work – the first (approximately 510 square metres) and third (approximately 790 square metres) floors in the 'New Mill'. These floors have high jack-arched vaulted ceilings and large window openings.

Specifications: Walls are solid brick (two sides) and plaster board (two sides) painted white. Flooring: old brick quarry tiles. Light: spots (approximately 30). Work can be hung on the walls, from picture rail or from ceiling pipes. Height: approximately 2.74 metres. Storage space available. The space is suitable for slide / video installations, large works and sculptures.

Access details: There is a small lift which can accommodate a wheelchair, and a number of wheelchair accessible toilets.

Exhibitions policy / 'ethos' of gallery: The gallery aims to provide an opportunity for artists to gain experience in exhibiting their work. As well as seasoned artists; new artists, students and community organisations are encouraged to make use of the facilities. No particular style of work is specified, the gallery prefers not to restrict the range of work.

What should interested artists do? Either call in or send in images. As the policy is to encourage new artists to exhibit, CVs are not too important. The gallery neither pays nor charges an exhibition fee. The only charge is for electrical usage (spots). Support for the artist/s exhibiting varies, depending on finances available, but may include funding for printing and postage, opening reception or office support such as catalogues, CVs and advice on hanging. The Gallery takes 10% commission. Sales depend on the work.

Management structure: Conway Mill is a community owned and managed project. It is run by a Management Committee which also oversees the Gallery.

The Tile Refinery Gallery

11 – 19 Blythe Street
Belfast BT12 5HU

Tel: +44 (0) 28 9023 2136
E-mail: david@davidscott-tiles.co.uk

Conversion of industrial space

Contact person / Director: David Scott

Person responsible for renovation to art space: David Scott

Housed on the fourth floor of an old warehouse and former clothing factory with excellent natural light and extensive views of North and West Belfast. The original building dates from around 1850, and The Tile Refinery Gallery has been in operation since 2003.

Number of rooms / galleries; area in square metres: One room at 500 square metres.

Specifications: High ceilings, lots of natural light; loft-style gallery space.

Access details: No disabled access at present. Planning permission has been sought for a new lift externally.

Exhibitions policy / 'ethos' of gallery: A sympathetic attitude to young artists.

What should interested artists do? Artists should send CV plus slides, CD, video etc plus exhibition proposal. Fees are negotiable, work sells in the space, and the gallery commission is 40%.

Management structure: Private.

Ulster Museum

Botanic Gardens
Stranmillis
Belfast BT9 5AB

Tel: +44 (0) 28 9038 3000
www.ulstermuseum.org.uk

Purpose-built space

Contact person / Director: S. B. Kennedy, Head of Fine and Applied Art; Chief Executive: Tim Cooke

Original Architect: James Cumming Wynne (1929)
Architect for the extension: Francis Pym (1972)

The Ulster Museum dates back, in various guises, to the 1830s. The present building has been in regular use since 1929 when the old part of building was opened; the 'new' extension was opened in 1972. The Ulster Museum is Northern Ireland's treasure house of the past and present, with 8,000 square metres of galleries, and rich collections of art, archaeology, local history and natural sciences. There is also a constantly changing programme of temporary exhibitions and events. From ancient Ireland to the South Pacific, from masterpieces of modern art to rare flowers, the museum is a window to the North of Ireland and a window on the world. The origins of the Museum can be traced back to Tuesday 5 June 1821, when eight young men met in Belfast to form a society for the study of natural sciences. The Belfast Natural History Society put its collections on public display in a handsome new building, which they described as "the first ever museum erected in Ireland by voluntary subscription", and which opened to the public, for a small admission charge, in 1833.

Number of rooms / galleries; area in square metres: Museum galleries and nine art galleries, for the display of the museum's fine and applied art collections, plus a large dedicated temporary exhibitions space of around 580 square metres.

Specifications: All galleries fully air-conditioned and environmentally controlled.

Access details: Disabled access and a loop system in the lecture theatre.

Exhibitions policy / 'ethos' of gallery: A mixture of the historic and the modern, but with little emphasis on the avant garde as such: "we are, after all, a museum".

What should interested artists do?
Exhibitions are by invitation in accordance with policy. The Ulster Msuem doesn't seek or accept submissions. Broadly speaking, in both fine and applied art, exhibitions are sought which will complement the permanent collections. Irish material is also a speciality. Selling exhibitions are not held.

Management structure: Run by the trustees of the National Museums & Galleries of Northern Ireland. It is funded in the main by government through the Department of Culture, Arts & Leisure in Northern Ireland.

Belfast Waterfront Hall

2 Lanyon Place
Belfast BT1 3WH

Tel: +44 (0) 28 9033 4400
Fax: +44 (0) 28 9024 9862
E-mail: turkingtona@waterfront.co.uk
www.waterfront.co.uk

Purpose-built multi-use venue

Contact person / Director: Adam Turkington

Architect: Robinson McIllwaine Partnership

Built in 1977, the Belfast Waterfront Hall is primarily a conference and concert venue with exhibition space in the front of house areas.

Number of rooms / galleries; area in square metres: One 42 m, wall-based gallery with a rod and hook hanging system and a number of spaces where board-based and 3D work can be displayed.

Specifications: Suitable for slide installations / video installations / large works on canvas, free-standing sculpture.

Access details: Access for all galleries.

Exhibitions policy / 'ethos' of gallery: The Waterfront Hall is not a commercial gallery and, as such, programming is from an aesthetic standpoint. Work from a community arts background is actively encouraged.

What should interested artists do?
Some representation of the work is essential, and along with a CV it helps to have some idea of why the artist wishes to exhibit specifically in the Hall and not somewhere else. The Hall takes 25% on work sold, although it is not a selling venue. The Hall does not pay an exhibition fee, but the space is available for hire, in which case commission is not charged on work sold. Where commission is being charged, the Hall will pay for invitations, professional installation, reception and list of works.

Management structure: Run by Belfast City Council.

Co Armagh

Armagh County Museum
The Mall East
Armagh BT61 9BE
Contact person: Catherine McCullough
Tel: +44 (0) 28 3752 3070
E-mail: acm.um@nics.gov.uk
www.armaghcountrymuseum.org.uk

The Market Place Armagh Theatre and Arts Centre (p. 174)
Market Street
Armagh City
Co Armagh BT61 7AT
Contact person: Jill Holmes
Tel: +44 (0) 28 3752 1820 Fax: +44 (0) 28 3752 1822
E-mail: admin@themarketplacearmagh.com
www.themarketplacearmagh.com

Millennium Court Arts Centre (p. 175)
William Street
Portadown
Co Armagh BT62 3NS
Contact person: Megan Johnston
Tel: +44 (0) 28 3839 4415 Fax: +44 (0) 28 3839 4483
E-mail: info@millenniumcourt.org
www.millenniumcourt.org

Prentice Gallery
20 Armagh Road
Craigavon BT62 3DP
Contact person: Paul Prentice
Tel: +44 (0) 28 3835 3377
info@theprenticegallery.com www.theprenticegallery.com

The Market Place Armagh Theatre and Arts Centre

Market Street
Armagh City
Co Armagh BT61 7AT

Tel: +44 (0) 28 3752 1820
Fax: +44 (0) 28 3752 1822
E-mail: admin@themarketplacearmagh.com
www.themarketplacearmagh.com

Purpose-built multi-use arts venue

Contact person / Director: Jill Holmes, Theatre Director

Architect: Glenn Howells Architects

Since March 2000, The Market Place Theatre and Arts Centre has been operating a year-long programme of performance and visual arts.

Number of rooms / galleries; area in square metres: One gallery (approximately 10 x 10 x 10 m), two multipurpose workshop rooms.

Specifications: Hanging is directly onto the wall (no hanging system). Natural light from roof lights is supplemented by electric lighting. Height allows large scale sculptures, but access is limited to heights of around 2.5 m. Video installations are possible, but natural light makes these difficult during the day.

Access details: Full access for wheelchair users. Auditorium and studio have infra-red systems for the hard-of-hearing.

Exhibitions policy / 'ethos' of gallery: No one 'ethos'. The gallery hosts avant-garde, contemporary, traditionalist etc. As broad a scope as possible is aimed for within the space.

What should interested artists do? The gallery can accept sub-missions in all forms, but photographs and / or CD ROM are the handiest. Gallery commission is 15% and sales are very much dependent of the subject matter. The gallery pays an exhibition fee of £100. An opening reception and invitations are provided as well as a basic list of prices and biographies.

Management structure: Local Authority owned and operated.

Millennium Court Arts Centre

William Street
Portadown
Co Armagh BT62 3NS

Tel: +44 (0) 28 3839 4415
Fax: +44 (0) 28 3839 4483
E-mail: info@millenniumcourt.org
www.millenniumcourt.org

MCAC is located within the town's old municipal market hall, a converted red-brick building (1929). MCAC houses facilities for artists working in the visual, verbal and multimedia arts. MCAC's exhibition programme has been running since March 2003.

Number of rooms / galleries; area in square metres: MCAC has two main exhibition spaces. Gallery One is approximately 260 square metres, with high ceilings and the original metal-trussed roof. Gallery Two is 168 square metres. There is also a sound / audio studio, video editing suite with full multimedia equipment, an education room, visual arts workshop space, a darkroom, and an artist-in-residence suite. There are also numerous alternative spaces for visual and sound installations.

Specifications: The main walls are masonry cavity walls and steel framing. In Gallery One the walls are plasterboard, approximately 3.7 m high, and specially constructed for hanging artworks. Floors are wood on a concrete substructure. A 'Powerpleat' blind system covers the 24 m long skylight for black-out conditions. Gallery Two has similar walls and neutral carpeting, it is also fitted for blackout. Both galleries have sound points, four audio points and two video points, all of which are controllable remotely. There is a suspended track lighting system with floodlighting and points for halogen spots; light intensity can be altered. Loading can be difficult for exceptionally large works.

Access details: Wheelchair access throughout, accessible toilets, induction loop system, MCAC guide available in large type and cassette on request.

Refurbishment of an historic building

Contact person / Arts Centre Manager: Megan Johnston

Architects for the conversion: Harry Porter Architects

Exhibitions policy / 'ethos' of gallery: 'altering perceptions'. MCAC aims to alter perceptions about contemporary art, about Portadown, and about people themselves. While all artforms are shown, MCAC particularly advocates art practice that involves new technologies and new media, as well as artists working in traditional disciplines in new and innovative ways. The goal is to provide a balanced and varied programme that is both contemporary and experimental, with works from both emerging and established artists.

What should interested artists do?
Interested artists should send a CV and portfolio in whatever format most fittingly represents their work. MCAC will accept slides, photographic prints, CD, DVD, mini DV, VHS or by e-mail (with CV). Exhibition proposals are continually evaluated. MCAC does sell some work, although this is secondary to the programming policy. Gallery commission is 25%. MCAC does not charge exhibition fees, and may offer a fee for some commis-

sioned projects. MCAC covers all costs of set-up. There is a full-time technician on staff; and in-house multimedia equipment is at the artist's disposal. Invitations, mailing and opening reception are provided, and in some cases, a catalogue.

Management structure: MCAC is run by Portadown 2000 Urban Regeneration Board. There is also an Arts Advisory Committee. MCAC is primarily financed through Craigavon Borough Council and the Arts Council of Northern Ireland.

Co Carlow

In process:
The lack of dedicated exhibition space for contemporary visual art here is to be addressed by **VISUAL** – *The National Centre for Contemporary Art & Performing Arts Centre for County Carlow.*

VISUAL aims to provide a space to display temporary exhibitions of contemporary art of national and international standing. The VISUAL project of 2,300 square metres will include Gallery 1, Gallery 2, gallery / workshop, gallery storage area, multi-media space, visual arts outreach / education space, entrance foyer, auditorium, side-stage, dressing rooms, performing arts outreach / rehearsal space, control room, entrance foyer and shared spaces: bar / café, toilets, offices and carpark. The site for the centre will be located in the same precinct as St. Patrick's College and Carlow Cathedral. Terry Pawson Architects (UK) have been appointed, and the design process is underway. Preliminary designs will be available in June 2005. This will be followed by the Part 8 planning process, with tender stage to be completed by late 2005 and a contractor appointed in early 2006.

Two gallery spaces will be provided and the centre will also act as an 'Art Factory' to foster artist in residence programmes where work can be explored, manufactured and exhibited in all visual mediums. VISUAL will contain new media technologies with digital equipment and projection facilities. *Visualise Carlow* has been developed in recent years as an advance programme to this new centre. The Carlow Local Authorities will also develop a separate Theatre / Performing Arts Centre on an adjoining site. The Theatre will receive touring productions as well as presenting locally produced work. It will comprise one performance space designed to ensure optimum and dynamic presentation of theatre, music, all types of dance, cinema and literary readings and associated workshop space.

Contact person: Sinead Dowling
Arts Officer, Carlow County Council
Athy Road
Carlow
Tel: +353 (0) 59 913 6237
E-mail: sdowling@carlowcoco.ie

Co Cavan

Cavan Co Council have undertaken a feasibility study to address the lack of facilites for the visual arts here. An integrated arts centre has been proposed.

Contact person: Caitriona Reilly
Arts Organiser
Cavan County Council
The Courthouse
Cavan
Tel: +353 (0) 49 437 2099
E-mail: artsoffice@cavancoco.ie   www.cavancoco.ie

Exhibitions, including some of contemporary visual art, are held at:

Cootehill Library and Arts Centre
Bridge Street
Cootehill
Contact person: Sinead Rice
Tel: +353 (0) 49 555 9873

Ballyhugh Arts and Cultural Centre
Belturbet
Contact person: Marian Bradley
Tel: +353 (0) 49 952 6044
E-mail: ballyhughart@eircom.net

Co Clare

Clare Library (p. 177)
Mill Road
Ennis
Contact person: Siobhán Mulcahy
Tel: +353 (0) 65 684 6267
E-mail: siobhan.mulcahy@clarelibrary.ie
www.clarelibrary.ie

Glór Irish Music Centre
Friar's Walk
Ennis
Contact person: Sinead Cahill
Tel: +353 (0) 65 684 3103
E-mail: info@glor.ie www.glor.ie

The Russell Gallery (p. 178)
New Quay
Burrin
Contact person: Stefania Russell
Tel: +353 (0) 65 707 8185
E-mail: russell@esatclear.ie
www.russellrakuceramics.com

In process:
The Courthouse Gallery and Studios. Due to open late 2005, this new facility is housed in a former courthouse, and will include artists' studios, a recording studio and a gallery space.

Parliament Street
Ennistymon
Contact person: Catherine Comer
Tel: +353 (0) 65 707 1569

Clare Library

Mill Road
Ennis

Tel: +353 (0) 65 684 6267
E-mail: siobhan.mulcahy@clarelibrary.ie
www.clarelibrary.ie

Housed in a former Presbyterian Church, built c. 1856 to a design by Joseph Fogarty of Limerick (at a cost of £570) the church was adapted to form a combined museum-library in 1975. The art space is annexed to the library. The space has been used as a gallery since 2000. Prior to this it fuctioned as the County Museum.

Number of rooms / galleries: One main exhibition area with a well / dip in the centre.

Specifications: White walls, carpet on floors.

Access details: There is disabled access to the gallery.

Exhibitions policy / 'ethos' of gallery: A mixture of professional, semi-professional and community art. Work does sell in the space, but mainly traditional painting.

Refurbishment of an historic building

Contact person / Director: Siobhán Mulcahy

Architects for the conversion: Anthony O'Neill

What should interested artists do? Artists interested in exhibiting should send slides, CD ROM, or e-mail with images – all plus CV. The gallery does not charge for exhibiting and charges no commission on work sold. Basic back up is provided in terms of receptions, but all costs are borne by the artist.

Management structure: Local Government.

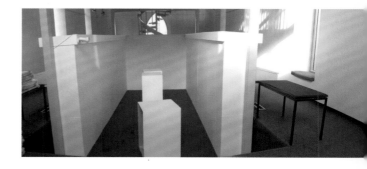

The Russell Gallery

Newquay
Burren

Tel: +353 (0) 65 707 8185
E-mail: russell@esatclear.ie
www.russellrakuceramics.com

Re-use of an historic building

Contact person / Director: Stefania Russell

Architects for the conversion: Self-conversion

crete floor. The little Gallery has white plasterboard walls and dark wood flooring. All spaces have daylight tubes or bulbs fitted. The main exhibition space is suitable for large canvas and free-standing sculptures.

Access details: There are two shallow steps to the main hall.

Exhibitions policy / 'ethos' of gallery: Contemporary art.

What should interested artists do? CD ROM, e-mail or photos and CV are required for artists to present their work. Reception and invitations are provided. Additional requests by negotiation. Work sells in the space, and the gallery commission is 33%.

Management structure: Private.

Located in a three storey stone building renovated from a 200 years old granary, the Russell Gallery is situated in Newquay, Co Clare and overlooking Galway Bay. The exact date of the building is unknown, but it appears on a map dated 1804. The renovation started in 1998 and progressed in stages. Initially a ceramic studio, the Russell Gallery began to show contemporary art in 2003 to make use of the building and to address a lack of art space in that part of Co Clare.

Number of rooms / galleries; area in square metres: Main hall 36 square metres and 5 m in height. Two additional space are available for exhibitions: the Conservatory 33 square metres and the Little Gallery (upstairs)18 square metres.

Specifications: The main hall has a white stone finishing, the conservatory is glass and stone finishing, both with con-

Co Cork

Alliance Française de Cork
36 Mary Street, Second Floor
Cork
Contact Person: Norah Callanan
Tel: +353 (0) 21 431 0677
E-mail: alliancefrancaisecork@eircom.net
www.alliancefrancaisecork.com

Briery Gap Cultural Centre
Main Street
Macroom
Contact person: Anne Dunne
Tel: +353 (0) 264 1793
E-mail: brierygap@eircom.net   www.brierygap.com

Cobh Library
The Arch Building
Casement Square
Cobh
Contact person: Anne-Marie Keneally
Tel: +353 (0) 21 481 1130
E-mail: cobhlibrary@eircom.net

Cork Vision Centre @ St. Peter's
North Main Street
Cork
Contact person: Lorraine Cahalame
Tel: +353 (0) 21 427 9925
E-mail: visioncentre@eircom.net
www.corkvisioncentre.com

Courtyard Craft and Exhibition Centre
Main Street
Midleton
Tel: +353 (0) 21 463 4644
E-mail: thecourtyardgallery@eircom.net
www.thecourtyardmidleton.com

Crawford Municipal Art Gallery (p. 181)
Emmet Place
Cork
Contact person: Peter Murray, Director; Dawn Williams,
Anne Boddaert, Assistant Curators
Tel: +353 (0) 21 427 3377
E-mail: crawfordexhibs@eircom.net
www.crawfordartgallery.ie

Cunnamore Galleries
Cunnamore Point
Skibbereen
Contact person: Diane Pitcher
Tel: +353 (0) 283 8483
E-mail: art@cunnamore.com   www.cunnamore.com

Fenton Gallery (p. 182)
5 Wandesford Quay
Cork
Contact person: Nuala Fenton
Tel: +353 (0) 21 431 5294 Fax: +353 (0) 21 491 7100
E-mail: nualafenton@eircom.net www.artireland.net

Form Gallery (p. 183)
Unit 2
Paul Street Shopping Centre
Cork
Contact person: Hazel Purcell, Kay Cogan
Tel: +353 (0) 21 427 1333
E-mail: form@affordableart-ireland.com

Gallery 44
Mac Curtain Street
Cork
Contact person: Rita Tighe
Tel: +353 (0) 21 450 1319

Gate Gallery
63 Townshend Street
Skibbereen
Contact person: Aidan Morris, Brenda Dodd, Michael
Stephens
Tel: +353 (0) 284 0666
E-mail: aidan@thegategallery.com www.thegategallery.com

Lewis Glucksman Gallery (p. 184)
University College
Cork
Contact person: Fiona Kearney
Tel: +353 (0) 21 490 1844 Fax: +353 (0) 21 490 1823
E-mail: info@glucksman.org www.glucksman.org

Catherine Hammond Gallery (p. 185)
Glengarriff
Contact person: Catherine Hammond
Tel: +353 (0) 276 3812
E-mail: info@hammondgallery.com
www.hammondgallery.com

Kent Gallery
Quayside
Kinsale
Contact person: Jennifer Goldstone
Tel: +353 (0) 21 477 4956 Fax: +353 (0) 21 477 4870
E-mail: info@kentgal.com www.kentgal.com

The Lavit Gallery (p. 186)
5 Father Mathew Street
Cork
Contact person: Avril Daly, Niall Foley
Tel: +353 (0) 21 427 7749
E-mail: thelavitgallery@eircom.net

The Lee Gallery
Lavitt's Quay
Cork
Contact person: Jerry O'Neill
Tel: +353 (0) 21 427 5204 Fax: +353 (0) 21 427 5205
E-mail: info@lee-gallery.com
www.lee-gallery.com

The Mall Arts Centre
Youghal Town Council
Mall House
Youghal
Contact person: Liam Ryan
Tel: +353 (0) 249 2926 Fax: +353 (0) 249 2690
E-mail: liam.ryan@corkcoco.ie
www.youghal.ie

Mill Cove Gallery (p. 187)
Mill Cove House
Castletownbere
Contact person: John Goode, John Brennan
Tel: +353 (0) 27 70393
E-mail: millcove@iol.ie www.millcovegallery.com

Sirius Arts Centre (p. 188)
Cobh
Contact person: Peggy Sue Amison
Tel: +353 (0) 21 481 3790
E-mail: cobharts@iol.ie www.iol.ie/~cobharts

Tig Filí
Thompson House
McCurtain Street
Cork
Contact person: Declan Barron
Tel: +353 (0) 21 450 9274
E-mail: info@tighfili.com
www.tigfili.com

Triskel Arts Centre (p. 189)
Tobin Street
Cork
Contact person: Penny Rae
Tel: +353 (0) 21 427 2022 Fax: +353 (0) 21 427 2592
E-mail: info@triskelart.com
www.triskelart.com

Vangard Gallery (p. 190)
Carey's Lane
Cork
Contact person / Director: John P. Quinlan
Tel: +353 (0) 21 427 8718
E-mail: vangard@eircom.net www.vangardgallery.com

West Cork Arts Centre (p. 191)
North Street
Skibbereen
Contact person / Director: Ann Davoren
Tel: +353 (0) 28 22090 Fax: +353 (0) 28 23237
E-mail: westcorkarts@eircom.net

Sarah Walker Art Gallery
The Pier
Castletownbere
Tel: +353 (0) 27 70387
E-mail: sarahwalker@eircom.net www.sarahwalker.ie

Crawford Municipal Art Gallery

Emmet Place
Cork

Tel: +353 (0) 21 427 3377
E-mail: crawfordexhibs@eircom.net
www.crawfordartgallery.ie

Conversion and extension of an historic building

Contact person / Director: Director: Peter Murray,
Assistant Curators: Dawn Williams, Anne Boddaert

Original Architect: (1724) Sir Edward Lovett Pearce (attributed)
Architects for the extension: (1884) Arthur Hill
Architects for the extension: (2000) Erick van Egeraat and Associates

The original Crawford Municipal Art Gallery building was constructed as the Custom House for Cork in 1724. A magnificent extension, housing studio and galleries was added in 1884 and in the year 2000, two 1,000 square metre galleries were built for temporary exhibitions. The 1724 Custom House is attributed to the architect Sir Edward Lovett Pearce, the 1884 extension was designed by Arthur Hill, of the firm Hill & Co., and finally the 2000 new Temporary Galleries were designed by Dutch architect company Erick van Egeraat and Associates. The building has been an arts space since 1850.

Number of rooms / galleries; area in square metres: 12 galleries – approximately 3000 square metres in total.

Specifications:
Galleries vary from 20 square metres to 500 square metres and are flexible to suit all media including slide installations / video installations / large works on canvas, free-standing sculpture.

Access details: Full wheelchair access and accessible toilet.

Exhibitions policy / 'ethos' of gallery:
Crawford Municipal Art Gallery is dedicated to a constantly evolving temporary exhibitions programme in tandem with displaying its permanent collection, which primary focuses on eighteenth century to contemporary art. The gallery also holds lectures in the lecture theatre and workshops in the galleries. The gallery ethos is to expose a wide audience to the significant role that art plays in contemporary culture and identity. It is committed to fostering recognition, critical assessment, and acknowledgement of contemporary and historical Irish and international art.

What should interested artists do? Post a comprehensive exhibition proposal consisting of CD ROM / slides / video etc. plus CV and artists statement. The Gallery is a non-commercial gallery. All exhibitions are

free to the public. Invitations, receptions, catalogues are available to artists at the discretion of the Gallery.

Management structure: Currently maintained by City of Cork V.E.C. and FÁS under the umbrella of the Department of Education.

Fenton Gallery

5 Wandesford Quay
Cork

Tel: +353 (0) 21 431 5294
Fax: +353 (0) 21 491 7100
E-mail: nualafenton@eircom.net
www.artireland.net

Conversion of an historic building

Contact person / Director: Nuala Fenton

Architects for the conversion: Self-conversion

Access details: Disabled access: gallery is on ground floor, double doors to side of building with removable ramp.

Exhibitions policy / 'ethos' of gallery: To show the best of contemporary art.

What should interested artists do?
Interested artists should send slides and CV. Work normally sells as the Fenton operates as a commercial gallery.
There is no fee charged and publicity for the shows (invitations, PR and opening receptions) is provided.

Management structure: Private.

The Fenton Gallery is housed in a 19th-century building, used originally as a warehouse. It was renovated as an arts space in 1999 by Nuala Fenton. The Fenton Gallery is a unique arts space, its size and open-plan feel allow for the exhibition: everything from large-scale paintings, to free-standing sculptures, to site specific installations and video works.

Number of rooms / galleries; approximate area in square metres: Main space: 185 square metres in size. Two adjencent vault-like spaces (additional).

Specifications: Average wall height from floor to ceiling: 2.46 metres. Lighting: wall washers and spots with soft tone / diffused bulbs. Flooring: bleached oak. Main loading doors: 1.60 x 2.11 metres approximately. Additional vaulted spaces: arched ceiling; maximum height of pieces: 1 metre. Highly suitable for installations, video or sculptural.

Form Gallery

Unit 2
Paul Street Shopping Centre
Cork

Tel: +353 (0) 21 427 1333
E-mail: form@affordableart-ireland.com

Re-use of existing space

Contact person / Director: Hazel Purcell, Manager / Curator
Kay Cogan, Director / Owner

Architects for the conversion: Self-conversion

Form Gallery has been in operation since June 2003. Located in a unit of a shopping complex (built 1985), the space originally functioned as a crèche. Form Gallery aims to provide a welcoming and helpful, calm space in a busy city centre location.

Number of rooms / galleries; area in square metres: The main space is a cube, with two ante rooms to the rear. Approximately 55 square metres.

Specifications: Painted white walls, aged concrete floor painted grey. Traditional hanging methods are used – putting the artwork directly on the wall rather than suspending it from the ceiling, the predominant lighting is artificial spotlighting but there is also indirect natural light. The gallery has storage space. Work enters through a doorway of 76 x 204 cm. At present the space is unsuitable for slide or video installations. Maximum canvas dimensions 2 x 5 m, free-standing sculpture 2.5 m height.

Access details: The gallery is located at ground level and is accessible to all.

Exhibitions policy / 'ethos' of gallery: Form is a forum for contemporary art in Cork.

What should interested artists do? Artists wishing to exhibit in the gallery should either forward slides or a CD ROM and a CV. The gallery neither pays nor charges an exhibition fee. An opening reception and invitations are provided, work sells in the space and gallery commission is 40%.

Management structure: Private.

Lewis Glucksman Gallery

University College Cork

Tel: +353 (0) 21 490 1844
Fax: +353 (0) 21 490 1823
E-mail: info@glucksman.org
www.glucksman.org

Purpose-built space

Contact person / Director: Fiona Kearney, Director; Nora Hickey, Curator of Education and Collections; Rene Zechlin, Curator of Exhibitions and Projects

Architects: O'Donnell + Tuomey

In the grounds of University College, Cork, the Lewis Glucksman Gallery is a purpose-built modern gallery that promotes the research, creation and exploration of the visual art. The gallery was opened in 2004. There is a book shop and the building also houses a public restaurant and private dining facilities.

Number of rooms / galleries; area in square metres: There are four exhibition spaces: 1. Lower Gallery: 350 square metres, linear run of display wall: 55 square metres, 4.9 m high; 2. Close Control Gallery: 63 square metres, linear run of display wall: 30 square metres, 5.05 m high; 3. Media Room: 21 square metres, linear run of display wall: 17 square metres, 2.4 m high; 4. Upper Gallery: 335 square metres, linear run of display wall: 67 square metres, 4.75 m high.

Specifications: Walls: white plaster; Heights: 4.7 m to 5 m; Floors: sawn oak boarding; Hanging: nails to wall, rails; Light: natural and artificial, controllable. Museum design conditions in close control galleries. Storage: Close control conditions in gallery store. Loading: Lift: L x W x H: 3.4 x 2. 5 x 2.4 m; Delivery bay and podium access.

Access details: Fully accessible.

Exhibitions policy / 'ethos' of gallery: The Glucksman's artistic mission is to explore all aspects of visual culture and present a range of innovative and intellectually-stimulating displays. The exhibitions programme at the Glucksman fosters scholarship in a new environment, placing particular emphasis on the unique role of visual media in communicating knowledge. Central to this is the creation of discursive relationships between academic disciplines and art practice. This is reflected in a wide range of exhibitions that span various media and historical periods.

What should interested artists do? The gallery is a non-commercial space and does not accept unsolicited materials.

Management structure: Private company wholly owned by University College Cork.

Catherine Hammond Gallery

Glengarriff
Co Cork

Tel: +353 (0) 27 63812
E-mail: info@hammondgallery.com
www.hammondgallery.com

Purpose-built space

Contact person / Director: Catherine Hammond

Architects for the conversion: Self-conversion

What should interested artists do? Send CV and slides, or Mac-compatible CD. The gallery has a contract with artists and provides marketing and publicity, invitations and other direct mail, as well as an opening reception. Work sells in the space, and gallery commission is 40%.

Management structure: Private, commercial gallery.

Open since March 2004, the Catherine Hammond Gallery is a purpose-built commercial gallery showing contemporary Irish and American art.

Number of rooms / galleries; area in square metres: Four different exhibition areas, approximately 155 square metres.

Specifications: Walls: 3.66 metres high, dry-wall with plaster skim backed by plywood; Flooring: Polished cement; Lighting: Museum-quality track wall washers. The space can accommodate large paintings, free-standing sculpture, video.

Access details: Wheelchair accessible.

Exhibitions policy / 'ethos' of gallery: The gallery shows contemporary art, particularly painting and works on paper, usually by mid-career and established artists.

The Lavit Gallery

5 Father Mathew Street
Cork

Tel: +353 (0) 21 427 7749
E-mail: thelavitgallery@eircom.net

Conversion of an existing building

Contact person / Director: Avril Daly / Niall Foley

Architects for the conversion: Self-conversion

Specifications: The walls are plastered, with facilities to hang paintings. At the moment all floors are carpeted. The ceilings are approximately 2.44 m high and would not easily accommodate very large paintings. Free standing sculpture can be accommodated if not too large.

In operation for over 40 years, The Lavit Gallery was originally based in Lavitts Quay. The name was kept when it was discovered that the Huguenot merchant, after whom the quay was named had lived in the area where the gallery is now based. It was also discovered that the correct spelling of his name was Lavit not Lavitt. Whilst the building has not been formally renovated, its shape and use has changed over its lifetime. Its history has been varied, ranging from a sweetshop with living accommodation overhead, a branch of the Cork College of Commerce to a factory producing plaster statues for local churches. During this period it was locally known as "The Chalky God Factory." The gallery was founded in 1963 in response to a lack of venues for artists to show their work in Cork city. The original ethos was and to a large extent still is: "To create and awareness of and appreciation of the visual arts". The Gallery awards an anual prize *The Student of the Year Award* to the student considered to have the most promise in the Crawford College of Art and Design.

Number of rooms / galleries; area in square metres: Two floors of exhibition space. Entrance is at street level. Each floor is approximately 75 square metres, one gallery on each floor.

Access details: No disabled access.

Exhibitions policy / 'ethos' of gallery: The policy of the board is to show the best of contemporary art. On the ground floor there is an ever evolving display of paintings, sculpture, ceramics, print and photography. In the upper gallery traditionally a range of one person or group shows, again by leading contemporary artists, both Irish and foreign are hosted. This policy is currently under review.

What should interested artists do? The Lavit Gallery is always interested in hearing from artists and initially potential exhibitors should submit their CV and original examples of their work. The gallery takes 40% commission on sales. When hosting exhibitions, fees are neither paid nor charged.

Management structure: The Lavit Gallery is a not-for-profit organisation and is a registered charity. It is run by a Board who answer to the membership, which currently stands at 250.

Mill Cove Gallery

Mill Cove House
Castletownbere

Tel: +353 (0) 27 70393
E-mail: millcove@iol.ie
www.millcovegallery.com

Conversion of an historic building

Contact person / Director: John Goode and John Brennan

Architects for the conversion: Self-conversion

Located in a 200 year old stone outhouse building in the grounds of Mill Cove House in West Cork, Mill Cove Gallery is 4 km from Castletownbere on the Glengarriff Road, overlooking Mill Cove and Bere Island. Mill Cove has been in operation since 2000. Prior to a gallery, the building had been used as office space.

Number of rooms / galleries; area in square metres: Four exhibition rooms. Total area: approximately 150 square metres.

Specifications: Stone and white wall / spotlights / dedicated storage room / VDU with catalogue presentation in foyer of gallery.

Access details: All on one floor, wheelchair friendly.

Exhibitions policy / 'ethos' of gallery: Irish contempory art; promotion of established and emerging artists.

What should interested artists do? Artists should complete the forms available on gallery website. Exhibition costs, invites, PR, reception, etc. are borne by the gallery.

Management structure: Private.

Sirius Arts Centre

Cobh

Tel: +353 (0) 21 481 3790
E-mail: cobharts@iol.ie
www.iol.ie/~cobharts

Renovation of an historic building

Contact person / Director: Peggy Sue Amison

Original Architect: Anthony Salvin
Conversion Architect: Alex White

Built in 1858 for the Royal Cork Yacht Club (the oldest yacht club in the world); this listed building is the only example of architect Anthony Salvin's work in Ireland. Renovated for use as an arts cantre in 1989, the Sirius became a full-time arts centre in the mid 1990s.

Number of rooms / galleries; area in square metres: Sirius has two gallery spaces which are located side by side, the galleries are multi-purpose. There is also an artist-in-residence studio. Square metres approximately: West Gallery 8.23 x 4.27 metres (one wall is all windows); Centre Gallery 7.47 x 6.10 metres (one wall is all windows).

Specifications: Being an historic listed building the galleries in Sirius Arts Centre have limits when it comes to installations in the building. There is a good hanging system for flat art. Lighting is spot lighting plus natural light. The floor is wood so there are restrictions on weight of pieces in the gallery. The galleries are very much about light, so video installations and other such installations that require black out are possible, but really take away from the Art Centre's most positive aspect, the view of Cork Harbour.

Access details: Wheelchair ramp for entry to the building.

Exhibitions policy / 'ethos' of gallery: Sirius is a multi-purpose arts centre exhibiting a wide range of contemporary work from painting to sculpture to photography and beyond. Contemporary artwork is shown as well as work of historical significance that ties directly into the area. Sirius also supports community arts events through outreach programming and exhibitions of work. Music concerts are held in the West Gallery every month, ranging from Irish traditional, to pop to classical music.

What should interested artists do? Artists interested in submitting an application for an exhibition should submit 10 slides or a CD ROM / CD of their work with an up-to-date CV and proposal. Exhibition fees are sometimes paid depending on funding. Normally Sirius pays for an opening reception and invitations. The Arts Centre has produced catalogues when it has received funding to assist in the production. Sirius Arts Centre's policy is to take 35% on work sold. Sirius is not strictly a commercial gallery but some exhibits have sold.

Management structure: Sirius Arts Centre is a limited company run by a Board of Directors. The staff is mostly FÁS-based, with a paid part-time administrator.

Triskel Arts Centre

Tobin Street
Cork

Tel: +353 (0) 21 427 2022
Fax: +353 (0) 21 427 2592
E-mail: info@triskelart.com
www.triskelart.com

Renovation of an historic building

Contact person / Director: Penny Rae

Most Recent Conversion Architect: Pat Higgison

Triskel is a multi-disciplinary contemporary arts centre incorporating seven flexible spaces which accomodate performance, visual presentations, residencies and film. The original building and site dates back to the early 1800's, when it was used as the City Livery. Since then it has been used for various purposes including grain stores and warehousing. The Triskel has been resident in the building for approximately twenty years. During its tenure, the Triskel has undergone a number of phased renovation projects, the most recent completed in Autumn 2004. The purpose of the latter was to generate more spaces with increased flexibility, and receptivity to the diversity of artistic activity.

Number of rooms / galleries; area in square metres: There are a total of seven spaces at the Triskel, with a total of approximately 335 square metres. Full details, measurements and floor plans are available on the Triskel website: www.triskelart.com

Specifications: Triskel spaces are receptive to a diversity of audio and visual presentations, inclusive of large-scale installation and object based work. Space 1 also has retractable seating for performance lecture, video, film.

Access details: Lift and outside ramps accommodate for visitors with special needs. Toilets are available to visitors with special needs while some exhibitions will provide induction loop systems.

Exhibitions policy / 'ethos' of gallery: The Triskel supports a diversity of new work through commission, residency and collaboration with communities, artists, local and international creative groups. Through its policy the Triskel: supports creativity,

develops creative skills, encourages participation, develops new forms of partnership, and undertakes ongoing research and development to identify, generate and engage new partnerships and creative projects in tandem with a diversity of groups.

What should interested artists do? Artists are encouraged to contact the Triskel to discuss proposals, joint partnerships and the most appropriate way of presenting work specific to individual working processes. Artists may contact either the Artistic Director, Penny Rae or the Programme Curator, Emma Johnston. The Triskel website can be referenced for past, current and forthcoming projects. Both selling and non-selling work are presented, and commission is 35% on sale of works. There is no set exhibition fee, due to the diversity of activity in the centre, however a base Artist's

Fee of €600 plus subsistence is offered for exhibitions. Exhibition openings are supported (minimum of invitation, reception and marketing).

Management structure: Run by a Board.

Vangard Gallery

Carey's Lane
Cork

Tel: +353 (0) 21 427 8718
E-mail: vangard@eircom.net
www.vangardgallery.com

Conversion of an historic building

Contact person / Director: John P. Quinlan

Architects for the conversion: Self-conversion

The Vangard gallery is situated on the second floor of a converted Huguenot warehouse building which retains many of its original features such as imposing beams and central pillars. Located in the Huguenot quarter of the city centre, the building was used as a warehouse. It was converted into an art space in 2000.

Number of rooms / galleries; area in square metres: The gallery is comprised of two rooms – the main gallery space measuring approximately 76.5 square metres, and another space measuring 24 square metres.

Specifications: Wall height varies from 2.44 to 2.74 metres interspersed with the original dramatic beams. The walls are both solid stone and stud partition with a textured plaster finish and painted white. The floor is exposed red deal finished with a dark stain. The lighting is provided by low voltage spot lights and the gallery has reasonable storage facilities. The space is suitable for multi-media, slide or video installation, large works on canvas and free-standing sculpture. A removable free-standing partition in the middle of the gallery floor creates a division of the space, enabling the exhibiting artist to tailor the space to suit the show.

Access details: No disabled access.

Exhibitions policy / 'ethos' of gallery: The Vangard holds monthly exhibitions of contemporary Irish art from emerging and established artists.

What should interested artists do? Any artist interested in exhibiting should send an e-mail with slides and a CV attached; alternatively a CD ROM or slides and a CV could be sent to the gallery. The gallery doesn't pay or charge an exhibition fee. Exhibiting artists can avail of an opening reception, invitation cards, postage, PR and administrative back-up. The Vangard is a commercial gallery and depends on the sale of work.

Management structure: Private.

West Cork Arts Centre

North Street
Skibbereen

Tel: +353 (0) 28 22090
Fax: +353 (0) 28 23237
E-mail: westcorkarts@eircom.net

Conversion of an existing building

Contact person / Director: Ann Davoren

Architects for the conversion: Donal Hoare

Originally a bank, then a school, the ground floor of this building was converted into galleries for the West Cork Arts Centre in 1985. The gallery comprises two galleries, workspace and office on the ground floor of the VEC-owned Sutherland Building. The exhibition programme resources many education and community programmes for children and for adults. The gallery spaces are also used for performances, book launches, film club etc.

Number of rooms / galleries; area in square metres: Gallery 1: 39 square metres; Gallery 2: 56.75 square metres.

Specifications: Wall finishes: white plastered stone; flooring, grey painted concrete; hanging: screws / mirror plates to wall; lighting track with spots and spreads; storage, small amount of storage; heights, 3.66 m in height to lighting track; loading doors 1.66 x 2.33 m.

Access details: The galleries, workspace and toilets have disabled access.

Exhibitions policy / 'ethos' of gallery: West Cork Arts Centre is a publicly-funded arts facility that creates opportunities for the people of West Cork to have access to, and engagement with, local and global arts practice of excellence. It supports a multi-disciplinary arts programme with a focus on modern and contemporary visual art and a range of education and community programmes. The space is suitable for slide installations / video installations / large works on canvas and free-standing sculptures.

What should interested artists do? Send slides plus CV; send CD ROM plus CV; send e-mail with images and CV attached

plus an artist's statement. The gallery pays an EPR fee and provides: opening reception, invitations, publicity and PR, occasional catalogue / pamphlet, hire of equipment for media works, insurance, transport, materials and technician for exhibition installation and take-down, artists' expenses when funds permit. Work does sell especially during the summer months and the gallery takes 33%.

Management structure: Run by a Board.

Co Derry

Cambridge Gallery
7 Market Street
Derry BT48 6EF
Contact person: Brian McCafferty
Tel: +44 (0) 28 7137 2237

Context Galleries (p. 193)
The Playhouse
5 – 7 Artillery St
Derry BT48 6RG
Contact person: Declan Sheehan
Tel: +44 (0) 28 7137 3538 Fax: +44 (0) 28 7126 1884
E-mail: contextgallery@yahoo.co.uk
www.derryplayhouse.co.uk

Eden Place Arts Centre
Rossville Street
Derry BT48 6LP
Contact person: Judi Logue
Tel: +44 (0) 28 7126 9418 Fax: +44 (0) 28 7137 3296
E-mail: judi_edenplaceartscentre@yahoo.co.uk

Flowerfield Arts Centre (p. 194)
185 Coleraine Road
Portstewart BT55 7HU
Contact person: Malcolm Murchison
Tel: +44 (0) 28 7083 1400 Fax: +44 (0) 28 7083 1432
E-mail: info@flowerfield.org www.flowerfield.org

Gallery 33
33 St Paul's Road
Coleraine BT51 4UP
Contact person: Justine Snowdon
Tel: +44 (0) 28 7084 9933
E-mail: info@irishgallery33.com   www.irishgallery33.com

Laneside Gallery
5 Stable Lane
Coleraine BT52 1DQ
Tel: +44 (0) 28 7035 3600
E-mail: info@lanesidegallery.com
www.lanesidegallery.com

McGilloway Gallery
6 Shipquay Street
Derry BT48 6DN
Contact person: Ken McGilloway
Tel: +44 (0) 28 7136 6011
E-mail: ken@themcgillowaygallery.com
www.themcgillowaygallery.com

Portstewart Galleries
49 & 85 The Promenade
Derry BT55 7AG
Contact person: Pauline Hughes
Tel: +44 (0) 28 7083 4600
E-mail: michael@irishartgroup.com
www.irishartgroup.com

Riverside Theatre
University of Ulster
Cromore Road
Coleraine BT52 1SA
Contact person: Sharon Kirk
Tel: +44 (0) 28 7032 3232
E-mail: riversidetheatre@ulster.ac.uk

Verbal Arts Centre (p. 195)
Stable Lane and Mall Wall
Bishop Street Within
Derry BT48 6PU
Contact person: James Kerr
Tel: +44 (0) 28 7126 6946 Fax: +44 (0) 28 7126 3368
E-mail: info@verbalartscentre.co.uk
www.verbalartscentre.co.uk

Void Art Centre (p. 196)
Old City Factory
Patrick Street
Derry BT48 7EL
Contact person: Maolíosa Boyle, Colin Darke
Tel: +44 (0) 28 7130 8080
E-mail: derryvoid@yahoo.co.uk

Context Galleries

The Playhouse
5 – 7 Artillery St
Derry BT48 6RG

Tel: +44 (0) 28 7137 3538
Fax: +44 (0) 28 7126 1884
E-mail: contextgallery@yahoo.co.uk

Conversion of an historic building

Contact person/Director: Declan Sheehan

Architects for the conversion: Self-conversion

Housed in a 19th Century hotel building, and former school, Context Galleries has been in operation since 1993. Context supports and encourages emerging fine and applied Irish artists, and aims to develop links between emerging artists from Ireland and other countries. The gallery's aim is to provide artists with a platform for their work. Twelve exhibitions, solo, grouped and themed are organised per year alongside several public art-based projects. Context continues to further develop its existing links to the local artistic community as well as opening the visual arts to every section of society through its Education and Outreach work.

Number of rooms / galleries; area in square metres: Two galleries. Gallery One: 2.79 x 2.23 m; ceiling 4.47 m high. Gallery Two: 4.11 x 7.32 m; ceiling 4.47 m high.

Specifications: Context has a large space suitable for all mediums – for slide installations / video installations / large works on canvas, free-standing sculpture, audio pieces. With the development of Gallery Two there is now also a space suitable as a process / smaller scale project room.

Access details: The gallery has disabled access, which is limited at present but is being improved.

Exhibitions policy / 'ethos' of gallery: Contemporary art by emerging artists in the visual and applied arts.

What should interested artists do? Send CD ROM, images, slides and CV by post. Context works with local festivals and with other arts organisations around Ireland on collaborative projects and exhibitions, which tour nationally. The gallery pays a fee to exhibiting artists, issues invitations and holds openings. The gallery also publishes catalogues for certain shows. Works sells occasionally and the gallery commission is 40%.

Management structure: Run by a Board, Context is a publicly funded charity.

Flowerfield Arts Centre

185 Coleraine Road
Portstewart BT55 7HU

Tel: +44 (0) 28 7083 1400
E-mail: info@flowerfield.org
www.flowerfield.org

Conversion and extension of historic building

Contact person / Director: Malcolm Murchison; Assistant Managers:
Deborah Logan, Anthony Toner

Original Architect: Samuel Orr (c. 1830)
Architects for the extension: Consarc Design Group (2003)

Established in 1990, Flowerfield
Arts Centre is Coleraine Borough
Council's dedicated arts facility. Centred
around a Georgian house, which has been
renovated and extended, it is a multi purpose arts centre specialising in providing
access to creative and participative activity.
The centre now also boasts a fine 150-seat
auditorium with multi-media capability,
four spacious teaching spaces for a variety
of disciples, four craft units for artists-in-
residence and a coffee shop/craft retail
area.

**Number of rooms / galleries; area in
square metres**: Gallery 1: 68 square
metres; Gallery 2: 39 square metres;
Gallery 3: 38 square metres.

Specifications: Wall finishes: white painted
plaster; flooring: carpet or wood; hanging:
nylon perlons; light: natural light and a
substantial number of low voltage spot
system lights; storage: very limited;
heights: 3.3 m. There are spaces suitable
for the exhibition of all types and sizes of
work.

Access details: Comprehensive access and
parking (lift, ramps etc.) as well as
Induction Loop.

Exhibitions policy / 'ethos' of gallery: The
gallery shows a very wide range of work
including contemporary, conceptual, craft,
amateur, non-elitist art.

What should interested artists do? Artists
should send CV plus slides, CD ROM or e-
mail with images attached. The gallery neither pays nor charges a fee. An opening
reception, invitations and catalogue are
provided. The commission taken by the
gallery is usually 20%, and work does sell
in the space, depending on the exhibition.

Management structure: Local Authority.

Verbal Arts Centre

Stable Lane and Mall Wall
Bishop Street Within
Derry BT48 6PU

Tel: +44 (0) 28 7126 6946
Fax: +44 (0) 28 7126 3368
www.verbalartscentre.co.uk

Conversion of an existing building

Contact person / Director: James Kerr

Original Architect: W.E. Pinkerton (1892)
Architects for the conversion: Stephen Hall: Hall, Black, Douglas (2000)

The Verbal Arts Centre is located on the site of the former First Derry National School which was built in 1892 to the designs of W.E. Pinkerton. The centre faces directly onto the Derry City Walls and is in an inner city location. The old building was renovated and converted with universal accessibility in mind. This award-winning building provides a rich and creative environment suitable for a wide range of activities. The conversion architect and client worked together to establish a narrative thread throughout the building, with commissioned works by leading Irish artists, sculptors and craftsmen providing a visual counterpoint to each floor. The Verbal Arts Centre provides Verbal Arts education for everyone through storytelling, creative writing, literacy, reading development and creative training courses. It is a unique organization located in an inspirational environment.

Number of rooms / galleries; area in square metres: 8 rooms for hire (including a recording studio). Building area: 844 square metres. The centre has an artist-in-residence flat that is available for exhibiting artists.

Specifications: Artists are advised to visit the website for dimensions and images of the available space, or telephone the Facilities Manager. The centre will work to accommodate the installation requests of any artists accepted to exhibit.

Access details: Fully accessible, including lift, Braille signage, induction loop, ramped areas.

Exhibitions policy / 'ethos' of gallery: To promote innovative interactions between the written and spoken word and contemporary art – where possible a preference is given to site specific work.

What should interested artists do? Send slides / CD ROM / Website / video etc as appropriate, include a CV and artist's statement outlining principles / values of practice as well as a proposal for the space. The centre does not take a percentage on work sold – work does not normally sell. The centre does not normally pay an exhibition fee, but can make exceptions at the discretion of the Executive Director. It does charge an exhibition fee. Services available to artists include documentation of work and inclusion on website.

Management structure: Private. Company limited by guarantee with charitable status.

Void Art Centre

Old City Factory
Patrick Street
Derry BT48 7EL

Tel: +44 (0) 287 130 8080
E-mail: derryvoid@yahoo.co.uk

Conversion of an indsutrial building

Contact person: Maolíosa Boyle, Colin Darke

Original Architect: Robert Young
Architects for the conversion: Michael Hegarty

Void Arts Centre is located in the basement of the old City Factory in Derry. The original building, built in 1861, was previously a shirt factory.

Number of rooms / galleries: Void houses two gallery spaces and six studios.

Specifications: The gallery space is adaptable and suitable for all media.

Access details: The gallery has disabled access.

Exhibitions policy / 'ethos' of gallery: Void aims primarily to promote the profile of international, national and local contemporary arists through its exhibition programme. Void aims to encourage critical discussion and appreciation of contemporary art practice through its exhibition programme.

What should interested artists do? Artists should send a proposal with CV in the form that best suits their work. The gallery pays an exhibition fee, which will vary depending on the exhibition. The gallery does not charge fees. An opening reception is held for each show.

Management structure: Void is an artist-led space. The Board of Directors is made up of two sub-boards: a professional board constructed from people with various backgrounds and expertise including finance, education, community involvement; and a curatorial board which has full curatorial control over decisions regarding the work to be exhibited.

Co Donegal

Cavanacor Gallery (p. 198)
Ballindrait
Lifford
Contact person: Joanna O'Kane
Tel / Fax: +353 (0) 74 914 1143
E-mail: art@cavanacorgallery.ie
www.cavanacorgallery.ie

Cristeph Gallery
Port Road
Letterkenny
Contact person: Niall O'Donnell
Tel: +353 (0) 74 912 6411

An Dánlann Dearg
No. 22 Carraig a' t'Seascain
Na Doirí Beaga
Leitir Ceanainn
Contact person: John White
Tel: +353 (0) 86 088 6003

An Gailearaí (p. 199)
Ceardlann na gCroisbhealach
Falcarragh
Contact person: Una Campbell
Tel/Fax: +353 (0) 74 916 5594
E-mail: ceardlann@eircom.net

Glebe Gallery (p. 200)
Church Hill
Letterkenny
Contact person : Adrian Kelly
Tel: +353 (0) 74 913 7071 Fax: +353 (0) 74 913 7461
E-mail: glebegallery@opw.ie

An Grianán Theatre (p. 201)
Port Road
Letterkenny
Contact person: Patricia McBride
Tel: +353 (0) 74 912 3288
E-mail: angrianan@eircom.net
www.angrianan.com

Letterkenny Arts Centre (p. 202)
Central Library
Oliver Plunkett Road
Letterkenny
Contact person: John Cunningham
Tel: +353 (0) 74 912 9186   Fax: +353 (0) 74 912 3276
E-mail: lkarts@eircom.net   www.donegalculture.com

Screig Gallery of Contemporary Irish Art
Fintown
Contact person: Patricia Sharkey
Tel: +353 (0) 86 825 6736
E-mail: info@searc.ie   www.searc.ie/screig.html

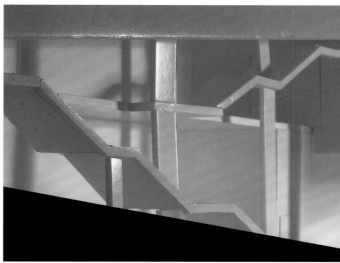
Model (detail) new Letterkenny Arts Centre, Magabhann Architects, 2004/05

Cavanacor Gallery

Ballindrait
Lifford

Tel / Fax: +353 (0) 74 914 1143
E-mail: art@cavanacorgallery.ie
www.cavanacorgallery.ie

Refurbishment of an historic building

Contact person / Director: Joanna O'Kane

Architects for the conversion: Antoin Mac Gabhainn

Cavanacor Gallery is located a mile and a half outside Lifford. It is situated in the courtyard at Cavanacor House, a seventeenth century plantation building, which is one of the oldest inhabited houses in Donegal. The historic house and gallery are set in ten and a half acres of mature grounds. The gallery is located in a restored two-storey stone building. The building was renovated as an art space in 1990 and also houses a small coffee shop, reception area and toilets.

Number of rooms / galleries: There are three rooms dedicated as gallery space, two upstairs and one downstairs. The reception room/café acts as a fourth auxiliary gallery space.

Specifications: The walls are white plaster finish and wood screens are positioned for display in three of the galleries. The flooring is stone on the ground floor and wood and carpet on the first floor. The spaces are spot lit and hanging is flexible for each individual show. There is a small amount of storage available. The gallery can cater for works on a scale up to 2 x 2 m. It is unsuitable for conceptual practise, ie video and slide installation. There is accommodation for free-standing sculpture.

Access details: There is disabled access to the two ground floor galleries, the café and the toilets.

Exhibitions policy / 'ethos' of gallery: Cavanacor Gallery is dedicated to increasing the audience for contemporary art and has established a professional, commercial venue, as an opportunity for exhibiting in the Northwest. The gallery hosts exhibitions by emerging and established national and international art. There is limited potential to exhibit installation art. Instead the gallery platforms high quality contemporary art of a non-conceptual nature, primarily drawing, painting, photography, printmaking and sculpture. The gallery is a professional commercial venue and represents exhibiting artists in terms of sales. Commission is decided in discussion with the artist and details are available on application. Cavanacor Gallery has been very successful since 1999, with excellent sales for many artists.

What should interested artists do? Artists are advised to submit exhibition proposals in the format that best reflects their practise. CVs should be accompanied by a selection of images: slides, CD ROM, transparencies, etc. The gallery does not pay, nor charge an exhibition fee. The gallery manages curation and installation of the exhibition. It provides an opening reception for the exhibiting artist(s), and also is responsible for production of invitation and postage.

Management structure: The gallery is private, managed by Eddie and Joanna O'Kane, both practising artists. The Curator is Marianne O'Kane.

An Gailearaí

Ceardlann na gCroisbhealach
Falcarragh
Co Donegal

Tel/Fax: +353 (0) 74 916 5594
E-mail: ceardlann@eircom.net

Conversion of an existing building

Contact person / Director: Una Campbell

Architects for the conversion: Self-conversion

Ceardlann na gCroisbhealach is situated in a two storey building, on the cross-roads of a village in Donegal, and has been in operation since 1999. A bank occupies the ground floor and the gallery occupies the first floor. The building was originally a family home above a drapery store.

Number of rooms / galleries; area in square metres: The art space is 11 x 5 m. There is also a studio space.

Specifications: White walls and a concrete floor. One wall is concrete, two are plasterboard. Another plywood wall has a window behind it, the plywood can be removed if the light is needed. There is a small light shaft in the middle of the ceiling. There are six fluorescent lights in the gallery space. The space has previously been used for large works on canvas and free-standing sculpture.

Access details: No disabled access.

Exhibitions policy / 'ethos' of gallery: An Gailearaí strives to maintain a policy of professionalism and quality. This informs its dealings with the artist/s, the public, how the work is presented and how the exhibition is planned, managed, publicised and hosted. Reflecting its location and cultural responsibility, all publications, notices and related material are presented in bilingual format. All artists are met, in person, well in advance of their exhibition date to agree content of show and possible requirements. Where applicable, artist/s are required to give talks, slide-shows or workshops on their work and practice.

What should interested artists do? Artists are invited to submit a proposal, 10 slides, photographs or a CD ROM along with a CV. Seven people make up the selection panel. The gallery pays an artist's fee subject to the Arts Council guidelines. The gallery also provides refreshments on the opening night and invitations. The gallery takes 20% commission on all work sold. Sales in the gallery are not high due to the nature of the artwork exhibited but usually one exhibition per year is hosted that sells well.

Management structure: Publicly funded gallery with a Management Committee.

An Grianán Theatre

Port Road
Letterkenny

Tel: +353 (0) 74 91 23288
Fax: +353 (0) 74 91 20665
E-mail: angrianan@eircom.net
www.angrianan.com

Purpose-built multi-use venue

Contact person / Director: Patricia McBride

Architects: Quinlan and Nolan Architects

Opened in 1999, An Grianán is a purpose-built multi-use venue, with the gallery occupying the upper and ground floor foyer areas. While there is an emphasis on the performance element of the venue, the gallery also operates a visual arts programme.

Number of rooms / galleries; area in square metres: Upstairs (foyer): temporary wall surface area: 11.52 square metres; side wall surface: 11.04 square metres; back wall surface: 13.44 square metres; floor area: 25.76 square metres. Downstairs (foyer): side wall surface: 7.68 square metres; back wall surface: 8.8 square metres; floor area: 34.16 square metres. The downstairs surface area is smaller because hanging drop to the radiators is 1.6 m.

Specifications: The walls are smooth and painted. There is a picture rail if need. The space is most suitable for two dimensional work. The areas are high and brightly lit because the building is glass fronted.

Access details: The lower exhibition area is fully wheelchair accessible, as is part of the upper level which can be reached by a lift. The upper foyer is split level and the highest part is not wheelchair accessible. The theatre also has an induction loop system.

Exhibitions policy / 'ethos' of gallery: An Grianán Theatre aims to reflect a diversity of work through a series of approximately eight exhibitions each year. The exhibition space at the theatre is most suitable for two-dimensional art. There is an emphasis on work from locally-based practitioners, but exhibitions are not exclusively so. The space available makes it ideal for one-person shows but this does not exclude the possibility of group shows. All styles of work are considered.

What should interested artists do? Artists interested in exhibiting their work should contact the Director by submitting a personal CV and colour images of their work. All work submitted to An Grianán Theatre is reviewed by a selection panel. The decision of the selection committee is final. A 20% commission is charged on all sales (or in lieu of sales commission, the artist may donate one of their painting to the theatre). The history of sales at the theatre is inconsistent, with some exhibitions achieving high levels of sales while other achieve none. An Grianán Theatre does not charge or pay an exhibition fee. The theatre pays for invitation postage, and covers the costs of an opening night reception. It does not produce dedicated invitations or catalogues. All exhibitions are publicised in the theatre's programme-of-events brochure.

Management structure: An Grianán Theatre is a company limited by guarantee and a registered charity, which is run by a voluntary Board of Directors.

Glebe Gallery

Church Hill
Letterkenny

Tel: +353 (0) 7491 37071
Fax: +353 (0) 7491 37461
E-mail: glebegallery@opw.ie

Conversion of an existing building

Contact person / Director: Adrian Kelly

Original Architect: DeBlacam
Architects for the conversion: OPW

The Glebe Gallery is housed in a renovated outbuilding, with exhibition spaces on two open-plan floors. The building dates from the 1830s but was completely refurbished by the Office of Public Works in the 1980s.

Number of rooms / galleries: Two gallery spaces.

Specifications: The walls are plastered stone, which can be drilled, there are also picture rails on all walls. The ground floor is stone with a wooden floor on the first floor. The entire space can be lit from movable lights on rails. It is difficult to block out light for slide or video installations and the space is not very suitable for large works.

Access details: Disabled access to the ground floor only.

Exhibitions policy / 'ethos' of gallery: The Glebe shows a mixture of contemporary and retrospective art. Exhibitions can either be curated inhouse, be touring shows, solo or group exhibitions. There is also an annual open submission exhibition which takes place each Easter.

What should interested artists do? Artists wishing to be considered for exhibition should send proposals including images and a CV. The Glebe mounts some selling shows, and traditionally sell around one third of the work displayed. Commission is 20%, and this is used to purchase work for the permanent collection. The Gallery does not pay or charge an exhibition fee , and will organise invitations and opening reception.

Management structure: Managed by the Office of Public Works.

Letterkenny Arts Centre

Central Library
Oliver Plunkett Road
Letterkenny

Tel: +353 (0) 74 9129186
E-mail: lkarts@eircom.net
www.donegalculture.com

Purpose-built space within Central Library
New building under construction

Contact person / Director: John Cunningham (Acting Director)

Original Architect: Niland Architects (1996)
Architects for the new building: Magabhann Architects

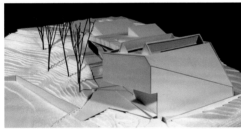

The Letterkenny Arts Centre (LAC) is situated in the basement of the Central Library in Letterkenny. LAC is currently in the final stages of the development of a new Arts Centre due to come on-line in 2006. (Images shown are an installation view at current gallery, and architects' drawing and model for the new centre.)

Number of rooms / galleries; area in square metres: Currently one large gallery space, divided into two rooms; approx 150 square metres in total.

Specifications: As the arts centre is presently situated in the basement of the Central Library, the gallery space has no natural light, though the lighting systems have adjustable levels for lux etc. The gallery is climate controlled and monitored by 24 hour CCTV and is very much a white cube with wooden floors: the walls are 3 m in height and hard-walled: there is an art store, large loading doors and an elevator to the gallery. The gallery is suitable for installations, slide / video / film

projections, performance, large works on canvas, large free-standing sculptures etc.

Access details: Elevator access to galleries.

Exhibitions policy / 'ethos' of gallery: LAC aims to develop contemporary cultural activity in County Donegal, to assist development in the County through the arts and to realise exceptional arts projects. With this is mind, LAC presents a year round programme of exhibitions and visual art events. LAC usually develops in-house productions ranging from large curated exhibitions (eg *Pre-Columbian Textiles* and *Form: 20th Century Sculpture*), to solo exhibitions by local, national and international artists.

What should interested artists do? LAC prefers proposals for specific exhibitions, along with slides / CD ROM, DVD and an up-to-date CV. LAC funds the cost of marketing, logistics, installation, reception, printing and postage. The LAC pays an exhibition fee, and (at this time) does not accept commission on works sold. Work normally sells in this space.

Management structure: Run by Donegal County Council.

Co Down

Ards Arts Centre (p. 204)
Town Hall, Conway Square
Newtownards BT23 4DB
Contact person: Eilís O Baoill
Tel: +44 (0) 28 9181 0803   Fax: +44 (0) 28 9182 3131
E-mail: arts@ards-council.gov.uk
www.ards-council.gov.uk/ardsarts.htm

Ava Gallery
Clandboye Estate BT19 1RN
Contact person: Dickon Hall
Tel: +44 (0) 28 9185 2263
E-mail: info@avagalleryclandeboye.co.uk
www.avagalleryclandeboye.co.uk

Bay Tree Pottery and Gallery
118 High Street
Holywood BT18 9HW
Contact person: Rozzy Allen
Tel: +44 (0) 28 9042 6414
www.baytreeholywood.com

Cleft Gallery
34 New Street
Donaghdee BT21 OAG
Contact person: Bill Morrison
Tel: +44 (0) 28 9188 8502
E-mail: thecleftgallery@whiteimage.com

Davison Gallery
53a High Street
Holywood BT18 9AB
Contact person: Martin Davison
Tel: +44 (0) 28 9754 3266 / +44 (0) 786 018 7530
E-mail: info@davisongallery.com
www.davisongallery.com

Down Arts Centre (p. 205)
2 – 6 Irish Street
Downpatrick BT30 6BN
Contact person: Cathie McKimm Arts Officer
Tel: +44 (0) 28 4461 5283 Fax: +44 (0) 28 4461 6621
E-mail: mail@downartscentre.com
www.downartscentre.com

Gallery 148
148 High St
Holywood BT18 9HS
Contact person: Leo and Hilary Donaghey
Tel: +44 (0) 28 9042 3386
E-mail: mail@gallery148.com   www.gallery148.com

Charles Gilmore Fine Art
31 Church Road
Holywood BT18 9BU
Contact person: Charles Gilmore
Tel: +44 (0) 28 9042 8555
E-mail: charles@charlesgilmore.com
www.charlesgilmore.com

Saint Patrick Centre / The Grove Gallery
53a Lower Market Street
Downpatrick BT30 6LZ
Contact Person: Dr Campbell
Tel: +44 (0) 28 4461 9000
E-mail: director@saintpatrickcentre.com
www.saintpatrickcentre.com

Sean Hollywood Arts Centre (p. 205)
1a Bank Parade
Newry BT35 6HP
Contact person: Mark Hughes
Tel: +44 (0) 28 3031 3180   Fax: +44 (0) 28 3026 6839
E-mail: jacqueline.turley@newryandmourne.gov.uk
www.newryandmourne.gov.uk

Imagos Art Gallery (p. 206)
4 Forthill Rd
Crieve
Newry BT34 2LP
Contact person: Damian Magee
Tel: +44 (0) 28 3083 4927
E-mail: info@imagosart.co.uk   www.imagosart.co.uk

Manor Fine Arts
18 Rathfriland Street BT32 3LA
Tel: +44 (0) 28 4062 3434
Contact person: Elizabeth McCrumlish
E-mail: info@manorfinearts.co.uk
www.manorfinearts.co.uk

Newcastle Art Gallery
1a Savoys Lane
Newcastle BT33 0SJ
Contact person: Dennis Murphy
Tel: +44 (0) 28 4372 3555

White Image
34 Lisburn Street
Hillsborough BT26 6AB
Contact person: Bill Morrison
Tel: +44 (0) 28 9268 9896
E-mail: info@whiteimage.com www.whiteimage.com

Ards Arts Centre

Town Hall, Conway Square
Newtownards BT23 4DB

Tel: +44 (0) 28 9181 0803
Fax: +44 (0) 28 9182 3131
E-mail: arts@ards-council.gov.uk

Conversion of an historic building

Contact person / Director: Eilís O Baoill, Arts Officer

Architects for the conversion: Knox & Markwell

Ards Arts Centre was originally built in 1777 as a market house. The architect was Ferdinando Stratford, based in Bath, and better known as an engineer, particularly of canals. The Georgian building now houses a multi-purpose arts centre, with performance as well as exhibition space. The building was renovated in 1999, although there has been an arts venue in Ards since 1975.

Number of rooms / galleries; area in square metres: Two galleries house the exhibition programme, the downstairs gallery (approximately 8 x 13 m) and the Sunburst gallery (8 x 5 m), each with large windows. The downstairs gallery is suited to large paintings and sculpture / installation; while the Sunburst gallery, with a low ceiling and sea-green walls, is more appropriate for smaller works, and those with light sensitivity.

Specifications: Wooden floors throughout. Dry lined walls present some difficulties in hanging heavy works. Hanging may be by means of brass rods or mirror plates. A limited number of plinths is available. Tall ceilings and doors allow for the installation of most works.

Access details: Two floors are universally accessible by means of a lift. Publicity is available in braille, on request.

Exhibitions policy / 'ethos' of gallery: Contemporary art, including interesting developments in traditional painting, Supportive of artists: agenda to bring art to life in Ards. Ards Arts Centre has shown solo shows of video, installation, performance, sculpture, print, painting, photography, craft, drawing and architecture. Priority is given to Northern Irish artists of importance and local emerging artists, with at least one historical exhibition per year. The centre is also involved in off-site projects such as Ards Art trail, Creative Peninsula project and international links with Sister City in Peoria.

What should interested artists do?
Submissions accepted with CV and images on slides, CD or by e-mail. Original works are not accepted. Submissions must be accompanied by a letter / proposal stating relevance to this building or Ards audience. Programming is at least one year in advance. The gallery takes 10% on works sold, although it is to be noted that buyers are a small proportion of visitors to the gallery. EPR is paid to established artists for solo exhibitions. The artist receives a preview reception (no speeches policy); invitations (500 – with artists given blank invites for personal use); photocopy price list including artist's statement and curator's comments. Artists are responsible for hanging their own work – no installation crew available, no transport provided.

Management structure: Local Government with Advisory Committee.

Down Arts Centre

2 – 6 Irish Street
Downpatrick
County Down BT30 6BN

Tel: +44 (0) 28 4461 5283
Fax: +44 (0) 28 4461 6621
E-mail: mail@downartscentre.com
www.downartscentre.com

In operation for ten years, Down Arts
Centre is in the Town Hall, Downpatrick.

Number of rooms / galleries: Two gallery
spaces: one for emerging artists; plus
main gallery space for touring exhibitions
and main gallery programme.

Specifications: White matt walls with picture rail (limits large scale canvas) dedicated lighting. Main Gallery is incorporated into reception space. Arts Room incorporates performance bar.

Conversion of an historic building

Contact person / Director: Cathie McKimm Arts Officer

Original Architect: DeBlacam
Architects for the conversion: Aonghus McCann

Access details: Access for those with
mobility impairment.

Exhibitions policy / 'ethos' of gallery:
Under review.

What should interested artists do? Send
CV plus slides, CD ROM, e-mail with
images. The gallery neither takes nor
charges a fee. Work sold varies with artist
and time of year, gallery commission is
15% plus 17.5% VAT. Opening reception,
invitations, catalogue provided.

Management structure: Local Authority.

Sean Hollywood Arts Centre

1a Bank Parade
Newry BT35 6HP

Tel: +44 (0) 28 3031 3180
Fax: +44 (0) 28 3026 6839
jacqueline.turley@newryandmourne.gov.uk

Multi-functional building that comprises a
rehearsal space, basement/workshop, two
galleries, café, 140 seater raked auditorium,
meeting rooms, and art and photographic
studios. It was established in 1980.

**Number of rooms / galleries; area in
square metres**: Carroll Gallery: 15.24 x 6.10
metres (93 square metres); Bell Gallery:
15.24 x 6.10 metres (93 square metres);
Studio: 51 square metres.

Specifications: Independent hanging system available. Spot lighting overhead. Bell
Gallery on first floor tiled. No storage facilities available, double door entry to both
galleries. Both galleries are suitable for large
canvas and free standing sculptural exhibitions.

Conversion of an existing building

Contact person / Director: Mark Hughes

Architect: J. L. O'Hagan

Access details: Ramped access, automatic
doors, lift facilities, induction loop at reception and in auditorium, wheelchair lift in
auditorium, Evac chairs, disabled toilets.

Exhibitions policy / 'ethos' of gallery: No
particular policy in place. Mostly traditional
painting.

What should interested artists do? Send
letter of introduction and slide/e-mail of
previous work. Gallery provides invitations
for 40 guests, opening (ie drinks), copy catalogues, invite press, advertise as part of the
Arts Centre's programme of activities. 25%
commission on sales for professional artists,
15% for amateur artists.

Management structure: Local Government.

Imagos Art Gallery

4 Forthill Rd
Crieve
Newry BT34 2LP

Tel: +44 (0) 28 3083 4927
Email: info@imagosart.co.uk

Re-use of an historic building

Contact person / Director: Damian Magee

Architects for the conversion: Self-conversion

The gallery, an old stone building, opened in 2002 and is set amid a farmyard. A former cattle byre and hayloft, it is a rural space in a rural environment.

Number of rooms / galleries; area in square metres: There are two rooms. The main gallery is 24 square metres. The smaller room measuring 8 square metres also doubles as an office space.

Specifications: White cement walls with wooden and carpeted flooring. The space is illuminated by three suspended halogen lights approximately 3 m high. There are two 3.5 m walls the rest are 2.3 m high. The gallery is best suited to house 2D and small 3D work.

Access details: Wheelchair accessible.

Exhibitions policy / 'ethos' of gallery: Traditional forms of painting as well as contemporary work.

What should interested artists do? Artists wishing to exhibit at the gallery should contact by telephone or e-mail. All exhibitions are promoted with a wine reception and PR. There are no fees. Between 30% and 40% commission is taken on all works sold. These are usually traditional landscapes.

Management structure: Private.

Co Dublin

15 Usher's Island Art Gallery:
The James Joyce House of *The Dead*
Usher's Island
Dublin 8
Contact person: Brendan Kilty
Tel: +353 (0) 86 157 9546
E-mail: info@jamesjoycehouse.com
www.jamesjoycehouse.com

Airfield Trust
Upper Kilmacud Road
Dundrum
Dublin 14
Contact person: Sancho Gallilei
Tel: +353 (0) 1 296 7609
E-mail: arts@airfield.ie www.airfield.ie

Alternative Entertainments Gallery Space (p. 211)
The Civic Theatre
Dublin 24
Contact person: Liam Morrissey
Tel: +353 (0) 1 452 0611
E-mail: altents@eircom.net

Axis
Ballymun
Dublin 9
Contact person: Ray Yeates
Tel: +353 (0) 1 883 2100
E-mail: brede.boyne@axis-ballymun.ie
www.axis-ballymun.ie

Bank of Ireland Arts Centre
Foster Place
Dublin 2
Contact person: Barry O'Kelly
Tel: +353 (0) 1 671 2261
E-mail: boi.arts@boimail.com www.boi.ie/artscentre

The Black Church Print Studio
4 Temple Bar
Dublin 2
Contact person: Avril Percival
Tel: +353 (0) 1 677 3629
E-mail: info@print.ie www.print.ie

The Bridge Art Gallery
6 Upper Ormond Quay
Dublin 7
Contact person: Deirdre Carroll
Tel: +353 (0) 1 872 9702
E-mail: mail@thebridgegallery.com
www.thebridgegallery.com

Blue Leaf Gallery
4a Pembroke Street Lower
Dublin 2
Contact person: Ciara Gibbon
Tel: +353 (0) 1 662 3682
E-mail: info@blueleafgallery.com www.blueleafgallery.com

Chester Beatty Library
Dublin Castle
Dublin 2
Contact person: Derval O'Carroll
Tel: +353 (0) 1 407 0750
E-mail: info@cbl.ie www.cbl.ie

Concourse
County Hall
Dún Laoghaire
Contact person: Sarah Searson
Tel: +353 (0) 1 205 4749
E-mail: arts@dlrcoco.ie www.dlrcoco.ie

Cross Gallery (p. 212)
59 Francis Street
Dublin 8
Contact person: Jane Byrne, Nicholas Gore-Grimes
Tel: +353 (0) 1 473 8978 Fax: +353 (0) 1 453 4190
E-mail: info@crossgallery.ie www.crossgallery.ie

Daffodil Gallery
Milverton
Skerries
Co. Dublin
Contact Person: Theresa Price
Tel: +353 (0) 1 849 2142 Fax: +353 (0) 1 849 2535
E-mail: daffodil@iol.ie www.daffodilgallery.com

Dalkey Art Gallery
19 Railway Road
Dalkey
Contact Person: Jennifer Voigt
Tel: +353 (0) 1 284 9663
E-mail: info@dalkeyarts.com www.dalkeyarts.com

Davis Gallery
11 Capel Street
Dublin 1
Contact person: Gerald Davis
Tel: +353 (0) 1 872 6969
E-mail: painter@iol.ie

Digital Hub Warehouse
10 – 13 Thomas Streeet
Dublin 8
Contact person: Elaine Parsons
Tel: +353 (0) 1 480 6200
E-mail: exhibit@thedigitalhub.com
www.thedigitalhub.com

Douglas Hyde Gallery (p. 213)
Trinity College
Dublin 2
Contact person: John Hutchinson
Tel: +353 (0) 1 608 1116 Fax: +353 (0)1 670 8330
E-mail: dhgallery@tcd.ie www.douglashydegallery.com

Draíocht (p. 214)
Blanchardstown
Dublin 15
Contact person: Carissa Farrell
Tel: +353 (0) 1 885 2610 Fax: +353 (0) 1 824 3434
E-mail: carissa@draiocht.ie   www.draiocht.ie

Dublin City Gallery The Hugh Lane (p. 215)
Charlemont House
Parnell Square North
Dublin 1
Contact person: Barbara Dawson, Christina Kennedy
Tel: +353 (0) 1 675 5550 Fax: +353 (0) 872 2182
info.hughlane@dublincity.ie www.hughlane.ie

Fire Station Artists' Studios
9/11 Lower Buckingham Street
Dublin 1
Contact person: Clodagh Kenny
Tel: +353 (0) 1 855 6735
E-mail: clodagh@firestation.ie   www.firestation.ie

William Frank Gallery
91 Monkstown Road
Monkstown Village
Co. Dublin
Contact person: Siobhán Bastable
Tel: +353 (0) 1 214 8547
E-mail: info@williamfrankgallery.com
www.williamfrankgallery.com

Gallery for One
5 Scarlet Row
Temple Bar
Dublin 2
Contact Person: Vaari Claffey
Tel: + 353 (0) 1 672 9534 / +353 (0) 87 641 0484
E-mail: fivescarletrow@language.ie

Gallery of Photography (p. 216)
Meeting House Square
Temple Bar
Dublin 2
Contact Person: Tanya Kiang
Tel: +353 (0) 1 671 4654 Fax: +353 (0) 1 670 9293
E-mail: gallery@irish-photography.com
www.irish-photography.com

Graphic Studio
Through the Arch, Cope Street
Temple Bar
Dublin 2
Contact person: Niamh McGrath
Tel: +353 (0) 1 679 8021 Fax: +353 (0) 1 679 4575
E-mail: gsg@iol.ie www.graphicstudiodublin.com

Green on Red Gallery (p. 217)
26 – 28 Lombard Street East
Dublin 2
Contact person: Jerome O Drisceoil
Tel: +353 (0) 1 671 3414 Fax: +353 (0) 1 672 7117
E-mail: info@greenonredgallery.com
www.greenonredgallery.com

Habitat
St. Stephen's Green
Dublin 2
Contact person: Deirdre Murphy
Tel: +353 (0) 1 677 1433
E-mail: deirdremurphy@habitat.ie

Hallward Gallery (p. 218)
65 Merrion Square
Dublin 2
Contact person: Mary Tuohy, Ruth McHugh
Tel: +353 (0) 1 662 1482 Fax: +353 (0) 1 662 1700
E-mail: hallward@indigo.ie   www.hallwardgallery.com

Helix
Dublin City University
Collins Avenue
Glasnevin
Dublin 9
Contact person: Marie Louise O'Donnell
Tel: +353 (0)1 700 7119
E-mail: info@thehelix.ie www.thehelix.ie

Hillsboro Fine Art (p. 218)
Anne's Lane
Dublin 2
Contact person: John Daly
Tel: +353 (0) 1 677 7905
E-mail: info@hillsborofineart.com
www.hillsborofineart.com

Holiday Inn
99 – 107 Pearse Street
Dublin 2
Contact person: Stephanie Howard
Tel: +353 (0) 1 670 3666
E-mail: info@holidayinndublin.ie
www.holidayinndublincitycentre.ie

Howth Harbour Gallery
6 Abbey Street
Howth
Contact person: Phyllis Grace
Tel: +353 (0) 1 839 3366
E-mail: gjb97@dial.pipex.com

Irish Museum of Modern Art (p. 219)
Royal Hospital
Military Road
Kilmainham
Dublin 8
Contact person: Monica Cullinane, Public Affairs Executive
Tel: +353 (0) 1 612 9900 Fax: +353 (0) 1 612 9999
E-mail: info@modernart.ie   www.modernart.ie

Jorgensen Fine Art
29 Molesworth Street
Dublin 2
Contact Person: Kevin Gaines
Tel: +353 (0)1 661 9758 Fax: +353 (0) 1 661 9760
E-mail: info@jorgensenfineart.com
www.jorgensenfineart.com

Kerlin Gallery (p. 221)
Anne's Lane
South Anne Street
Dublin 2
Contact person: Darragh Hogan, David Fitzgerald,
John Kennedy
Tel: +353 (0) 1 670 9093 Fax: +353 (0) 1 670 9096
E-mail: gallery@kerlin.ie www.kerlin.ie

Kevin Kavanagh Gallery (p. 222)
66 Strand Street Great
Dublin 1
Contact person: Kevin Kavanagh
Tel: +353 (0) 1 874 0064   Fax: +353 (0) 1 874 9486
E-mail: kevinkavanaghgallery@eircom .net
www.kevinkavanaghgallery.ie

Leinster Gallery
27 South Fredrick Street
Dublin 2
Contact person: Loretto Meagher
Tel: +353 (0) 1 679 0834
E-mail: art@leinstergallery.com www.leinstergallery.com

Lemonstreet Gallery
24 – 26 City Quay
Dublin 2
Contact person: Catherine Hall
Tel: +353 (0) 1 671 0244 Fax+ +353 (0) 1 671 0240
E-mail: info@lemonstreet.com www.lemonstreet.com

Molesworth Gallery
16 Molesworth Street
Dublin 2
Contact person: Ronan Lions
Tel: +353 (0) 1 679 1548 Fax: +353 (0) 1 679 6667
E-mail: molegall@indigo.ie www.molesworthgallery.com

National Gallery of Ireland
Merrion Square West
Dublin 2
Contact person: Valerie Keogh, Press and
Communications
Tel: +353 (0) 1 661 5133 Fax: +353 (0) 1 661 5372
E-mail: info@ngi.ie www.nationalgallery.ie

Office of Public Works (p. 223)
51 St. Stephen's Green
Dublin 2
Contact person: Anne O'Shea
Tel: +353 (0) 1 647 6135 Fax: +353 (0) 1 661 9897
E-mail: anne.oshea@opw.ie

Oriel Gallery
17 Clare Street
Dublin 2
Contact person: Mark Nulty
Tel: +353 (0) 1 676 3410
E-mail: oriel@eircom.net www.theoriel.com

Origin Gallery (p. 223)
83 Harcourt Street
Dublin 2
Contact person: Noelle Campbell-Sharp
Tel: +353 (0) 1 478 5159 Fax: +353 (0) 1 478 5826
E-mail: origingallery@eircom.net

Original Print Gallery (p. 224)
4 Temple Bar
Dublin 2
Tel.: +353 (0) 1 677 3657
Contact: Cróna Connolly
E-mail: info@originalprint.ie www.originalprint.ie

Pallas Studios + Pallas Heights (p. 225)
17 Foley Street
Dublin 1
+ Nos 25, 28, 29, 30 Seán Tracey House
Buckingham Street
Dublin 1
Tel: +353 (0) 1 856 1404
Contact person: Mark Cullen, Brian Duggan
E-mail: info@pallasstudios.org www.pallasstudios.org

Project Arts Centre (p. 226)
39 East Essex Street
Temple Bar
Dublin 2
Contact person: Grant Watson
Tel: +353 (0) 1 881 9613/14
E-mail: info@project.ie www.project.ie

The Return: Goethe-Institut (p. 227)
7 Merrion Square
Dublin 2
Contact person: Barbara Ebert
Tel: +353 (0) 1 661 1155 Fax: +353 (0) 1 661 1358
E-mail: goethe@iol.ie www.goethe.de/dublin

**Royal Hibernian Academy Gallagher Gallery
+ Ashford Gallery (p. 228)**
15 Ely Place
Dublin 2
Contact person: RHA: Patrick T. Murphy;
Contact person: Ashford Gallery: Mark St. John Ellis
Tel: +353 (0) 1 661 2558
www.royalhibernianacademy.com

Rubicon Gallery of Contemporary Art (p. 229)
10 Saint Stephens Green
Dublin 2
Contact person: Josephine Kelliher, Cate Kelliher
Tel: +353 (0) 1 6708055
E-mail: www.rubicongallery.ie info@rubicongallery.ie

Solomon Gallery
Powerscourt Townhouse
South William Street
Dublin 2
Contact Person: Suzanne MacDougald
Tel: +353 (0) 1 679 4237 Fax: +353 (0) 1 671 3262
E-mail: info@solomongallery.com
www.solomongallery.com

Stone Art Gallery (p. 230)
70 Pearse Street
Dublin 2
Contact person: Cleo Fagan
Tel.: +353 (0) 1 675 2165 Fax: +353 (0) 1 675 2166
E-mail: cleo@lomancusack.com www.stoneartgallery.com

Taylor Galleries (p. 231)
16 Kildare Street
Dublin 2
Contact person: John Taylor, Patrick Taylor
Tel: +353 (0) 1 676 6055 Fax: +353 (0) 1 676 6642

Temple Bar Gallery and Studios (p. 232)
5 – 9 Temple Bar
Dublin 2
Contact Person: Marian Lovett
Tel: +353 (0) 1 671 0073 Fax: +353 (0) 1 677 7527
E-mail: info@templebargallery.com
www.templebargallery.com

Temple Gallery
56 Temple Road
Blackrock
Contact Person: Thomas Murphy
Tel / Fax: +353 (0) 1 278 1151
E-mail: info@temple-gallery.com
www.temple-gallery.com

Tramyard Gallery
14 Castle Street
Dalkey
Contact person: Clodagh Hannon
Tel: +353 (0) 1 235 1346
E-mail: clodagh2@ireland.com www.tramyardgallery.com

United Arts Club
3 Upper Fitzwilliam Street
Dublin 2
Contact person: Margo Banks
Tel: +353 (0) 1 661 1411
E-mail: office@www.dublinarts.com www.dublinarts.com

The Workroom (p. 233)
36 – 40 Upper Dominick Street
Dublin 7
Contact Person: Alison Pilkington
Tel: +353 (0) 1 830 3211
E-mail: alisonpilkington@eircom.net

Alternative Entertainments Gallery Space

The Civic Theatre
Tallaght
Dublin 24
Tel: +353 (0) 1 4520611

E-mail: altents@eircom.net

Purpose-built multi-use venue

Contact person / Director: Liam Morrissey

Architect: Eddie Conroy

The Alternative Entertainments Gallery space is located on the upper floor walk-through area at the Civic Theatre Tallaght. The Civic Theatre and Gallery were built and opened in 1999.

Number of rooms / galleries: One room.

Specifications: Narrow gallery space that opens into a wider square area. Plain white concrete walls, lift accessible, have had video and CD installations. Room for large work on canvas but very little room for free standing sculpture. Very little storage space.

Access details: Disabled access via lift.

Exhibitions policy / 'ethos' of gallery: Art work of recognised excellence from contemporary, emerging and traditional artists. All work is submitted to the committee and shows are selected by them.

What should interested artists do? Send CV, slides and / or CD images via e-mail or post. Up to eight exhibitions per year. Gallery commission is 30% on work sold, and sales vary. The gallery pays an exhibition fee and artists are provided with an opening reception and invitations.

Management structure: Run by a Board.

Cross Gallery

59 Francis Street,
Dublin 8

Tel: +353 (1) 473 8978
Fax: +353 (1) 453 4190
E-mail: info@crossgallery.ie
www.crossgallery.ie

Conversion of existing building

Contact person / Director: Jane Byrne and Nicholas Gore-Grimes

Architects for the conversion: Self-conversion

Housed in a building dating from approximately 1830, the Cross Gallery was set up in 1999 as a progressive new space to showcase contemporary art by both established and up-and-coming artists. The gallery has been designed to be informal and relaxed for both first-time buyers and collectors. The space has been previously used as a bakery and an antiques arcade. The end room of the gallery was constructed by a previous owner in the 1980s.

Number of rooms / galleries: There are four rooms in the gallery, each leading directly into the next. The basement is under renovation as a further exhibiting space.

Specifications: The walls are solid block in front three rooms, and plaster board in the fourth room. All walls/ceiling and wood work are painted matt white with the exception of the Victorian architrave surround in the front room which is natural wood. The front three rooms have a dado rail, and the front two rooms have a high picture rail. The front two rooms have a floating wood floor with a honey pine finish; the third and fourth rooms have a concrete floor which was painted wine at some point, now wearing to achieve an industrial warehouse look in contrast to the elegance of the front two rooms. The front door is the only loading entrance. Work is hung using nails and screws, sculptural pieces are displayed on plinths

and have in the past been hung from the ceiling and walls. A track and spot light system is currently used in the front three rooms and a floating wire track with spot lights is used in the fourth room. This art space is suitable for slide installations, video installations, large works on canvas, free standing sculpture, wall and ceiling-hanging sculptures etc.

Access details: No disabled access.

Exhibitions policy / 'ethos' of gallery: One exhibition a month with a Summer group show usually in July and a Christmas group show in December. The gallery showcases contemporary art, however during group shows the gallery includes some more classical works by artists such as Polly Lui.

What should interested artists do? Artists interested in exhibiting with the gallery should forward slides / CD and CV together with a stamped self-addressed envelope. E-mails with images and CV attached are accepted, however slides or CDs are preferred. All info will be returned to artist by the gallery. Artists are also welcome to ring or call in to the gallery to ask advice on any of the above. The gallery neither pays nor charges a fee. Services available to artists are as follows: advice about framing and presentation of work, professional hanging and lighting of exhibition, invitations (printed and posted), catalogue, opening reception, press and PR. The gallery takes 45 – 50% on work sold.

Management structure: Private.

The Douglas Hyde Gallery

Trinity College
Dublin 2

Tel: +353 (0) 1 608 1116
Fax: +353 (0)1 670 8330
E-mail: dhgallery@tcd.ie
www.douglashydegallery.com

Built in 1977/8, the Douglas Hyde
Gallery was officially opened in March
1978. The Douglas Hyde is a purpose-
built gallery, and plays a leading role in
the visual arts in Ireland, with major exhibitions by Irish and international artists.
Gallery 2 was built in 2001 (within the
store room of the original gallery building). There is also a bookshop which
stocks all Douglas Hyde Gallery publications as well as art and culture magazines
and periodicals.

**Number of rooms / galleries; area in
square metres**: There are two exhibition
areas within The Douglas Hyde Gallery.
Gallery 1 measures 158.02 square metres,
while Gallery 2 measures 24.12 square
metres. Gallery 1 includes a balcony viewing area as well as exhibition areas off the
main space.

Specifications: Walls: concrete, painted
white. Floor: grey concrete. Hanging: nails
in wall, mirror plates. Light: some natural
(can be blocked out); tungsten, spotlight
rig. Loading doors: 8 x 3 m; close parking
but steep (3 m) flight of steps. The gallery
space is suitable for slide installations /
video installations / large works on canvas
as well as free-standing sculpture.

Access details: There is disabled access to
the gallery via an elevator.

Exhibitions policy / 'ethos' of gallery: The
Douglas Hyde is committed to exploring
cultural issues that are relevant at the
beginning of the 21st century. The gallery
shows most forms of contemporary art,
averaging 6 – 7 exhibitions a year. There is
an active education policy, with lectures,
gallery tours and artists' talks.

Purpose-built space

Contact person / Director: John Hutchinson, Director

Architects: The Gallery was designed by Paul Koralek of Ahrends Burton
and Koralek. McCullough Mulvin Architects designed Gallery 2,
incorporated into the original structure (2001).

What should interested artists do?
Almost all exhibitions are originated by
the Director and artists should not apply
individually. The gallery is non-commercial. A nominal fee is usually paid, but generally fees are paid to artists in the form of
an exhibition catalogue. Every exhibition
has a formal opening reception for which
invitations are posted to a mailing list. A
catalogue generally accompanies each
show in the main gallery space.

Management structure: The Douglas
Hyde Gallery is jointly funded by the Arts
Council and Trinity College Dublin. The
Gallery is run by a Board of Directors.

Draíocht

Blanchardstown
Dublin 15

Tel Box Office: +353 (0) 1 885 2622
Admin: +353 (0) 1 885 2610
Fax: +353 (0) 1 824 3434
E-mail: carissa@draiocht.ie
www.draiocht.ie

Purpose-built venue

Contact person / Director: Carissa Farrell, Visual Arts Officer

Architect: David O'Connor, with Fingal County Council

Built during 2000 and opened to the public in January 2001, Draíocht is housed in one half of a new complex of civic buildings. These include a new library and local authority offices, the two halves (arts venue and offices) are joined by a first floor corridor. Draíocht comprises two gallery spaces on the ground and first floors, a 280 seater theatre plus a 100 seater theatre which can be divided into two smaller spaces, a large workshop space, a bar with a kitchen backing on to it, dressing rooms etc.

Number of rooms / galleries; area in square metres: The ground floor gallery has 30 metres of hanging space, approximately 140 square metres, and is a dedicated visual arts space, with floor-to-ceiling glass covering one whole wall of the gallery facing on to the street (triple height); half the gallery is covered by a mezzanine. The first floor gallery exists as part of a throughway to the first floor of the building, although 90% of the space is unused and therefore dedicated to visual arts most of the time.

Specifications: Walls: matt white, mostly masonary, with a few small patches of stud wall and a small skirting between wall and floor. Hanging is to the walls, drilled with plates, d-rings, screws. Floor: laid with large ceramic tiles, light beige, 70 x 70 cm. Half the gallery is covered by a mezzanine, ceiling height of 2.7 m, the other half the ceiling height is three floors above. Under the mezzanine there are two long runs of clean wall space, one 9 m, the other 5 m, as well as two shorter runs of 3 m and 2 m.

There is one long space with triple height, 6 m which suits large canvases. Draíocht has its own supply of plinths (approximately 25) in three sizes. The glass wall makes video installation difficult, however the gallery has been blacked out with some success, and smaller rooms can be constructed under the mezzanine. There is a very open policy of adapting the gallery.

Access details: The building is fully accessible. The theatre has Induction Loop.

Exhibitions policy / 'ethos' of gallery: To support artists and innovation and present a broad range of contemporary and modern art practice which includes both the traditional fine arts of painting and sculpture in addition to new media such as multi-media art, video and photography. Draíocht presents the work of young emerging artists as well as established artists and seeks to include both local, national and international artists and audiences.

What should interested artists do? Artists are requested to forward a letter, CV, colour slides or photographs and a description of their proposed show. CD ROMs are discouraged. There is no exhibition fee for artists. The gallery pays for and organises transport of artworks, professional installation, a preview card, reception, expenses for artists travelling from abroad or outside Dublin and a PR service. The gallery charges a 30% commission on sales of works.

Management structure: Draíocht is currently governed by a Board of Directors and is a company limited by guarantee, however this is due to change shortly to being a municipal facility supported by Fingal County Council.

Dublin City Gallery The Hugh Lane

Charlemont House
Parnell Square North
Dublin 1

Tel: +353 (0) 1 675 5550
Fax: +353 (0) 872 2182
E-mail: info.hughlane@dublincity.ie
www.hughlane.ie

The Municipal Gallery of Modern Art first opened to the public in Harcourt Street in 1908. The Gallery has been located in Charlemont House since 1933. Charlemont House, which houses the Hugh Lane collection was commissioned by James Caulfeild (1728 – 1799), 4th Viscount Charlemont and later 1st Earl of Charlemont. In 1746, aged 18, Charlemont went on the grand tour which was favoured by the aristocracy in the eighteenth century, thus developing his lifelong interest in the Classical arts. In 1763 Charlemont commissioned the young Scottish born architect William Chambers (1723 – 96), whom he had met in Rome, to design his new town house at the top of Parnell Square, formerly Rutland Square. Because of the smaller scale of investment in Dublin, the squares and streets lacked the uniformity of design found in the grand squares in English cities. However, the design for Charlemont House was unique in that it provided a majestic centrepiece for the streetscape and was unrivalled in Irish Georgian squares. Charlemont House is stone-clad and set back from the street, framed by curved walls with rustic details. The house and its interior are designed on strict Classical lines. In 1929 the gardens of the house were built upon to accommodate the Gallery. In 1933 Charlemont House opened as the permanent location of the Hugh Lane Municipal Gallery of Modern Art with purpose-built galleries. In May 2001 the reconstructed studio of Francis Bacon housed in the Francis Bacon studio complex opened to the public. Dublin City Gallery The Hugh Lane is now undertaking a major extension on the site of the former National Ballroom, designed by architects Gilroy McMahon and due for completion in late 2005.

Conversion of an historic building

Contact person / Director: Barbara Dawson

Original Architect: William Chambers (1765)
Architects for the Francis Bacon Studio complex: David Chipperfield with Mitchell and Associates (2001)
Architects for the extension: Gilroy McMahon (2004/05)

Number of rooms / galleries:
15 gallery spaces including entrance hall and sculpture hall.

Specifications: Suitable for paintings, sculpture, slide installations, video installations.

Access details: Lift access to the upper first floor galleries as well as in the Bacon studio complex. Wheelchair ramp to entrance and in the Bacon studio complex. All wall labels and painting guides written in large font.

Exhibitions policy / 'ethos' of gallery: Dublin City Gallery The Hugh Lane is a municipal gallery of modern and contemporary art. The Gallery has a dynamic temporary exhibitions programme which encourages contemporary dialogue, often encompassing the permanent collection, as well as exploring new expression in multimedia. The Gallery also stages historical and retrospective exhibitions, particularly of Irish art.

What should interested artists do? Slides and CVs may be sent to Barbara Dawson, Director or Christina Kennedy, Head of Exhibitions. As Dublin City Gallery The Hugh Lane is a public art gallery work is not for sale. Exhibitions are usually accompanied by an opening reception, invitations and catalogue as well as a programme of education related events.

Management structure: Municipal gallery funded by Dublin City Council.

Gallery of Photography

Meeting House Square
Temple Bar
Dublin 2

Tel: +353 (0) 1 671 4654
Fax: +353 (0) 1 670 9293
E-mail: gallery@irish-photography.com
www.irish-photography.com

Purpose Built Space

Contact person / Director: Tanya Kiang, Director

Architect: John Tuomey (O'Donnell Tuomey + Group 91)

In operation since 1978, the Gallery of Photography has occupied its current purpose-built space since 1996. The gallery is Ireland's leading centre for contemporary photography, with exhibitions, darkroom facilities (traditional and digital), on- and off-site workshops and a bookshop. The gallery is also available for hire to organisations.

Number of rooms / galleries; area in square metres: Six exhibition spaces (some very small); on two levels, total 62 square metres.

Specifications: Walls: MDF with scrim. Some walls concrete with scrim. Painted white throughout. Flooring: mainly light maple boards. Some lino carried through from stairwells. Lighting: basic, consists of 'wall washer' spots with limited directionality; some fluorescents. Storage: none, even for crates. Heights: varies from double-height atrium main space, to lowest ceiling height of 2.13 m. Loading: lift doors are 2.4 x.8 m. Some spaces relatively easy to black out for video and other installations.

Access details: Disabled access (also for darkrooms).

Exhibitions policy / 'ethos' of gallery: Policy is to exhibit the best of critical fine art practice in lens-based media. Ethos: 'contemporary photography', though the gallery also shows video work.

What should interested artists do? Send CD by post after making initial contact by email to check relevance of proposed work. Gallery pays EPR. Can also offer budgets (of about €3,000) towards artists' production costs, depending on the circumstances. Gallery pays for invitations, mailout, reception. Catalogues made where funding is available. Gallery takes 20% commission on sales. VAT is charged at 21% on the commission element. The Gallery is not known as a commercial gallery, though particular exhibitions can be good sellers.

Management structure: Private limited company. Run by a non-executive Board of Directors.

Green On Red Gallery

26 – 28 Lombard Street East
Dublin 2

Tel: +353 (0) 1 671 3414
Fax: +353 (0) 1 672 7117
E-mail: info@greenonredgallery.com
www.greenonredgallery.com

In operation for twelve years, the Green On Red Gallery is now located in a refurbished, early 19th century hayloft in city centre, Dublin (original building 1814, conversion to gallery 1997). The main galleries are situated in a double-height room at first floor level of the two storey building. Daylight fills the main gallery space from the glazed Lombard Street East façade.

Number of rooms / galleries; area in square metres: The main gallery occupies the large first floor loft (13 x 10 x 4 m). Exposed original oak beams support a 4 m high pitched roof. Ancillary spaces include street level glazed lobby and a first floor reception hall (10 x 2.2 x 2.6 m).

Specifications: Main gallery space consists of three walls measuring 9 x 0.2 x 4 m, 11 x 0.2 x 4 m and 12 x 0.2 x 4 m respectively. All walls of timber, plywood and plasterboard construction ideal for hanging large and small canvases and as a backdrop for large free-standing sculptural or installation work. Slide, video and film installations are a regular feature of the gallery's programme. The floor is of soft-wood board construction. Lighting is provided by a combination of natural light and low voltage spot lighting held on tracks running the length of the three aforementioned walls. The fourth, east-facing wall is the concrete block façade with nine, 6 m wide x 3 m high windows. Storage is housed in two first floor rooms fitted with painting racks and two open plan mezzanine rooms. The gallery office is situated in the third mezzanine. Access is through a ground floor square arch 0.95 wide x 2.26 high x 0.5 m deep.

Access details: No disabled access.

Conversion of an industrial building

Contact person / Director: Jerome O Drisceoil (Proprietor)

Architects for the conversion: Micheál O Drisceoil and Simon O Drisceoil

Exhibitions policy / 'ethos' of gallery: The gallery exhibits exclusively contemporary art from Ireland and abroad. All media are shown including painting, sculpture, photography, film, multi-media and installation work.

What should interested artists do? The gallery will look at submissions in January of each year on CD and / or CD ROM or slides. Gallery covers all exhibition and installation expenses.

Management structure: Private.

Hallward Gallery

65 Merrion Square
Dublin 2

Tel: +353 (0) 1 662 1482 / 3
E-mail: hallward@indigo.ie
www.hallwardgallery.com

Conversion of Georgian building

Contact person / Director: Mary Tuohy / Ruth McHugh

Architects for the conversion: Self-conversion

Hallward is a basement gallery in a fine Georgian house showing contemporary Irish art. The house was renovated in 1972, and first used as a gallery in 1991.

Number of rooms / galleries; area in square metres: Three spaces. One: 5.3 x 7.2 m; Two: 4.25 x 8.4 m; Three: 2.25 x 7.3 m.

Specifications: Plaster walls painted white. Grey painted floor. Spotlights and strip fluorescent lighting as well as natural daylight. The main space has two large clear walls and is divided from the two ancillary spaces by three arches. The second space can also hold large works and features a curved wall with two windows at the end. The third space is a narrow vault, which works well for smaller works and studies.

Access details: No disabled access.

Exhibitions policy / 'ethos' of gallery: Contemporary art.

What should interested artists do? Send slides and CV. The gallery provides exhibiting artists with an opening reception and invitations.

Management structure: Private.

Hillsboro Fine Art

3 Anne's Lane, South Anne Street
Dublin 2

Tel: +353 (0) 1 677 7905
E-mail: info@hillsborofineart.com
www.hillsborofineart.com

Use of a Contemporary Building

Contact person / Director: John Daly

Architects for the conversion: Self-conversion

Hillsboro Fine Art has been in operation since 1995, and moved to its present space in 2003. The gallery, which shows and sells the work of Irish and international contemporary artists is located in a two-storey contemporary building dating from the 1970s.

Number of rooms / galleries; area in square metres: 93 square metres.

Specifications: White rendered walls, wooden flooring, not suitable for very large wall-mounted work.

Access details: No disabled access.

Exhibitions policy / 'ethos' of gallery: The gallery exhibits 20th century and contemporary painting, drawing, sculpture and graphics, with a special interest in St Ives 'middle generation' artists. One-person exhibitions by contemporary Irish, European and US artists are at the core of the exhibition schedule, and special exhibitions are programmed to coincide with museum exhibitions, retrospectives, etc.

What should interested artists do? Interested artists should contact the gallery by email. Gallery commission is by arrangement. No fees are paid or charged to artists; opening reception, invitations, catalogues are provided.

Management structure: Private.

Irish Museum of Modern Art

Royal Hospital
Military Road
Kilmainham
Dublin 8

Tel: +353 (0) 1 612 9900
Fax: +353 (0) 1 612 9999
E-mail: info@modernart.ie
www.modernart.ie

Conversion of an historic building

Contact person / Director: Enrique Juncosa, Director,
Monica Cullinane, Public Affairs Executive (contact person)

Original Architects: Royal Hospital Kilmainham (1680/84): William
Robinson, Official State Surveyor General.
Restoration Architects: John Costello & Associates, under the supervision
of the Office of Public Works (1980/85).
Conversion Architects: Shay Cleary Architects, under the supervision of
the OPW (1990/91). Restoration and conversion of Deputy Master's
House (New Galleries) (1996/2000) OPW, consultant architects, Shay
Cleary Architects.

The Irish Museum of Modern Art is
Ireland's leading national institution for
the collection and presentation of modern
and contemporary art. The Museum's mission is to foster within society an awareness, understanding and involvement in
the visual arts, through policies and programmes which are excellent, innovative
and inclusive. The Museum presents a
wide variety of art in a dynamic programme of exhibitions, which regularly
includes bodies of work from its own collection and its award-winning Education
and Community Department. It also creates more widespread access to art and
artists through its Studio and National
programmes.

The building: The Museum is housed in
the Royal Hospital Kilmainham, the finest
17th-century building in Ireland. The
founder of the Royal Hospital was James
Butler of Kilkenny Castle who was Duke of
Ormonde, and Viceroy to King Charles ll.
Inspired by Les Invalides, then rececntly
opened as Louis XIV's home for his army
pensioners in Paris, Ormonde obtained a
charter from King Charles to create a similar type building in Kilmainham. He laid
the foundation stone in 1680 and presided
over its completion four years later. The
Royal Hospital continued in that use for
almost 250 years. The RHK was formally
handed over to the Irish Free State Army
in 1922 when most of its existing pensioners and the contents of the building were
removed to the Royal Hospital in Chelsea.
From 1931 to 1950 the RHK became the
headquaters of the Garda Síochana.
Restoration work on the building began in

1980 and it opened as the National Centre
for Culture and the Arts in 1985. In 1989
the decision was taken to establish the new
Irish Museum of Modern Art at the Royal
Hospital. The Museum officially opened in
May 1991.

**Number of rooms / galleries; area in
square metres**:
First Floor Galleries: East Wing – Long
Galleries: 68 x 4 m – 272 square metres; 23
x 4 m – 92 square metres; 12 rooms each:
5.7 x 5.2 m – 356 square metres; Annex:
6.7 x 2.5 m – 17 square metres. West Wing:
Long Galleries: 50 x 4 m – 200 square
metres; 23 x 4 m – 92 square metres; 7
rooms each: 5.7 x 2.9 m – 215 square
metres; 1 Annex: 5.7 x 2.9 m – 17 square
metres; 1 Long room: 5.7 x 12.5 m – 71
square metres; Landing area: 19.5 x 10 m –
195 square metres. Ground Floor Galleries:

East Wing: 127 square metres; West Wing: square metres; New Galleries: 320 square metres. Total Main Building Gallery space = 1,824 square meters.

Specifications: Spaces are suitable for all media.

Access details: With the exception of the Ground Floor East Wing Gallery, where access is limited, the Museum is wheelchair accessible. There is a wheelchair available on request.

Exhibitions policy / 'ethos' of gallery: Exhibitions: The Museum's temporary exhibition programme regularly juxtaposes the work of leading, well-established figures with that of younger-generation artists, to create a debate about the nature and function of art and its connection with the public. IMMA originates many of its exhibitions but also works closely with a network of international galleries and museums. The Collection: The Collection of the Irish Museum of Modern Art, which comprises some 4,500 works, has been developed since 1990 through purchase, donations and long-term loans, as well as by the commissioning of new works. The Museum purchases contemporary art but accepts donations and loans of more historical art objects with a particular emphasis on work from the 1940s onwards. Loans to the Collection include an important body of work by Outsider, or self-

taught, artists in the Musgrave Kinley Outsider Collection.

What should interested artists do? Artists should send in a short CV with an example of three slides of their work. The fee is negotiated for every exhibition, as each artist or group show exhibition is treated on an individual basis. The Museum supplies the opening reception, invitation and catalogue, and organises talks and lectures around the exhibition through the education department. IMMA does not sell work.

Management structure: IMMA is a national cultural institution, funded by the State through the Department of Arts, Sport and Tourism. The Minister for Arts, Sport and Tourism appoints the Chairperson and the 14 other Board members who in turn are responsible for the appointment of the Director.

Kerlin Gallery

Anne's Lane
South Anne Street
Dublin 2

Tel: +353 (0) 1 670 9093
Fax: +353 (0) 1 670 9096
E-mail: gallery@kerlin.ie
www.kerlin.ie

Purpose-built space

Contact person / Director: Darragh Hogan, David Fitzgerald and John Kennedy

Architect: John Pawson

Kerlin Gallery is a contemporary arts space. In operation for seventeen years, Kerlin moved into its current space in 1994.

Number of rooms / galleries; area in square metres: One main gallery, approximately 138 square metres.

Specifications: The space is suitable for slide installations / video installations / large works on canvas, free-standing works. Walls: 4.1 m high, white painted plaster board. Lighting: diffused daylight, electric wall washers and neon srips behind wall washers (spotlights also available). Floor: concrete.

Access details: No disabled access.

Exhibitions policy / 'ethos' of gallery: To exhibit Irish and international contemporary art.

What should interested artists do? Send slides plus CV plus return paid postage. The gallery neither pays nor charges a fee. Opening reception and invitations are provided.

Management structure: Private.

Kevin Kavanagh Gallery

66 Strand Street Great
Dublin 1

Tel: +353 (0) 1 8740064
Fax: +353 (0) 1 8749486
kevinkavanaghgallery@eircom .net
www.kevinkavanaghgallery.ie

Conversion of an industrial building

Contact person / Director: Kevin Kavanagh

Architects for the conversion: Self-conversion

Previously the Jo Rain Gallery (February 1994 to December 1998) in Temple Bar, (Kevin Kavanagh Gallery is on the ground floor of an industrial space which was converted to use as a gallery in 1998.

Number of rooms / galleries; area in square metres: One exhibition area, three walls, concrete floor, door and large window at front. Small office/store at back. Approximately 60 square metres in total.

Specifications: Mainly concrete walls and floor, fixed low voltage lighting.

Access details: Ground floor gallery, shallow step.

Exhibitions policy / 'ethos' of gallery: Don't have one.

What should interested artists do? Don't send anything. Generally it's a waste of time. Fees neither paid or charged.

Reception, invites provided. Work sells in the space and commission is 40/45%.

Management structure: Private.

Office of Public Works

51 St. Stephen's Green
Dublin 2

Tel: +353 (0) 1 647 6135
Fax: +353 (0) 1 661 9897
E-mail: anne.oshea@opw.ie

Conversion of a Georgian space

Contact person / Director: Anne O'Shea

Architects for the conversion: OPW

The Office of Public Works' exhibition area is in a converted atrium space. The space, in the former courtyard in a Georgian building, is available for hire.

Number of rooms / galleries; area in square metres: Main space: 16 x 15 m, 3 m at the surrounding walls and 7.4 m in the central area (3.7 x 8 m). Lowest obstructionn: 2.7 m. Surrounding walls have windows. Adjoining corridor (20 m) provides additional space for exhibits.

Specifications: Walls on three sides: original masonry walls with windows. Roof: fully glazed with green Sun-guard solar control double-glazing. Floor: off-white lino-finished raised timber floor.

Access details: Access for wheelchair users.

Exhibitions policy / 'ethos' of gallery: The space is available for hire, but no commercial exhibitions are accepted.

What should interested artists do?
E-mail information about exhibition and requirements. Hire fee €1,200. Exhibition duration 2 / 3 weeks, including setting up and dismantling. Hirer responsible for arranging opening reception, invitations, catalogue etc. Services available: advance set up of screens; extra lighting; sculpture stands; PA system; plasma screen.

Origin Gallery

83 Harcourt Street
Dublin 2

Tel: +353 (0) 1 478 5159
Fax: +353 (0) 1 478 5826
E-mail: origingallery@eircom.net

Re-use of historic space

Contact person / Director: Noelle Campbell-Sharp

Architects for the conversion: Self-conversion

The Origin Gallery is located in bright double rooms in a Georgian building in central Dublin. There is also a Private Member's Arts Club (open to non-members after openings). The space is related to the Cill Rialaig Retreat in South West Kerry which was founded by gallery owner Noelle Campbell-Sharp (*see p. 240*).

Number of rooms / galleries; area in square metres: Two rooms: approximately 178 square metres.

Specifications: The gallery is suitable for all forms of art, although floors are not equiped for very heavy sculpture.

Access details: No disabled access.

Exhibitions policy / 'ethos' of gallery: Irish and international contemporary art.

What should interested artists do? Artists should send slides and CV. The gallery provides an opening reception and 50% towards invitations and catalogue. Work sells in the space, and the gallery commission is 50%.

Management structure: Private.

Original Print Gallery

4 Temple Bar
Dublin 2

Tel: +353 (0) 1 677 3657
E-mail: info@originalprint.ie
www.originalprint.ie

Purpose-built space

Contact person / Director: Cróna Connolly

Architects: McCullough Mulvin

In the Temple Bar area of Dublin, the Original Print Gallery is a contemporary, custom-built space, exhibiting framed and unframed original prints. The gallery has been in operation for ten years. The building houses both the Original Print Gallery and the Black Church Print Studio.

Number of rooms / galleries; area in square metres: One large room and mezzanine. 700 square metres.

Specifications: Concrete ceilings and floor, white walls, steel stair-case and large window onto street level.

Access Details: Complies with specifications for disabled access.

Exhibitions policy / 'ethos' of gallery: The gallery specialises in contemporary Irish printmakers' work. There are 6 – 8 designated exhibitions a year, as well as shows of artists' work from gallery portfolios. More than 150 artists currently have work in the portfolios.

What should interested artists do? Send CV plus slides, CD ROM or e-mail with images attached. Preference is given to artists who have built a relationship with the gallery. There are no fees. Gallery provides reception, invitations, postage and promotion. Work sells in the space and gallery commission is 45%.

Management structure: Private.

Pallas Studios + Pallas Heights

17 Foley Street, Dublin 1
+ Nos 25, 28, 29, 30 Sean
Tracey House, Buckingham St.
Dublin 1

Tel: +353 (0) 1 856 1404
+353 (0) 87 957 2232
+353 (0) 87 967 7394
E-mail: info@pallasstudios.org
www.pallasstudios.org

Re-use of existing space

Contact person: Mark Cullen, Brian Duggan

Architects for the conversion: Self-conversion

Pallas Studios' core business is the provision of studio space to contemporary artists in Dublin's inner city. Pallas currently runs three art studios. Now in its seventh year of operations, over one hundred artists have had studios with Pallas Studios Ltd. Pallas Studios also facilitates and organises exhibitions, enabling the production and fermentation of experimental artwork unrestricted by the conventions of commercial and established spaces. Over one hundred and twenty contemporary artists have exhibited with Pallas Studios Ltd. Pallas Studios have set up a new space, and a new studio on Buckingham St, in a block of semi-derelict apartments awaiting demolition. This innovative new space, which is housed amongst local residents on the top level, is Pallas Heights. Sean Tracey House, a municipal housing block overlooking Dublin, provides an excellent context for keeping art on the agenda within the living quarters of the inner city. Pallas Heights links the past histories of Dublin 1 with its future aspirations. Pallas Heights is being developed in partnership with Dublin City Council. The exhibition space is run independent of the studio program. Pallas Studios is housed in a 1940s knitware factory, while Pallas Heights is in 1950-60s social housing block of flats.

Number of rooms / galleries; area in square metres: Studios: 30 rooms 600 square metres; gallery: 48 square metres

Specifications: The walls are plaster finished, there are no loading doors. The Heights are accessed via a public stairwell which can accommodate large 2-D work but would pose problems for large sculpture. There are black out rooms available for light-based work video or slide. Storage is available.

Access Details: No disabled access.

Exhibitions policy / 'ethos' of gallery: To show the best of contemporary art in a unique and challenging context.

What should interested artists do?
Preferably, artists should send e-mail with images, CV and artist's statement /proposal, although slides / CD-ROM are also acceptable. All services are negotiable depending on the show and funding available. All Pallas activities are well documented on the website. Commission is 30 – 40% negotiable.

Management structure: Private.

Project Arts Centre

39 East Essex Street
Temple Bar
Dublin 2

Tel: +353 (0) 1 881 9613/14
E-mail: info@project.ie
www.project.ie

Purpose-built venue

Contact person / Director: Grant Watson, Visual Arts Curator

Architects: Shay Cleary Architects

In operation in various venues since 1966, Project settled in the former Dollard Printing Works at East Essex Street in 1974. The building was later demolished (1998) and rebuilt in 2000.

Number of rooms / galleries; area in square metres: One permanent visual art gallery (total floor area: 12.94 x 8.42 x 45 m). On occasion the Cube space is used to host exhibitions, dimensions for total floor area and auditorium: 11.8 m x 8.8 x 4.5 m.

Specifications: Suitable for all types of work.

Access Details: Project is completely accessible for wheelchair users. Wheelchair patrons should inform Project staff of their needs when booking. Performance spaces are also fitted with the Loop system to assist those with hearing impairment.

Exhibitions policy / 'ethos' of gallery: Project exists in order to encourage and support emerging and established artists in creating innovative work, and to engage the public in a dynamic encounter with that work. Programming includes all contemporary art forms by Irish and interna-

tional artists; encouraging and facilitating new audiences to engage with the work; commissioning new work; generating informed and critical debate about the work of artists in contemporary society; evaluating the relationship between the public and the artwork presented in the context of Project.

What should interested artists do?
Project welcomes proposals and information on artists and their work. Send a letter of introduction to the curator of visual arts. A short written statement outlining: a) the ideas, sources and themes behind your work b) your working methods and medium c) reasons for wanting to show at Project. Do not send visual material eg. slides. Project pays a production fee. Provided are: technical assistance, administrative, marketing and publicity services including opening reception, invitations, newspaper listings, inclusion in the season brochure and on the website, display poster at front of building and catalogue where possible. Works are generally not made available for sale in Project.

Management structure: Run by a Board.

The Return: Goethe-Institut

7 Merrion Square
Dublin 2

Tel: +353 (0) 1 661 1155
Fax: +353 (0) 1 661 1358
E-mail: goethe@iol.ie
www.goethe.de/dublin

Use of space within Georgian building

Contact person / Director: Barbara Ebert / Dr. Matthias Müller-Wieferig

Original Architect: DeBlacam
Architects for the conversion: Aonghus McCann

Located on the first floor return of a Georgian building. The house was built around 1750, with various renovations over the centuries. The gallery space, formerly used as the reception, was turned into a gallery in 2002.

Number of rooms / galleries; area in square metres: One room, approx 14 square metres.

Specifications: Walls painted white, but can be painted any colour; floor painted charcoal; no hanging facilities; spotlights; storage in Goethe-Instituts storerooms; height c. 3.50 m, wide glass door.

Access Details: No disabled access.

Exhibitions policy / 'ethos' of gallery: Specialising in contemporary artists, mainly site specific work, often with a German connection.

What should interested artists do? Send CV plus slides, CD ROM or e-mail with images attached. Interested artists should view the space before making an application. The gallery is non-commercial. Usually invitation cards and opening reception are provided, also subsidy towards artist's expenses.

Management structure: run by the Goethe-Institut Dublin with an advisory board of three curators.

RHA Gallagher Gallery & Ashford Gallery

15 Ely Place
Dublin 2

Tel: +353 (0) 1 661 2558
E-mail: rhagallery@eircom.net
www.royalhibernianacademy.com

Purpose-built gallery

Contact person / Director: RHA: Patrick T. Murphy; Ruth Carroll, Curator Ashford Gallery: Mark St. John Ellis

Architects: Original Architect: Raymond McGrath, completed by Arthur Gibney

The Royal Hibernian Academy was established in 1823. Building work commenced on the RHA Gallagher Gallery in the 1970s and was finished in 1989. The gallery shows contemporary individual and group exhibitions, and is dedicated to serving artists in Ireland at all stages of their career, and to contextualizing this with international programming.

Number of rooms / galleries; area in square metres: Main Gallery 600 square metres; two additional galleries each 150 square metres; Ashford Gallery 100 sqaure metres

Specifications: Main Gallery: 96.3 m running wall, 5.3 m high, wooden floors, daylight, fluorescent wash and incandescent spots; Gallery 2: 50 m running wall, 4.1 m high; wooden floors, fluorescent wash and incandescent spots wooden floors; Gallery 3: 44.2 m running wall, 3.8 high; fluorescent wash incandescent spots, wooden floors. All spaces are adaptable for any style of presentation.

Access details: Disabled access is available, though building needs modification to make access easier.

Exhibitions policy / 'ethos' of gallery: Contemporary art recognizing traditional and innovative methods of practice. The gallery is interested in work that values method of production as much as content.

Content ambitious (non ironic).

What should interested artists do? Studio visits are encouraged as part of the curatorial ethos at the Academy. Exhibitions are by invitation only. Open access for Annual exhibition, adjudicated by Academy members. Academy offers an exhibition fee and provides full professional service for all exhibitions. Selling opportunities are confined to the Annual Exhibition (25% commission) and to the Ashford Gallery Programme (40% commission).

Management structure: Governed by members of the Academy in association with Programme Board that is jointly appointed with the Arts Council.

Rubicon Gallery of Contemporary Art

10 Saint Stephens Green
Dublin 2

Tel: +353 (0) 1 670 8055
E-mail: info@rubicongallery.ie
www.rubicongallery.ie

Conversion of space in a Georgian building

Contact person / Director: Josephine Kelliher / Cate Kelliher

Architects for the conversion: O'Carroll / O'Riordan & Suzanne Freeney architects

Established in 1990 on Upper Mount Street, Rubicon has been located in its current space, in a Georgian building adjacent to Grafton Street, since 1995. The first floor provides views of Saint Stephens Green. It is a bright, modern, minimal exhibition space with a well-regarded contemporary programme.

Number of rooms / galleries; area in square metres: One room approx 75 square metres.

Specifications: Modern, minimal, interior. White walls, erco light-fittings, beech veneer floor, tall and wide oak doors. Gallery space adapts well to various art-forms.

Access Details: No disabled access.

Exhibitions policy / 'ethos' of gallery: Irish and International contemporary artists, all media.

What should interested artists do? Consult web site for current procedures.

Rubicon Gallery provides full exhibition support and services for scheduled artists. It is a commercial gallery and activities are funded through sales.

Management structure: Private.

Stone Gallery

70 Pearse Street
Dublin 2

Tel: +353 (0) 1 671 1020
Fax: +353 (0) 1 675 2166
E-mail: art@stonegallery.ie
www.stonegallery.ie

Conversion of a commercial premises

Contact person / Director: Cleo Fagan, Andrew McQuillan

Architects for the conversion: Chris Ryan Architects

Opened in 2005, the Stone Gallery is a contemporary commercial gallery designed to showcase by Irish and international artists in an intelligently-designed sympathetic space.

Number of rooms / galleries; area in square metres: Single ground floor space with approximately 35 square metres of gallery space. There is an ancillary storage area in the basement which is accessed via a floor hatch from the gallery above.

Specifications: Walls: mixture of rough 'sacked' brickwork and smooth plaster panels.Lighting: low voltage directional lights on adjustable tracks from ERCO. Flooring: white vinyl flooring with banked skirting. Floor-to-ceiling height: 2.6 m. Works access: via the front door of the gallery. Sculpture: small plinths available for smaller pieces. Mac available for interactive installations.

Access details: No disabled access.

Exhibitions policy / 'ethos' of gallery: A new space for contemporary art, exhibiting a cross-selection of contemporary painting, prints and sculpture by established and emerging artists. The aim is to produce an exhibition programme which is stimulating, exciting, engaging and accessible.

What should interested artists do?
Prospective exhibitors should contact Cleo Fagan with slides/CD/email and CV to arrange a portfolio viewing. Stone is a commerical gallery, so work does sell. No fees are paid to artists, and opening reception and invitations are provided. Catalogues are by arrangement. Gallery commission is 40%.

Management structure: Privately run with a Board of Directors.

Taylor Galleries

16 Kildare Street
Dublin 2

Tel: +353 (0) 1 676 6055
Fax: +353 (0) 1 676 6642

Conversion of a Georgian building

Contact person / Director: John and Patrick Taylor

Architects for the conversion: Ross Cahill O'Brien

The Taylor Galleries are located in a Georgian building, with exhibition space over two floors. The Taylor Galleries are a commercial gallery with an established reputation. The Galleries have been in operation since 1978, and in this location since 1996. The space was formerly an antique showroom.

Number of rooms / galleries; area in square metres: Four rooms, encompassing 154 square metres.

Specifications: Wooden floors, off-white walls. Battery of light bulbs in centre ceilings. Height: 3.75 m; door: 2.14 x 1 m.

Access details: Access to the ground floor only.

Exhibitions policy / 'ethos' of gallery: The Taylor Galleries' policy is to exhibit the best available art, contemporary and modern, to as wide an audience as possible in an Irish context.

What should interested artists do? The gallery prefers to source its artists. Gallery commission is 40% and a full range of services is provided.

Management structure: Private.

Temple Bar Gallery and Studios

5 – 9 Temple Bar
Dublin 2

Tel: +353 (0) 1 671 0073
Fax: +353 (0) 1 677 7527
E-mail: info@templebargallery.com
www.templebargallery.com

Conversion of an industrial building

Contact person / Director: Marian Lovett

Architects for the conversion: McCullough Mulvin

Temple Bar Gallery and Studios is a city centre arts venue dedicated to promoting, presenting and mediating contemporary visual art. The building features an on-street gallery and has four floors of artist's studios. These studios are non-residential work spaces with 24 hour access for artists. The building was first used as an art space in 1983; prior to this it had been a clothing factory (constructed in the early part of the 20th century). A full renovation of the building as a dedicated arts space took place in 1994.

Number of rooms / galleries; area in square metres: The building features one main gallery space (approximately 12 x 12 m) plus an internal atrium area over four floors which is equipped for use as an exhibition space. There are also 30 artist's studios of various sizes.

Specifications: Ceiling height: 3.3m, so suitable for large works on canvas or other works of significant stature. Main entrance point from street reaches to the full ceiling height, making access for large work straightforward. Lighting: fourteen tracks to meet specific needs. Floor: polished concrete surface. Walls: three plastered concrete; one plasterboard. Large windows looking onto street; these can be blocked out if a dark space is needed. In addition, temporary walls, divisions or internal spaces are often constructed to facilitate particular projects. As such the space can easily accommodate either video installations or wall-based work.

Access details: the entire building meets the 1993 NRB standards for disability access.

Exhibitions policy / 'ethos' of gallery: Temple Bar Gallery and Studios is dedicated to presenting an innovative and outward looking programme of contemporary art with an emphasis on featuring young and emerging talents alongside more recognised figures drawn from Ireland and the international arena.

What should interested artists do? Artists wishing to exhibit may send in slides or CDs of images, plus a CV and statement. While every effort will be made to view work, there is no guarantee that unsolicited submissions will be considered for exhibitions. The Director seeks to develop the artistic programme through active ongoing research into contemporary practice on both a local and international level. TBG&S pays an exhibition fee of €450. In addition TBG&S will provide substantial installation support, also a full-colour invitation card with postal mail-out (up to 500 arts and media contacts, plus an e-mail mail-out to around 800 contacts); and reception. TBG&S also frequently initiates and supports publishing projects in relation to exhibitions. Talks and events are integrated with the gallery programme. Selling work is not the primary aim, though work is often sold through the gallery. The percentage is generally 33%.

Management structure: the Board of Management generally comprises nine directors, four drawn from the business world, four nominated by the membership and if possible one arts professional with expert knowledge of contemporary art practice. This board appoints an Executive Director and staff report to the Director.

The Workroom

36 – 40 Upper Dominick Street
Dublin 7

Tel: +353 (0) 1 830 3211
E-mail: alisonpilkington@eircom.net

Conversion of an industrial space

Contact person / Director: Alison Pilkington

Architects for the conversion: Self-conversion

The Hendron building is a fine example of 1950s industrial architecture with a light-diffusing glass brick façade. The Workroom gallery is on the second floor behind this façade. There are five artists using the studio spaces in the Workroom. The Workroom was set up in January 2002 to provide an alternative visual arts venue for artists in Dublin, and to provide studio spaces and facilities for artists. The Workroom is dedicated to providing a platform for exhibition and debate on the visual arts within the artistic community and, equally importantly, dedicated to engaging with, and including, the local community and wider public in general.

Number of rooms / galleries; area in square metres: The Workroom consists of a gallery space of approximately 80 square metres which is made up of a main exhibition space with a smaller room attached which is usually used for installation and video display. There are also three other studios, a kitchen area and offices.

Specifications: The gallery space is flexible and can host work in all media. The floating L-shaped gallery walls are MDF panels, the floor is reinforced concrete. Gallery

lights are fluorescent strips.

Access details: No disabled access.

Exhibitions policy / 'ethos' of gallery: The gallery exhibitions policy is to show contemporary art in various media. The workroom has shown solo shows of painting and drawing as well as curated group shows of mixed media, sculpture, video, printmaking drawing and painting.

What should interested artists do? Artists who are interested in exhibiting should send slides or proposals to Alison Pilkington. Gallery commission: 30% on all works sold. Exhibitions are usually of three weeks duration, with an opening reception and full colour invitation provided.

Management structure: Private.

Co Fermanagh

Ardhowen Theatre
Dublin Road
Enniskillen BT74 6BR
Contact person: Eamonn Bradley
Tel: +44 (0) 28 6632 3233 Fax: (028) 6632 7102
E-mail: ardhowen.theatre@fermanagh.gov.uk
www.ardhowentheatre.com

The Basement Gallery
Dunbar House
Loughshore Road
Enniskillen BT74 5NN
Contact person: George and Emma Moore
Tel: +44 (0) 28 6632 5798
E-mail: info@basement-gallery.com
www.basement-gallery.com

The Higher Bridges Gallery (p. 234)
The Clinton Centre
Queen Elizabeth Road
Enniskillen BT74 6AA
Contact person: Diane Henshaw
Tel: +44 (0) 28 6632 5050 Fax: +44 (0) 28 6632 8991
E-mail: diane.henshaw@fermanagh.gov.uk
www.fermanagh.gov.uk

Clanart Gallery
25 Darling Street
Enniskillen BT74 7DP
Contact person: Nat Lunny
Tel: +44 (0) 28 6632 3285
E-mail: clanartgallery@btconnect.com

Share Arts
Smiths Strand
Co Fermanagh BT92 OEQ
Contact person: Majella Flanagan
Tel: +44 (0) 28 6772 2122 Fax: +44 (0) 28 6772 1893
E-mail: arts@sharevillage.org www.sharevillage.org

The Higher Bridges Gallery

The Clinton Centre
Queen Elizabeth Road
Enniskillen BT74 6AA

Tel: +44 (0) 286 632 5050
E-mail: diane.henshaw@fermanagh.gov.uk
www.fermanagh.gov.uk

Purpose-built multi-use venue

Contact person / Director: Diane Henshaw

Architect: Richard Pierce

Built in 2002, The Higher Bridges Gallery is a modern space, promoting the arts on a local, national and international scale. The building is situated on the site of the former St. Michael's Reading Rooms, which was demolished in the Enniskillen Remembrance Day bomb of 1997.

Number of rooms / galleries; area in square metres: One room, approx 34 square metres.

Specifications: White plaster board walls, Cement blackened floor. Lit with spots throughout. Limited storage available.

Suitable for installations, large canvas work and free-standing sculpture.

Access details: Fully accessible.

Exhibitions policy / 'ethos' of gallery: Contemporary and community art

What should interested artists do? Send CD ROM or JPEGS by email with CV and cover letter. Work sells in the space, and gallery commission is 20%. Hire fee for gallery is £100 per week; commissioned shows are free of hire costs and PR and reception /opening are provided.

Management structure: Local Government.

Co Galway

Áras Éanna (p. 236)
Inis Oírr
Contact person: Val Ballance
Tel: 353 (0) 997 5150
E-mail: araseanna@eircom.net

Atlantic Art Gallery and Studio (p. 236)
Clifden Station House
Clifden
Contact person: Siobhán Ní Ghallchóir, Mo West
Tel: +353 (0) 952 2871
E-mail: info@atlantic-art.com www.atlantic-art.com

Bold Art Gallery (p. 237)
Merchants Road
Galway
Contact person: Hazel Hendy
Tel: +353 (0) 9153 9900 Fax: +353 (0) 9153 1497
E-mail: info@boldartgallery.com www.boldartgallery.com

Clifden Art Gallery
Main Street
Clifden
Contact person: Delores Dowling
Tel / Fax: 353 (0) 952 1788
E-mail: dwyse@eircom.net www.connemaraart.galway.net

Galway Arts Centre (p. 237)
47 Dominick Street
Galway
Contact person: Michael Dempsey
Tel: +353 (0) 9156 5886 Fax: +353 (0) 9156 8642
E-mail: info@Galwayartscentre.ie www.galwayartscentre.ie

Kenny Gallery
High Street
Galway
Contact person: Karen Golden
Tel: +353 (0) 9153 4760
E-mail: art@kennys.ie www.kennys.ie

Lavelle Art Gallery
Main Street
Clifden
Contact Person: Gavin Lavelle
Tel: +353 (0) 952 1882
E-mail: gavinlavelle@eircom.net
www.lavelleartgallery.ie

Norman Villa Gallery
86 Lower Salthill
Galway
Contact person: Mark Keogh
Tel: +353 (0) 9152 1131
E-mail: enquiry@normanvillagallery.com
www.normanvillagallery.com

University Art Gallery
NUI Galway
University Road
Galway
Contact Person: Fionnuala Gallagher
Tel: +353 (0) 9151 2062
E-mail: ahoary@nuigalway.ie
www.nuigalway.ie/arts_office/gallery.html

Áras Éanna

Inis Oírr
Co na Gaillimhe

Tel: 353 (0) 997 5150
E-mail: araseanna@eircom.net

Conversion of an industrial building

Contact person / Director: Val Ballance, Director

Original Architect: DeBlacam (1982)
Architects for the conversion: Aonghus McCann (2000)

Converted in 2000, Áras Éanna was originally a weaving factory.

Number of rooms / galleries; area in square metres: 13 rooms in total; approximately 650 square metres; Gallery is on the first floor: walls: 7.92 m long x 2.59 m high; 3.96 m x 3.66 m; 3.35 m x 3.66 m; panel wall 2.74 m x 1.52 m.

Specifications: Walls: block, MDF and plaster; flooring: carpet; lighting: spots and washes on rails; storage in office space; entrances are 2.13 m high, 1.22 m wide.

Access details: No disabled access to the gallery; access to ground floor only.

Exhibitions policy / 'ethos' of gallery: Nearly all work shown is produced by artists who have had residencies in the arts centre. Ethos is contemporary.

What should interested artists do? Send e-mail with images and CV attached. Gallery takes 20%. No exhibition fee, no exhibition charge. The gallery provides opening reception, invitations, catalogue. Work sold varies from artist to artist.

Management structure: Private company. Run by a Board of Directors.

Atlantic Art Gallery and Studio

Clifden Station House
Clifden

Tel: +353 (0) 952 2871
E-mail: info@atlantic-art.com
www.atlantic-art.com

Use of shop-style building

Contact person / Director: Siobhán Ní Ghallchóir – Administrator
Mo West - Director

Architects for the conversion: Self-conversion

Opened in 2001, Atlantic Art is a combined gallery and studio space located at the Clifden Station House. Atlantic Art provides a platform for local and visiting artists. The Atlantic Artists work together to share the administration of the gallery. The use of the studio space by these members ensures vibrancy in the gallery all year round.

Number of rooms / galleries; area in square metres: 13 x 6 m.

Specifications: Painted walls. Space for video installations, large works on canvas and free standing sculpture.

Access details: Disabled access.

Exhibitions policy / 'ethos' of gallery: Contemporary; innovative and challenging art. The gallery is co-managed by a co-operative of local artists.

What should interested artists do? Send e-mail with images and CV attached or send CD ROM and CV via post. Exhibition policy currently under review. Work sells well in this space due to central Clifden location.

Management structure: Run by the Atlantic Artists Co-operative.

Bold Art Gallery

Merchants Road
Galway

Tel: +353 (0) 91 53 9900
E-mail: info@boldartgallery.com
www.boldartgallery.com

Conversion of existing space

Contact person / Director: Hazel Hendy

Builders for the conversion: M.J. Conroy & Sons / Hazel Hendy

The Bold Art Gallery opened in Galway in 2003, in a centrally located building formerly used as office space.

Number of rooms / galleries; area: one L-shaped room 130 square metres.

Specifications: white limestone floor. Walls: white, with one painted magenta. Hanging: perlon line from bar system in ceiling. Light: natural daylight, also low voltage dual track wire system.

Access details: Wheelchair accessible to front and rear entrances.

Exhibitions policy / 'ethos' of gallery: a relaxed and friendly environment where a mixture of contemporary and traditional work is shown.

What should interested artists do?
Send disk or e-mail, or call in person. Presently showing groups, with plans to run solo exhibitions. Percentage by arrangement.

Management structure: Private.

Galway Arts Centre

47 Dominick Street
Galway

Tel: +353 (0) 9156 5886
E-mail: info@Galwayartscentre.ie
www.galwayartscentre.ie

Refurbishment of an historic building

Contact person: Curator of Art and Community programmes: Michael Dempsey; Director: Tómas Hardiman

Architect responsible for renovation: John Yeats

Galway Arts Centre was established in 1982, initially operating out of a former Presbyterian Church at 23 Nun's Island. In 1988, Galway Arts Centre took over 47 Dominick Street which houses the art galleries, workshop/studios and offices. The house was built in the 1840's as a residence for the Persse family, the whiskey makers (the most famous member of which was Lady Augusta Gregory, playwright and patroness of the Irish literary revival). In 1998, the Arts Centre completed a major refurbishment.

Number of rooms / galleries; area: Three floors of galleries: first and second floors have three rooms and the top floor has one room. 798 square metres in total.

Access details: No disabled access.

Exhibitions policy / 'ethos' of gallery:
All forms: contemporary art, traditional painting etc. The Art + Community Programme aims to develop new audiences to the arts by widening its access points where artists and writers can interact with people and meaningful exchange can take place.

What should interested artists do?
Submissions are reviewed quarterly. Send slides and CV; or CD ROM and CV. Galway Arts Centre does not charge an exhibition fee. Opening reception and invitations are provided. Galway Arts Centre takes 35% comission on work sold.

Management structure: Run by a Board.

Co Kerry

Bín Bán Gallery
124 Lower Rock St.
Tralee
Contact person: Helen Shanahan
Tel: +353 (0) 66 712 2520
E-mail: info@binbanart.com www.binbanart.com

Frank Lewis Gallery
6 Bridewell Lane
off New Street
Killarney
Contact person: Frank Lewis
Tel: +353 (0) 643 4843 Fax: +353 (0) 643 1570
E-mail: info@franklewisgallery.com
www.franklewisgallery.com

Greenlane Gallery
Green Street
Dingle
Contact person: Susan Callery
Tel: +353 (0) 66 915 2018 Fax: +353 (0) 66 915 2047
E-mail: info@greenlanegallery.com
www.greenlanegallery.com

Killarney Art Gallery
Plunkett Street
Killarney
Contact person: Declan Mulvany
Tel: +353 (0) 643 4628
E-mail: art@irishartcollector.com
www.irishartcollector.com

Siamsa Tíre Theatre and Arts Centre (p. 239)
The Gallery / An Danlann
Town Park
Tralee
Contact person: Ciaran Walsh
Tel: +353 (0) 66 712 3055 Fax: +353 (0) 66 712 7276
E-mail: siamsagallery@eircom.net www.siamsatire.com

Siopa Chill Rialaig (p. 240)
Dun Geagan
Ballinskelligs
Co Kerry
Contact person: Ger O'Connell
Tel: +353 (0) 66 947 9277 Fax: +353 (0) 66 94 79324
E-mail: cillrialaig@esatclear.ie

St. John's Art Centre
The Square
Listowel
Contact person: Jules Murphy
Tel: +353 (0) 682 2566
E-mail: stjohnstheatre@eircom.net
www.stjohnstheatrelistowel.com

Wellspring Art Gallery
16 Denny Street
Tralee
Contact Person: Louise O'Donnell
Tel: +353 (0) 66 712 1218 Fax: +353 (0) 66 714 4919
E-mail: wellspring@eircom.net

Siamsa Tíre Theatre and Arts Centre

The Gallery / An Danlann
Town Park
Tralee
Co Kerry

Tel: +353 (0) 66 712 3055
E-mail: siamsagallery@eircom.net
www.siamsatire.com

Purpose-built multi-use venue

Contact person / Director: Ciaran Walsh, Visual Arts Director
Marianne Kennedy, General Manager

Architect: Paddy O'Sullivan, O'Sullivan Campbell

Opened in May 1991, Siamsa Tíre is a theatre and arts centre with galleries. Siamse Tíre is a public sector exhibition space within an arts centre attached to the National Folk Theatre.

Number of rooms / galleries; area in square metres: interlocking exhibition spaces on left of main entrance to theatre building /arts centre.

Specifications: Space 1: Round Gallery (78.5 square metres): rotunda 30 m across, with cone shaped roof 8 m high in centre; walls 3 m high x 20 metres and 6 m long; top lit by skylight and artificially by 12 sided lighting track 4 m high, 1 m from wall. Entrances / exits from foyer (stepped) and Long Gallery (ramped). Long Gallery: 5 x 10 m curved space, space partitioned in three with semi permanet ply partition. Access Corridor 5 m x 3 m (ramped). Artificial light only. Walls: sand /cement and partition. Centre Section adjoining round gallery. Natural /artificial light. Walls: sand /cement and partition. Projection Space: partitioned space suitable for projection. Artificial light only. Walls: sand /cement and partition. Multimedia: Siamsa does not own any digital projection or multimedia equipment. This is acquired on a rental basis.

Access details: Disability: Fully compliant with national standards for access (physical). Facilities: automatic front door; ramped access to all public areas; wheelchair accessible toilet: Induction loop, one wheelchair bay in theatre.

Exhibitions policy / 'ethos' of gallery: Current programming is built around a concern for the persistence of folk culture, and related issues of cultural identity as themes in contemporary visual arts prac-

tice. This is complemented by an arts centre functioning in support of professional arts practitioners in the county and region. Participation / Access programmes are limited but comprise two or three visual arts based events a year.

What should interested artists do?
Siamsa originates most of the exhibitions on its own, or in collaboration with other galleries or visual arts agencies. It does not, as a rule, operate an open submission policy. This reflects the role of the centre as defined by its relationship with the National Folk Theatre. Artist-originated exhibitions are considered: an initial 'Proposal For An Exhibition' should be submitted in writing / e-mail with support material provided in graphic or digital media formats. These form the basis for subsequent interview / discussion. Siamsa provides artists with Exhibition Payment Rights along with an agreed schedule of fees for installation, travel, subsistence and other work connected with exhibitions. All other costs (transport, technical, curatorial and marketing – including opening) are covered by Siamsa. Exceptional requirements (digital media etc) are negotiated.

Management structure: Managed by the Office of Public Works.

Siopa Chill Rialaig

Dun Geagan
Ballinskelligs

Tel: +353 (0) 66 947 9277
Fax: +353 (0) 66 947 9324
E-mail: cillrialaig@esatclear.ie

Purpose-built mixed-use space

Contact person / Director: Noelle Campbell Sharp, Founder and Honorary Managing Director; Ger O'Connell, Gallery Manager

Architect: Roger Foxall

Cill Rialaig was established in 1996 in the beautiful, remote Kerry countryside, close to the sea and stunning coastlines. The area has a unique history and culture and was the land base for the monks that lived on Skellig Rock, eight miles out in the Atlantic Ocean. Siopa Chill Rialaig is linked to the Cill Rialaig Artists Retreat (located 3.2 km away) where artists come and stay free of charge to paint, compose or write. Much of the art comes directly from the gallery's association with the artists who stay at the Retreat. The gallery part of the building is modelled on an old Irish 'crannóg' building with a triangular, vaulted thatched roof set on a cylindrical base. The gallery, therefore, is a circular room with a high, wooden-beamed ceiling. The rest of the building, including the exhibition room, café and workshop, is a single story construction adjoined to the gallery. The façade of the building is in stone, to blend in with the local houses and cottages that are traditionally fronted in this way.

Number of rooms / galleries: Gallery, two workshops, exhibition room, café / restaurant area.

Specifications: Modest exhibition space. Floors: wooden and stone / slate (concrete painted standard flooring in exhibition room). Stone wall finishing on outside and inside of foyer and restaurant, brick walls in gallery, exhibition room and rest of building. Spot lighting and neon lighting in gallery, neon lighting in exhibition room and standard lighting everywhere else. Most paintings are hung by nail on wall. One storeroom and storage available in workshops. Slide and video installations would be suitable in exhibition room. Plenty of space in gallery and throughout for displaying large works on canvas and sculpture. High ceilings.

Access details: Full access: no steps inside or around the building, disabled toilet.

Exhibitions policy / 'ethos' of gallery: Exhibitions are held only with artists who have stayed on the International Artists and Writers Retreat, along with selected local artists. In general the gallery accepts and exhibits a combination of all artistic styles in contemporary art, from representational to abstract. This includes paintings, ceramics, sculptures, glass-work, metal-work.

What should interested artists do? Send slides + CV, send CD ROM + CV, or send e-mail with images and CV attached. No exhibition fees charged or paid. Free admission to all. The gallery provides opening receptions, catalogues, mailing invitations, posters and publicity.

Management structure: Run by a Board, community project, not for profit.

Co Kildare

Kilcock Art Gallery
School Street
Kilcock
Contact person: Breda Smyth
Tel: +353 (0) 1 628 7619 Fax: +353 (0) 1 628 4293
E-mail: info@kilcockartgallery.ie
www. kilcockartgallery.com

Maynooth Exhibition Centre
St. Patrick's College
Maynooth
Contact person: Dominic McNamara
Tel: +353 (0) 1 628 5222 Fax: +353 (0) 1 708 3954
www.kildare.ie/arts/housing/maynooth-
exhibition-centre.htm

Riverbank Arts Centre
Mainstreet
Newbridge
Contact person: Sinead Redmond
Tel: +353 (0) 4544 8314 Fax: +353 (0) 4543 2490
E-mail: artscentre@riverbank.ie www.riverbank.ie

Co Kilkenny

Butler Gallery (p. 242)
Kilkenny Castle
Kilkenny
Contact person: Anna O'Sullivan
Tel: +353 (0) 56 776 1106
E-mail: info@butlergallery.com www.butlergallery.com

County Hall
John Street
Kilkenny
Contact Person: Mary Butler
Tel: 353 (0) 56 779 4135 Fax: +353 (0) 56 779 4004
E-mail: mary.butler@kilkennycoco.ie

National Craft Gallery
Castle Yard
Kilkenny
Contact person: Vincent O'Shea
Tel: +353 (0) 56 776 1804
E-mail: ncg@ccoi.ie www.ccoi.ie

No. 72 John Street
Kilkenny
Correspondence address:
County Hall
John Street
Contact Person: Mary Butler
Tel: +353 (0) 56 779 4135 Fax: +353 (0) 56 779 4004
E-mail: mary.butler@kilkennycoco.ie

Watergate Theatre: Upstairs Gallery
Parliament Street
Kilkenny
Contact Person: Polly Donnellan
Tel: +353 (0) 56 779 4135 Fax: +353 (0) 56 779 4004
E-mail: polly.donnellan@kilkennycoco.ie

Butler Gallery

The Castle
Kilkenny

Tel: +353 (0) 56 776 1106
Fax: +353 (0) 56 777 0031
E-mail: info@butlergallery.com
www.butlergallery.com

Refurbishment of an historic building

Contact person / Director: Anna O'Sullivan

Architects for the conversion: William Robertson

The Butler Gallery is situated in the basement of a castle, which was built in 1820. The Butler Gallery has been in Kilkenny Castle since 1982, however it has been in opperation as the Kilkenny Art Gallery Society since 1942.

Number of rooms / galleries; area in square metres: The gallery has five thick walled chambers of varying dimensions with connecting archways. Five rooms in total give a floor area of 120 square metres. Each room has a window with natural light. Windows can be blocked off, depending on installations.

Specifications: Given the gallery's accommodation in Kilkenny Castle, door heights and widths are extremely limited. The height of the ceiling in the gallery is three metres throughout, the floor is a neutral grey and the walls white.

Access details: No disabled access.

Exhibitions policy / 'ethos' of gallery: Exhibitions or projects may be group or solo, and curated internally by curatorial staff or externally by a freelance curator. The policy must reflect current visual art practice on a local, national and international circuit. There is an emphasis on previewing new work by new and established artists. Occasionally the gallery mounts retrospectives of mature or non living arists. The gallery seeks out exciting and innovative modes of collaboration off site and on site. Curated group exhibitions are given equal priority to solo exhibitions. The gallery increases international collaborations by bringing significant artists from around the world to the attention of national and local audiences. The Butler Gallery also has an acclaimed contemporary collection of Irish and international art. Education and outreach projects are programmed on site and off site.

What should interested artists do? Artists and groups can submit work in whatever medium best represents their practice, however no original artwork should be submitted. The programming committee usually meets once a year in Autumn; a call for submissions is advertised in CIRCA Art Magazine and the SSI. The fee to artists is €350 for a solo project. Invite cards, accommodation, insurance, reception, and transport costs are provided for each exhibition. In some cases catalogues are produced, depending on funds. Artists are not charged a fee. The Butler is not a commercial gallery and the programme is not dictated by sales, however sales are made depending on the work; in this case the Butler Gallery takes a 30% commission.

Management structure: non-profit public gallery with charitable status. Governance is through a Board of Directors.

Co Laois

Dúnamaise Arts Centre (p. 243)
Portlaoise
Contact person: Louise Donlon
Tel: +353 (0) 502 63356 Fax: +353 (0) 5026 3357
E-mail: dunamaise@eircom.net www.dunamaise.ie

Dúnamaise Arts Centre

Portlaoise

Tel: +353 (0) 5026 3356
E-mail: dunamaise@eircom.net
www.dunamaise.ie

Dúnamaise is a multi-purpose arts centre
(theatre and gallery), built in 1999 by
Laois County Council. There is a main
gallery space upstairs, and the foyer and
restaurant area are also used for exhibitions. Prior to its conversion to an arts
centre, the building housed the County
Council offices, and before that, the
County Gaol.

**Number of rooms / galleries; area in
square metres**: Two spaces approximately
8 x 5 m.

Specifications: The space is suitable for
large works on canvas and free-standing
sculpture, but not for slide and video
installations. Full specifications are
available from the gallery on request.

Access details: Full disabled access, lift
etc. Braille signage, induction loop in
theatre.

Exhibitions policy / 'ethos' of gallery:
The arts centre aims to provide the
best in local, national and international performing and visual arts to the
people of Laois and the surrounding
counties. With regard to the visual
arts, exhibitions are primarily of contemporary visual arts – painting,
sculpture, photography. The centre
also hosts an open art competition
each year for amateur artists.

Conversion of an historic building

Contact person / Director: Louise Donlan

Architects for the conversion: Rory Milligan, Milligan Reside Larkin

What should interested artists do? Artists
and should send submissions by email
with images and CV attached. The gallery
pays a fee to exhibiting artists. Gallery
commission is 25% on works sold. Some
work does sell in this space. Opening
reception and invitations are provided.

Management structure: Run by a Board.

Co Leitrim

In process:
Leitrim Co Council is in the process of developing the Courthouse, Manorhamilton as an arts centre to address the lack of exhibition facilites for the visual arts here.

Contact:
Caoimhin Corrigan, Arts Officer
Leitrim County Council
Carrick-on-Shannon
Co. Leitrim
Tel: +353 (0) 71 965 0335
E-mail: artoff@leitrimcoco.ie
www.leitrimcoco.ie/Services/arts/arts.htm

Exhibitions are also held at:

Glens Centre
New Line
Manorhamilton
Contact person: Anna Legge
Tel: +353 (0) 71 985 5833 Fax: +353 (0) 71 985 6063
E-mail anna@theglenscentre.com www.theglenscentre.com

Co Limerick

Belltable Arts Centre
69 O'Connell Street
Limerick
Contact person: Peter McNamara
Tel: +353 (0) 61 31 5871 Fax: +353 (0) 61 41 8552
E-mail: info@belltable.ie www.belltable.ie

Bourn Vincent Gallery (p. 245)
Foundation Building
University of Limerick
Contact person: Yvonne Davis, Dr. John Logan
Tel: +353 (0) 61 21 3052 Fax: +353 (0) 61 31 3617
E-mail: bournvincentgallery@ul.ie

Church Gallery
Limerick School of Art and Design
Clare Street
Limerick
Contact person: Bob Baker
Tel: +353 (0) 6120 8870
E-mail: bob.baker@lit.ie www.lit.ie

Gallery 75
75 O'Connell Street
Limerick
Contact person: Sarah Marshall
Tel: +353 (0) 6131 5650

Hunt Museum
Custom House
Rutland Street
Limerick
Contact person: Virginia Teehan
Tel: +353 (0) 6131 2833 Fax: +353 (0) 6131 2834
E-mail: info@huntmuseum.com www.huntmuseum.com

Limerick City Gallery (p. 246)
Carnegie Building
Pery Square
Limerick
Contact person: Mike Fitzpatrick
Tel: +353 (0) 61 31 0633 Fax: +353 (0) 61 31 0228
E-mail: lcgartzz@iol.ie www.limerickcity.ie/lcga

Moulin Gallery
5 Cornmarket Court
Upper Denmark Street
Limerick
Contact person: Mary Hannon
Tel: +353 (0) 6131 8700
E-mail: moulingallery@msn.com

Bourn Vincent Gallery

Foundation Building
University of Limerick
Limerick

Tel: +353 (0) 6121 3052
Fax: +353 (0) 61 31 3617
E-mail: bournvincentgallery@ul.ie

Purpose-built space

Contact person / Director: Curator: Dr John Logan
Administrator: Yvonne Davis

Original Architect: Pat Whelan (engineer)

The Bourn Vincent gallery is located in the Foundation Building, at the University of Limerick. The Foundation Building was completed in the early 1990s, and the gallery was opened in 1993.

Number of rooms / galleries; area in square metres: The gallery is a single space, 162 square metres with 28.56 m of available wall hanging space.

Specifications: Walls: white. Hanging space is 28.56 m. Windows, covered with blinds. Near blackout available. Tungsten ceiling lighting and track spot lighting. Wooden floor. Ceiling height is 2.57 m. There is one free standing wall 6.7 m and this stands in front of a glass wall 10.7 m. The gallery is equipped to show slide installations, video installations, DVDs, free-standing sculpture. Access only to a standard commercial lift. All doors are of standard height and width.

Access details: The building is accessible to disabled users. In order to gain access after 5.30pm, prior notice must be given, as access to the lifts is by code only to a limited group of users. Notice is required in order to ensure that security will be available to open the relevant areas.

Exhibitions policy / 'ethos' of gallery: The gallery is dedicated to showing the work of professional Irish artists, and is equally interested in showing the work of emerging artists as well as those longer established in their practise. The gallery will exhibit single or multi-media work.

What should interested artists do? Send a letter by way of introduction and examples of work in either slide or digital format. It is preferable to include a copy rather than

original documentation. It should arrive at the administrator's office no later than 1 September and will be considered by the Bourn Vincent Gallery committee who meet annually. The gallery commits to buying a work from the exhibition. It neither charges or pays an exhibition fee. The gallery offers the following: an exhibition typically for two months; an invitation; poster; opening reception with press in attendance; e-mail notification to arts and media listings.

Management structure: The gallery is managed by a committee comprising the Curator, Administrator, and three invited members, two from University staff and one member external to the University. It is entirely supported by the University and is not in receipt of external sponsorship or funding.

Limerick City Gallery of Art

Carnegie Building
Pery Square
Limerick

Tel: +353 (0) 61 310 633
Fax: +353 (0) 61 310 228
E-mail: lcgartzz@iol.ie

Conversion of an historic building

Contact person / Director: Mike Fitzpatrick

Original Building: Carnegie Library
Architects for the conversion: John A O'Reilly Architect, in association with Murray O'Laoire

LCGA houses a permanent collection of works by 19th and 20th century Irish artists, tracing the development of modern Irish art in painting, sculpture and drawing. The collection, begun in 1948, continues to grow and also includes the National Collection of Contemporary Drawing. LCGA also runs a contemporary exhibition programme by Irish and International artists which includes EV+A, Ireland's premier annual exhibition. The gallery also hosts events including poetry readings, seminars, concerts and lectures. Built in 1906 as a Carnegie Library, with the permanent collection gallery added in 1848, the gallery has occupied the entire building since 1985.

Number of rooms / galleries; area in square metres: 650 square metres of exhibition space on two floors, five rooms on ground floor, with the largest space being 10 x 10 m. Three rooms and an atrium upstairs.

Specifications: The gallery has exhibited all forms of visual art, including installa-

tions, video projections, the space is extremely flexible for all forms of display.

Access details: Temporary ramp available as required.

Exhibitions policy / 'ethos' of gallery: Contemporary art and design.

What should interested artists do? Any format welcome but colour printouts and material that is not required to be returned is best. The gallery pays a fee and normally provides a reception and invites.

Management structure: Local Authority.

Co Louth

Basement Gallery (p. 247)
Town Hall
Crowe Street
Dundalk
Contact person: Marie Gray
Tel: +353 (0) 42 939 6437 Fax: +353 (0) 42 935 1539
E-mail: dundarts@eircom.net www.dundalktown.ie

Droichead Arts Centre (p. 248)
Stockwell Street
Drogheda
Contact person: Tony Conaghy, Paul O'Hanrahan
Tel: +353 (0) 41 983 3946 Fax: +353 (0) 41 984 2055
E-mail: info@droicheadartscentre.com
www.droicheadartscentre.com

Basement Gallery

Town Hall
Crowe Street
Dundalk

Tel: +353 (0) 42 939 6437
E-mail: dundarts@eircom.net
www.dundalktown.ie

Refurbishment of an historic building

Contact person / Director: Marie Gray, Arts Officer

Architects for the renovation: Jan Van Dijk, Van Dijk Architects

The Gallery is in the basement of the Town Hall, the original architect of which was John Murray. The building was completed in the 1860s. The space was formerly a gaol, and has been in operation as the Basement Gallery since 1990. In 2003, the galley was refurbished as part of a refurbishment of the Town Hall Office buildings and Theatre. This has tripled the size of the gallery.

Number of rooms / galleries; area in square metres: Main space with vaulted ceiling, and four adjacent spaces. There is also workshop space. Central Space: 24 m x 3.75 m approx. Three side spaces: each 8.5 m x 2.5 m approx. Fourth space: 7.5 m x 7.5 m approx.

Specifications: Walls: stone painted white. Flooring: tiled in places, original stone flagging in places, and painted concrete in others. Hanging: flexible hanging system for 2D works. Light: adjustable focus spots on adjustable track. Storage: adequate storage for one to two shows depending on scale. Heights: average height in gallery space is three metres. Loading doors: easy access to gallery through double doors.

Access details: A ramp is in place in the main entrance to the building from the street. Access to the gallery by means of a lift from the main ground floor level of the Town Hall. Ramps also exist within the

Gallery space, where there are split-level floors.

Exhibitions policy / 'ethos' of gallery: Primary consideration is given to freedom for the exhibiting artist. A range of activities accompanies most exhibitions, including workshops and artists' talks. The Gallery is particularly suited to installations, being made up of separate rooms with no natural light. There is space for large works on canvas and freestanding sculpture, but artists should note the ceiling height (3 metres approx).

What should interested artists do? Artists should send a maximum of six slides, or CD ROM, or VHS, plus CV and artist's statement. Post is preferable to e-mail. Include a S.A.E. and indicate if you require material to be returned. The Gallery provides opening reception; design, print and mailing of invitations and publicity. The Gallery does not pay or charge a fee. The Arts Office, on behalf of the Town Council, usually purchases a piece from each exhibition.

Management structure: the Gallery is part of the Town Hall building and is run by Local Government: The Arts Office of Dundalk Town Council manages and programmes the Basement Gallery.

Droichead Arts Centre

Stockwell Street
Drogheda

Tel: +353 (0) 41 983 3946
Fax: +353 (0) 41 984 2055
E-mail: info@droicheadartscentre.com
www.droicheadartscentre.com

Purpose-built space

Contact person: Tony Conaghy: Gallery; Paul O'Hanrahan: Director

Architect responsible for renovation: Facilities for visitors with special needs: Pat Weafer

In operation since 1995, the Droichead Arts Centre is a multi-use arts venue with a purpose-built gallery, 160 seated theatre, 2 changing rooms, a workshop area, office and reception area and storeroom with loading bay.

Number of rooms / galleries; area in square metres: Two galleries. The main gallery is 10 square metres. Height from floor to ceiling is 4 m but increases to 7 m in height by the large window.

Specifications: Space suitable /adaptable for slide installation /video /large works on canvas /standing sculptures. White concrete walls, wooden floor, natural and track lighting.

Access details: Lift: 1.8 x 1.4 m, capable of carrying 630 kg plus one toilet for the disabled.

Exhibitions policy / 'ethos' of gallery: To show a variety of work by established and up-and-coming artists, both professional and non professional. To produce a gallery programme that is exciting, accessible, challenging and relevant.

What should interested artists do? Artists should send slides / CD ROM / e-mail plus CV and artist's statement. The gallery takes 20% commission on work sold. The selling of work depends on the show. An exhibition fee is paid to artists, and the gallery does not charge any fees for exhibiting. An opening reception, invitations and transport are provided. Catalogues can be produced, by arrangement.

Management structure: Municipal Building, run by Board of Directors, Droichead Arts Centre Ltd.

Co Mayo

Ballina Arts Centre
Market Square
Ballina
Contact person: Sally O'Leary
Tel: +353 (0) 967 3593
E-mail: ballinaartscentre@eircom.net

Ballinglen Arts Foundation
Main Street
Ballycastle
Contact person: Una Ford, Margo Dolan
Tel: +353 (0) 964 3184
E-mail: baf@iol.ie

Custom House Studios (p. 249)
Westport Quay
Westport
Contact person: John Mc Hugh
Tel: +353 (0) 982 8735
E-mail: customhouse@eircom.net

Linenhall Arts Centre (p. 250)
Castlebar
Contact person: Marie Farrell
Tel: +353 (0) 94 902 3733 Fax: +353 (0) 94 902 6162
E-mail: info@thelinenhall.com www.thelinenhall.com

Town Hall Arts Centre
Barrack Street
Charlestown
Contact person: Sarah Craig
Tel: +353 (0) 94 925 5812
E-mail: thac@eircom.net

Western Light Art Gallery
The Sandybanks
Keel
Achill Island
Contact Person: Seán, Margaret or Paul Cannon
Tel: +353 (0) 984 3325
E-mail: artgallery@eircom.net www.art-gallery-ireland.com

Custom House Studios

Westport Quay
Westport

Tel: +353 (0) 98 28735
E-mail: customhouse@eircom.net

In operation since 2000, The Custom House Studios and Gallery is a refurbished pre-famine building, set at street level on a prominent site on Westport Quay, the gallery attracts a non-art audience as well as those specifically interested in art. There is a good international audience too. Prior to conversion as a gallery, the building functioned (as the name suggests) as a Customs House.

Number of rooms / galleries; area in square metres: There are two exhibition rooms at street level,with a total area 67 square metres.

Specifications: Concrete walls, tiled floors, spot lighting, good natural light, suitable for most types of works.

Access Details: The gallery has disabled access and disabled toilet facilities.

Conversion of an historic building

Contact person / Director: John McHugh

Architects for the conversion: Carr Architects

Exhibitions policy / 'ethos' of gallery: The gallery exhibits contemporary art from Custom House Studios as well as other artists with group and solo shows. The gallery neither pays nor charges a fee. An opening reception, invitations, and PR are provided. Work does sell in the space, and the gallery commission is 25%.

What should interested artists do? Artists should send slides, photographs, or CDs. The gallery does not accept submissions made by e-mail.

Management structure: Not for profit, run by a Board.

Linenhall Arts Centre

Linenhall Street
Castlebar

Tel: +353 (0) 94 902 3733
Fax: +353 (0) 94 902 6162
E-mail: linenhall@eircom.net
www.thelinenhall.com

Conversion of an historic building

Contact person / Director: Marie Farrell, Director

Architect responsible for renovation: Recent renovations by Tom Carr Architects

In operation since 1990, The Linenhall Arts Centre is based in an 18th century Linen Hall which was renovated in 2000 to serve as a multi-disciplinary arts centre. The building was originally built in 1790 as a clearing house for flax and linen.

Number of rooms / galleries; area in square metres: There is one main gallery space on the first floor measuring approx 105 square metres. There is additional exhibition space in the foyer and stairwell areas.

Specifications: White plasterboard walls, light grey carpet, natural light and spotlights, no storage, maximum height 2.75 m. There are spaces in the building suitable for slide and video installations and large works, there are a selection of plinths for free-standing sculptures.

Access details: Disabled access on the ground floor to the arts workshop, foyer and performance space, but not to the first floor.

Exhibitions policy / 'ethos' of gallery: The Linenhall reflects contemporary arts practice and concerns, working with both Irish and international artists.

What should interested artists do? Artists who are interested in exhibiting may apply at any time, by sending a proposal to include CV and up to ten images (slides, or CD ROM preferably in jpeg format). The gallery does not pay an exhibition fee but endeavours to cover all of the costs related to the show, excluding making and framing the work. The gallery organises printing and mailing of invitation and press release, hosts an opening reception and arranges for collection of work. Gallery commission is 30%.

Management structure: The Linenhall is a company limited by guarantee with a Board of Directors.

Co Meath

Toradh Gallery (p. 251)
Meath County Council Offices
Duleek
Contact person: Denis Boyle
Tel: +353 (0) 1 824 0000
E-mail: toradhgallery@meathcoco.ie
www.meath.ie/arts_office

Boltown Gallery
Kells
Contact person: Paul Bowers
Tel: +353 (0) 46 924 3605
E-Mail: somervillestudios@eircom.net
www.boltowngallery.com

In process:
A new arts centre, the Navan Arts Centre, is presently being planned. For further information contact:

Meath County Council Arts Office
Dunshaughlin Library
Main Street
Dunshaughlin
Contact person: Denis Boyle, Arts Officer
Tel: +353 (0) 1 824 0000
E-mail: artsoffice@meathcoco.ie
www.meath.ie/arts_office

Toradh Gallery

Meath County Council Offices
Duleek

Tel: +353 (0) 1 824 0000
E-mail: toradhgallery@meathcoco.ie
www.meath.ie

Located within purpose-built multi-use building

Contact person / Director: Denis Boyle

Architect: Burke-Kennedy Doyle

Toradh is Meath's first publicly-funded art gallery, programmed and administered by the local authority arts office, and contained in Meath county council's first 'one-stop-shop', which was built in 1999.

Number of rooms / galleries; area in square metres: Two lobby areas on the ground and first floors connected by an open staircase. Hanging space 24.4 square metres approx.

Specifications: Toradh gallery is restricted mainly to painting, with little facilities for installation art or sculpture. There is a great deal of natural light.

Access details: Disabled access: elevator and toilets.

Exhibitions policy / 'ethos' of gallery: Traditional and contemporary art.

What should interested artists do?
Exhibitions are by advertised requests for submissions (local and national), and number about ten a year. Sales attract a 20% commission, and the gallery provides an opening reception, invitations and a catalogue for exhibiting artists. It is the Toradh Gallery's policy to purchase, where possible, a piece from an exhibiting artist in lieu of an exhibition payment, for the Meath County Council Art Collection. Meath County Council's online catalogue can be viewed at www.meath.ie

Management structure: Local government.

Co Monaghan

Monaghan County Museum
1 – 2 Hill Street
Monaghan
Contact Person: Liam Bradley
Tel: +353 (0) 478 2928
E-mail: comuseum@monaghancoco.ie
www.monaghan.ie/museum/services.asp

The Market House
Market Street
Monaghan
Contact person: Joanne Behan
Tel: +353 (0) 473 8162 Fax: +353 (0) 477 1113
E-mail: themarkethouse@eircom.net
www.themarkethouse.ie

Co Offaly

Birr Theatre and Arts Centre
Oxmantown Hall
Birr
Contact person: Emma Nee Haslam
Tel: +353 (0) 509 22911
E-mail: birrtheatre@eircom.net
www.birrtheatre.com

Co Roscommon

Roscommon Arts Centre (p. 253)
Circular Road
Roscommon
Contact person: Jacinta Lynch
Tel: +353 (0) 90 662 5993
E-mail: roscartscentre@eircom.net
www.roscommonartscentre.ie

Roscommon Arts Centre

Circular Road
Roscommon
Co Roscommon

Box Office: +353 (0) 90 662 5824
Admin: +353 (0) 90 662 5993
E-mail: roscartscentre@eircom.net
www.roscommonartscentre.ie

Purpose-built venue

Contact person / Director: Jacinta Lynch

Senior Engineer: Kieran Madden

Operating since 2002, Roscommon Arts Centre is a multi-disciplinary contemporary arts space. The building itself is an A-frame construction, and budgets have been invested in the equipment, rather that in an elaborate, expensive building. This has proved very successful in the development of the space, allowing for the operation of a greater number of facilities for artists in all areas.

Number of rooms / galleries; area in square metres: The gallery space is on the first floor (14.7 m x 5.35 m) – a large industrial space, with a raised roof on one side (5.1 m) and lower on opposite wall (4 m). The project space is also on the first floor, parallel and opposite to the gallery space (14.7 m x 5.35 m). Artists are given the freedom to alter the space specific to the installation of their works, subject to agreement with the Director. The space is suitable for all forms of installation.

Specifications: Visual arts space / gallery is fitted with a halogen spot lighting system and a series of overhead daylight fluorescent fittings. Natural light is available on lower wall section, running lengthways within the space.

Access details: Ground floor disabled access, developments underway to include upper floor access.

Exhibitions policy / 'ethos' of gallery: Professional facilities, services, support and advice to exhibiting artists within a fresh context that aims to increase touring opportunities for visual artists in Ireland. International collaborations are an integral part of the exhibitions programme. The opportunity for visual artists to explore their work in a non-commercial environment increases the visibility of visual

artists in a space that is not driven by commercial interests. The exhibition policy of the gallery is to promote the understanding of visual arts practice in Ireland, enhance career development for artists and provide opportunities for the public to engage with professional visual artists working in all media.

What should interested artists do? Artists interested in submitting proposals for the visual arts gallery, should send CV, artist's statement and either 35 mm transparencies, CD ROM, DVD, VHS, or catalogue / photographs. Access to the gallery is by open submission and by invitation. The gallery neither pays nor charges a fee. All services are made available to the artist: opening reception, invitations, press and publicity; local and national press listing; invited speakers at openings; technical support. Gallery takes commission of 30% on sale of all artworks. Work generally does sell, there is an interested buying public in the area. Catalogues are subject to budgets and collaborations.

Management structure: Local Government, and a non-executive advisory panel of invited members.

Model Arts and Niland Gallery

The Mall
Sligo

Phone: +353 (0) 71 914 1405
Fax: +353 (0) 71 914 3694
E-mail: info@modelart.ie
www.modelart.ie

Renovation of an historic building

Contact person / Director: Sarah Glennie

Original Architect: James Higgins Owens
Architects for the conversion: McCullough Mulvin (2000)

On The Mall, overlooking the town, the Model Arts and Niland Gallery is a unique arts venue in Ireland. The refurbished gallery houses the internationally important Sligo Municipal Art Collection, and the contemporary galleries have an established reputation as one of Ireland's foremost contemporary art spaces. There is also a performance space, an education facility, artists' studios and a café. Housed in a former school, the Model Arts Centre was begun in 1990.

Number of rooms / galleries; area in square metres: Six contemporary galleries, two on the ground floor and four on the first floor. Galleries 1 and 3 (9.5 m wide x 5 m long, 47.5 square metres); Galleries 2 and 4 (5.5 m wide x 5 m long, 27.5 square metres); Gallery 5 (13 m wide x 6.7 m long, 87.1 square metres); Gallery 6 (6 m wide x 11m long, 66 square metres); The Niland Collection is housed in two purpose-built galleries (200 square metres). Large atrium.

Specifications : Contemporary Galleries: All spaces suitable for slide / video installations, large works on canvas and for free-standing sculpture. White rendered walls. Galleries 3 and 4 have plaster ceilings at 3.25 m high and 3.1 m high. Door sizes are 2.2 m high x 0.8 m / 1.3 m wide. Galleries 5 and 6 have vaulted ceilings and exposed wooden truss beams at 3.1m high. ERCO lighting tracks are at 2.75 m height throughout. Old sash windows, wooden shutters and floorboards. All galleries have access to natural light. Loading door heights are 2.2 m high. Storage is available in the Municipal Storeroom and in the basement. Black Box performance space for music, literary events and film (35mm projection). Niland Gallery: to UK Museums and Galleries Commission standards of environmental control; north-facing etched glass roof lights provide shadowless daylight.

Access details: Disabled access, ramps leading up to both front and rear entrances, elevator, audio as well as visual information incorporated. Disabled toilet facilities.

Exhibitions policy / 'ethos' of gallery: The arts centre facilitates the contemporary arts, with a major focus on the visual arts. The centre strives to make its activities accessible to the public and to increase an understanding and appreciation of our contemporary culture and heritage. Local to international level work is undertaken, Interdisciplinary interactions through the music and literary festivals and through the permanent collection of Irish art are encouraged. The Arts Centre has an active ArtReach programme which provides means for the public to interact with the programme.

What should interested artists do? Send a cover letter stating the nature of your work, ten slides or photographs, CD ROM

is acceptable, and CV. The gallery pays an exhibition fee. Accommodation is provided to artists for the night of the opening by prior arrangement and for installation period, if necessary. Also: transportation and security; invitations, reception, and PR; catalogues for specific exhibitions. Work normally sells in this space and the gallery takes 30%.

Management structure: Limited company; a partnership between the Model Arts and Niland Gallery and Sligo Local Authorities, with staff and a volunteer Board.

Sligo Art Gallery

Yeats Memorial Building,
Hyde Bridge
Sligo

Tel: +353 (0) 71 914 5847
Fax: +353 (0) 71 914 7426
E-mail: sagal@iol.ie
www.sligoartgallery.com

Conversion of an historic building

Contact person / Director: Robbie McDonald

Architects for the conversion: Self-conversion

Located in the Yeats Memorial Building at Hyde Bridge, in a building dating from 1900, the Gallery was founded in 1977 under the auspices of the Yeats Society to provide exhibition facilities for all art forms. From this committee the Sligo Art Gallery evolved into an independent incorporated charity and educational foundation. The Gallery does not have a permanent collection but hosts up to 20 exhibitions and artistic events each year, most of them initiated by the Gallery itself. In 1990 the Gallery held its first Iontas Small Works Open Submission Exhibition, which offers generous financial rewards to artists and is now well established as an annual event. Another initiative was the Solo Exhibition Opportunity which is open to all artists normally resident in Ireland and Irish nationals living abroad who have not mounted a solo exhibition at a publicly funded art gallery. The Gallery invites submissions in the categories of painting, print, sculpture, drawing and photography, or a number of these media.

Number of rooms / galleries: Three rooms plus one hallway.

Specifications: The space has no loading doors, but is suitable for installations.

Access details: Access for wheelchairs is to ground floor only. Gallery is situated on first floor.

Exhibitions policy / 'ethos' of gallery: Contemporary art with emphasis on emerging artists and on education.

What should interested artists do? Artists interesting in exhibiting should send slides CV / CD ROM, or by e-mail with images attached. No exhibition fee is paid or charged. The gallery provides opening reception, invitations, catalogue, publicity and invitation. Gallery commission is 30%.

Management structure: Run by a Board of Directors.

Co Tipperary

Nelson Street
Clonmel
Contact person: Brendan Maher
Tel: +353 (0) 52 27877 Fax: +353 (0) 52 27866
E-mail: stac@eircom.net   www.southtipparts.com

In Process: Thurles Civic Centre

Designed by McCullough Mulvin Architects, Thurles Civic Centre is an integrated Civic Centre, which incorporates a new art branch library facility and an arts centre. The arts element of the project includes a 230 seat fully-equipped theatre with backstage facilities, and an exhibition space of 145 square metres. There will also be a café and a community space. The exhibition space, which will be equipped for digitally and installation-based works, is to be shared, and the Library service and arts centre will each programme 50% of the annual exhibition programme, with the opportunity for joint programming of certain projects. A formal policy is currently being developed. Thurles Civic Centre is due to open in 2006.

For further information contact: Melanie Scott
Arts Officer
North Tipperary County Council
Civic Offices
Nenagh
Tel: +353 (0) 674 4852
E-mail: artsoffice@northtippcoco.ie
www.northtippcoco.ie/services/arts.htm
[*see also pp. 43-44.*]

South Tipperary Arts Centre

Nelson Street
Clonmel

Tel: +353 (0) 52 27877
E-mail: stac@eircom.net
www.southtipparts.com

Conversion of an existing building

Contact person / Director: Brendan Maher

Architects for the conversion: Unknown

Located in a 1950s former bus station and Credit Union, the South Tipperary Arts Centre has been in operation for nine years.

Number of rooms / galleries; area in square metres: Two interconnected spaces: Gallery one (14 m x 3 m) and Gallery 2 (3.5 m x 3.5 m). Total space: 54.25 square metres.

Specifications: Large glass fronted reception area leads to a lower-ceilinged exhibition area. Long wall space with good natural light, links with a smaller room for display. Hard floor finish (grey), white panel wall, suitable for all forms of work.

Access details: Wide doors, building level with path.

Exhibitions policy / 'ethos' of gallery: Mixture of contemporary art with some traditional. Slight tendency towards debut or early exhibitions by young artists, but broad-based choices made by Visual Arts Committee annually.

What should interested artists do? Artists should send slides, CV and letter of intent re: work to be exhibited; Some sales are made, gallery commission is 30%. The gallery pays a fee to artists and provides invitations, reception and, occasionally, a catalogue.

Management structure: Company Limited by Guarantee, run by a Board.

Co Tyrone

Burnavon Arts and Cultural Centre (p. 257)
Burn Road
Cookstown BT80 8DN
Contact person: Tony McCance
Tel: +44 (0) 28 8676 7994 Fax: +44 (0) 28 8676 5853
E-mail: burnavon@cookstown.gov.uk
www.burnavon.com

Gormley's Art Gallery,
3/4 Dromore Road,
Omagh BT78 1RE
Contact person: Oliver Gormley
Tel: +44 (0) 28 8224 7738
E-mail: info@gormleys.ie
www.gormleys.ie

Spires Art
2 Brookmount Rd
Omagh BT78 5HZ
Contact person: Declan McLoughlin
Tel: +44 (0) 28 8224 6613
E-mail: info@spiresart.com   www.spiresart.com

Burnavon Arts and Cultural Centre

Burn Road
Cookstown BT80 8DN

Tel: +44 (0) 28 8676 7994
E-mail: burnavon@cookstown.gov.uk
www.burnavon.com

Purpose-built multi-use venue

Contact person / Director: Tony McCance, Manager

Architect: McCormick, Tracey & Mullarkey

Operating since 1999, the Burnavon Arts & Cultural Centre acts as a catalyst and focal point for arts and cultural activity in the Mid Ulster Region. Hosting a wide range of arts and cultural events such as exhibitions, pantomimes, dramas, comedies and concerts. The Burnavon places an emphasis on the promotion of local artists and performers, affording them the opportunity to present their productions / exhibitions within the venue. As the only venue of its type in mid-Ulster, the Burnavon is a key contributor towards audience development for arts and culture in the region.

Number of rooms / galleries; area in square metres: One auditorium space with full retractable seating: capacity 351 seats; one gallery: 52 square metres.

Specifications: Gallery provides for wall hangings only, hanging rods are provided suitable for all sizes of work. Spot lighting is provided.

Access details: The Gallery is on the first floor, lift facility available from ground floor to first floor. Induction loop system available in auditorium area only.

Exhibitions policy / 'ethos' of gallery: Open.

What should interested artists do?
Contact the Manager by telephone or e-mail. Booking in advance of up to one year. Maximum usage is for 1 month. No fees paid or charged, but 10% commission is taken on work sold. Opening reception, can be arranged, but costs are borne by the artists. Success of exhibition depends upon time of year and type of exhibition.

Management structure: Local Authority.

Co Waterford

In Process:
Lismore Castle Arts
Lismore
Tel: +353 (0) 585 4424

Designed by Gareth O'Callaghan from Jack Coughlan and
Associates Architects, Lismore Castle Arts is a new contemporary gallery within the walls of a 17th century tur-
reted Keep overlooking the River Blackwater. The gallery
itself comprises two large 'white cube' spaces, and an
additional circular Project Room occupying a tower in the
oldest part of the castle. Plans for Lismore Castle Arts are
to exhibit and support the development of new contemporary artworks and artistic collaborations, and to work
closely with schools, colleges and the local community.
The aim is to make use of the space to show, share and
enjoy contemporary art, and to further the understanding
of it. In addition, the intention is to facilitate the creation
of new art, and this will be augmented in the future by a
planned programme of artists' residencies.
Dimensions: Gallery 1: 26.5 x 6.8 square metres, height
3.5 m to wall plate; Gallery 2: 6 x 6.8 square metres,
height 3.5 metres to wall plate; Project Room: 4 square
metres approx).

Lismore Castle Arts will open in September 2005.

**Joan Clancy Gallery
/ Dánlann Shiobhán Uí Fhlannchadha (p. 259)**
Mullinahorna
Ring
Dungarvan
Contact person: Joan Clancy
Tel: +353 (0) 584 6205
E-mail: jclancy1@eircom.net

Dye House Gallery
Mary Street
Waterford
Contact person: Liz McCay, Oliver Dempsey
Tel: +353 (0) 5184 4770 Fax: +353 (0) 5185 0399
E-mail: info@dyehouse-gallery.com
www.dyehouse-gallery.com

Garter Lane Arts Centre (p. 260)
5 O'Connell Street
Waterford
Contact person: Caitlin Doherty, Caroline Senior
Tel: +353 (0) 5187 7153 Fax: +353 (0) 5187 1570
E-mail: artswave@garterlane.ie www.garterlane.com

Greyfriars Municipal Gallery
Greyfriars Street
Waterford
Contact Person: Conor Nolan
Tel: +353 (0) 5184 9856
E-mail: arts@waterfordcity.ie

Lismore Arts Centre
Dromore
Cappoquin
Contact person: Wishy Martin
Tel: +353 (0) 585 4630

Old Market House Art Centre
Dungarvan
Contact person: Elaine Bowe, Assumpta Nugent
Tel: +353 (0) 584 8944
E-mail: artscentre@waterfordcoco.ie
www.waterfordcoco.ie

[above left and left:]
Lismore Castle Arts

Joan Clancy Gallery / Dánlann Shiobhán Uí Fhlannchadha

Mullinahorna
Ring
Dungarvan

Tel: +353 (0) 584 6205
E-mail: jclancy1@eircom.net

Purpose-built space

Contact person / Director: Joan Clancy

Architect: Damien Dillon & Co

Joan Clancy Gallery is located in the Ring Gaeltacht, overlooking Dungarvan Bay and the Comeragh and Knockmealdown Mountains. Part of the Clancy family, Joan's husband Tom was a founding member of The Clancy Brothers and they lived in New York and Los Angeles for seventeen years, before returning to live permanently in Ireland. The art space has been in operation since 2001. Before that, paintings were sold from the drawing room for several years. The gallery was built onto the existing house in the Ring Gaeltacht, overlooking Dungarvan Bay.

Number of rooms / galleries; area in square metres: One room, plus foyer space and stairwell: 860 square metres.

Specifications: Wall finishes are smooth brilliant white plaster. Floor is maple. Lighting: 26 directional lights. The gallery space is most suited to wall mounted paintings, no bigger than 180 x 180 cm.

Access details: No disabled access.

Exhibitions policy / 'ethos' of gallery: Exhibiting paintings from young and established contemporary artists.

What should interested artists do?
Artists who are interested in exhibiting should send slides or CD ROM, CV, statement and SAE, or e-mail with images and CV attached. The gallery neither pays or charges an exhibition fee. Opening reception, invitations and catalogue are provided. The gallery takes 30% commission on work sold. Work normally sells in the space.

Management structure: Private with grant from Udaras na Gaeltachta. Advisors: Blawnin Clancy and Rayleen Clancy.

Garter Lane Arts Centre

5 O'Connell Street
Waterford

Tel: +353 (0) 51 87 7153
Fax: +353 (0) 51 87 1570
E-mail: artswave@garterlane.ie
www.garterlane.com

Conversion of an historic building

Contact person / Director: Caitlin Doherty, Visual Art Coordinator;
Caroline Senior, Artistic Director

Architects for the: C J Falconer and Associates

Established as the Barker Arts Centre Ltd., the Garter Lane Arts Centre was officially opened in 1984, the Centre is housed in a late 18th century townhouse, also believed to have housed the Provincial Bank of Ireland in the mid 19th Century. The building was used as the Waterford Municipal Library until 1983.

Number of rooms / galleries; area in square metres: Front Gallery: front wall (windows) 8.26 m, wall inside door on R.H.S. 6m, wall opposite windows 6.2 m, end outside wall 6 m. Back Gallery: wall inside door on L.H.S. 3.2 m, back wall (windows) 8.26 m, end outside wall 6.1 m, wall around corner from entrance on R.H.S. 2.9 m, inside wall-opposite windows 6.2 m. Plus Children's Room and artists' studios.

Specifications: Two separate gallery rooms off new lobby entrance with plaster finish and picture rail. Natural light in both rooms from the almost floor to ceiling Georgian windows. Front Gallery: painted timber floorboards. Walls have been drylined to picture-rail level (timber picture-rail); plaster cornice intact; timber sash windows to front have architraves and panelled shutters. Rear Gallery: painted timber floorboards; plaster cornice; square-headed door-case to hall with timber and glass panelled doors with brass pull-handles; six sash windows with architraves and panelled shutters, which align with glazing pattern.

Access details: No disabled access.

Exhibitions policy / 'ethos' of gallery:
Garter Lane has a broad-based visual arts programme, which encourages applications for exhibitions in all media and styles. Individual artists and groups exhibit, with a local, national and international standing.

What should interested artists do? Artists are asked to submit a proposal, this should include a current CV, a brief artist's statement and images of current work in slide, photographic or digital format. The gallery takes 25% on work sold, and fees are not charged. The gallery pays an EPR of €318 per exhibition to professional artists. Press, admin, invitations provided.

Management structure: Company limited by guarantee, with charitable status. Board includes two Waterford City Council nominees.

Co Westmeath

Belvedere House and Gardens
Tullamore Road
Mullingar
Contact person: Bartle D'Arcy
Tel: +353 (0) 444 9060 Fax: +353 (0) 444 9002
E-mail: info@belvedere-house.ie
www.belvedere-house.ie

Dean Crowe Theatre and Arts Centre
Athlone
Contact person: Fionnuala O'Connell
Tel: +353 (0) 90 649 2129
E-mail: deancrowetheatre@eircom.net
www.deancrowetheatre.com

Mullingar Arts Centre (p. 261)
Mount Street
Mullingar
Contact Person: Sean Lynch
Tel: +353 (0) 444 7777 Fax: +353 (0) 444 7783
E-mail: mac@westmeathcoco.ie
www.mullingarartscentre.ie

Reeves Art Studio
33 Church St.
Athlone
Contact Person: Lavina Reeves
Tel: +353 (0) 90 647 8507
E-mail: info@reevesartstudio.com
www.reevesartstudio.com

Tuar Ard Arts Centre
Church Street
Moate
Contact person: Maire Farrell
Tel: +353 (0) 90 648 2042
E-mail: tuarard@eircom.net

Mullingar Arts Centre

Mount Street
Mullingar

Tel: +353 (0) 444 7777
E-mail: lmimnagh@westmeathcoco.ie
www.mullingarartscentre.ie

Mullingar Arts Centre opened in 1999. The Arts Centre is contained in the refurbished County Hall (originally built in 1913), and comprises a 407 seat theatre, two art workshops and an art gallery. The workshops cater for all art forms.

Number of rooms / galleries; area in square metres: Gallery: 288 square metres, and can be divided into three smaller sections by the use of sliding panels.

Specifications: Plaster walls, wooden flooring, assorted hanging, low voltage 35 watt / 50 watt lighting, art store room: 3.3 m high, standard loading doors. The space is suitable for slide installations / video installations / large works on canvas and free-standing sculpture.

Access details: Disabled access with a ramp, double entry and exit doors, lift.

Conversion of an existing building, multi-use venue

Contact person / Director: Sean Lynch, Centre Director

Architects for the conversion: Murray O'Laoire

Exhibitions policy / 'ethos' of gallery: To bring more people in contact with the visual arts. To make exhibition and installation facilities available in order to exhibit a wide range of art. To foster public awareness and sensitivity to art and to the business of professional artists.

What should interested artists do? Submit a CV accompanied by pictures, slides or a CD containing images of work. The Gallery does not pay or charge an exhibition fee. Opening reception and invitations are provided and commission is 10% for local guilds and 25% for professional artists. Local work sells well, while the sales of other work varies.

Management structure: Run by a Board.

Co Wexford

Cockle Shell Arts Centre
The Fort
Duncannon
New Ross
Contact person: Francis Delaney
Tel: +353 (0) 51 38 9990
E-mail: cockleshellartscentre@eircom.net

Greenacres Art Gallery
Selskar
Wexford
Contact person: Marianne Jackman
Tel: +353 (0) 532 3343 Fax: + 353 (0) 532 4905
E-mail: info@greenacres.ie   www.greenacres.ie

hopewire (p. 262)
Ryland Road
Bunclody
Contact person: David Begley, Marie Tumilson
Tel: +353 (0) 547 6588
E-mail: hopewire@eircom.net www.hopewire.com

Newtownbarry House
Bunclody
Contact Person: Clody Norton
Tel: +353 (0) 547 6383
E-mail: gallery@newtownbarry.com
www.newtownbarryhouse.com

The Norman Gallery (p. 263)
Monksgrange
Rathnure
Enniscorthy
Contact person: Jeremy Hill
Tel: +353 (0) 545 5071 Fax: +353 (0) 545 5146
E-mail: sales@normangallery.com
www.normangallery.com

Pigyard Gallery @ Spectrum Print
13 Selskar Street
Wexford Town
Contact person: Tony Robinson
Tel/Fax: +353 (0) 532 2019
E-mail: tonyrobinson@oceanfree.net

Wexford Arts Centre
Cornmarket
Wexford Town
Contact Person: Anne Comerford
Tel: +353 (0) 532 3764 Fax: +353 (0) 532 4544
E-mail: wexfordartscentre@eircom.net
www.wexfordartscentre.ie

hopewire

Ryland Road
Bunclody

Tel: +353 (0) 547 6588
E-mail: hopewire@eircom.net
www.hopewire.com

Re-use of an existing building

Contact person / Director: David Begley, Marie Tumilson

Architect: Unknown

Located in north Wexford, the hopewire building comprises of combined gallery space, studios, photographic darkroom, video production and graphic design facilities for artists, as well as accommodation. hopewire has been in operation since 2002, and the building was originally built as artists' studios (Bunclody Studios).

Number of rooms / galleries; area in square metres: Main gallery space: 31.5 square metres; second gallery: 13.5 square metres

Specifications: Walls: white plasterboard; flooring: grey painted concrete; hanging: directly onto walls; light: large front window giving natural light as well as fluorescent (spot lighting to be added); storage: small stockroom catering for small-to-large canvases; heights: 3 metres; loading doors: 2.5 metres height x 2 metres wide with van and truck access. The space is suitable for all types of work.

Access details: The gallery has limited disabled access: adequate door width; ground level with no stairs in the gallery; car parking.

Exhibitions policy / 'ethos' of gallery: The intention of hopewire is to provide an exhibition space for emerging, contemporary Irish and international artists, including recent graduates.

What should interested artists do?
Submissions are accepted from artists working in all media. CD ROM, prints and C.V on submission. The gallery does not pay or charge fees. hopewire provides an opening reception, invitations, posters and publicity for exhibitions. Artists may be invited to give public talk for which a fee is paid. A series of short video documentaries are currently being made about exhibiting artists at hopewire. The gallery commission is 35% on all sales of fine art.

Management structure: Independent.

The Norman Gallery

Monksgrange
Rathnure
Enniscorthy

Tel: +353 (0) 545 5071
E-mail: sales@normangallery.com
www.normangallery.com

Conversion of an historic building

Contact person / Director: Jeremy Hill

Architect: Edward Richards-Orpen (1912 section)
Architects for the conversion: Self-conversion

The Norman Gallery is situated in a wing of the house at Monksgrange. The main house was built in 1769, and the gallery wing was begun in 1912 to a design by Edward Richards-Orpen. The building was renovated as an artspace in 2003.

Number of rooms / galleries; area in square metres: The gallery has one main room of 110 square metres and one room of 45 square metres.

Specifications: Two-storey main space. Fifty percent of the main gallery roof is clear sheeting which, along with the windows, allows natural light to flood the space. The gallery walls are natural stone. Flooring is poured concrete with dark green carpeting. Paintings up to five metres high and four metres wide can be hung. Two hectare garden for outdoor sculpture of all scales. The space is suitable for slide and video installation. Loading is by the ground-level door.

Access details: The gallery is accessible to the disabled; it has adequate door widths

and is on the ground level with no steps or stairs. Immediately adjacent car parking.

Exhibitions policy / 'ethos' of gallery: The Norman Gallery displays both contemporary and traditional art from local, national and international artists. As a relatively new art space, the gallery aims to uphold a high standard for all its exhibitions, as well as create an informative and approachable space for the public.

What should interested artists do?
Send images (slides, CD ROM or by e-mail) along with CV. Services such as opening receptions, invitations and a slide projector are available to artists. The gallery takes 30% commission, and past exhibition sales from the gallery, and from the stockroom have been successful. The gallery does not charge admission fees.

Management structure: Privately owned and run.

Co Wicklow

Courthouse Art Centre (p. 264)
Main Street
Tinahely
Contact person: Sharon Corcoran
Tel: +353 (0) 4023 8529
E-mail: tinahely@iol.ie www.tinahely-courthouse.ie

Mermaid Arts Centre (p. 265)
Bray
Contact person: Artistic Director
Tel: +353 (0) 1 272 4302
E-mail: info@mermaidartscentre.ie
www.mermaidartscentre.ie

OS|B Art Gallery (p. 266)
Church Hill
Enniskerry Village
Contact person: Ian Bewick, John O'Sullivan
Tel: +353 (0) 1 286 2065
E-mail: info@osbgallery.com www.osbgallery.com

Signal Arts Centre
1A Albert Avenue
Bray
Contact person: Claire Flood
Tel: +353 (0) 1 276 2039
E-mail: signalartscentre@eircom.net

Courthouse Art Centre

Main Street
Tinahely
Co Wicklow

Tel: +353 (0) 4023 8529
www.tinahely-courthouse.ie

Conversion of an historic building

Contact person / Director: Sharon Corcoran

Architect responsible for the renovation: Paul Bodkin and Conor Maguire both contributed to the renovation.

The Courthouse Arts Centre is a multi-disciplinary arts centre, with one main space for exhibitions and performances. Built in 1843 and renovated in the late 1980s, the building was originally a courthouse, used for a while as a community centre, before becoming totally derelict. The arts centre has been in operation since 1996

Number of rooms / galleries; area in square metres: The main exhibition space (10.85 m x 6.77 m) consists of two floors, the first floor being a gallery overlooking the main space on three sides. There is,

in addition, a smaller gallery (4.28 m x 3.83 m) appropriate for smaller works.

Specifications: Walls in the main space are 3 m high, and are panelled to a height of 1m downstairs. Radiators limit the size of works able to be hung in certain places. Mirror plating is used to hang works on the plaster walls. Flooring is stone on the ground floor, pine on the upstairs gallery. Lighting is halogen track in the main space, and 120-W floods upstairs, where there is also natural light from the six large windows. Large works on canvas can be shown, as well as free-standing sculpture and video installations. There is no storage space.

Access details: Ramp into the building, and wheelchair-accessible toilet on the ground floor. The first floor gallery space is only accessible by stairs.

Exhibitions policy / 'ethos' of gallery: Courthouse exhibitions span a broad range of styles and media, from print to painting, sculpture to video installation. The visual arts programme is dedicated to showing the work of emerging and established professional artists. Summer months (June, July and August) are reserved for three-dimensional exhibitions, or installations.

What should interested artists do?
Submit CV and images in any format. The current exhibition schedule is online at the arts centre website. Commission is taken on sales, and work does sell in the space. When funding allows, the Courthouse have paid Exhibition Payment Right, although that is not current practice. No exhibition fee is charged. Invitation, postage, and opening reception provided.

Management structure: The arts centre is run by full-time staff, reporting to a Board.

Mermaid Arts Centre

Bray
Co Wicklow

Tel: +353 (0) 1 272 4302
E-mail: info@mermaidartscentre.ie

Purpose-built multi-use venue

Contact person: Aideen Howard, Artistic Director

Architects: Burke-Kennedy Doyle

Just off the Main Street in Bray, Co Wicklow, Mermaid is a multi-disciplinary venue comprising a theatre, gallery space and café / bar. Housed in a new purpose-built building, Mermaid opened in 2002.

Number of rooms / galleries; area in square metres: One gallery space in an L-shape. Total floor space; 165 square metres.

Specifications: The space is L-shaped and is bordered on one and a half sides by a glass curtain wall. At the corner of the L there is a 5 square metre open area with a canopy ceiling at 5 m high. Otherwise the ceiling is 2.55 m. The floor is carpet-tiled throughout. Hanging walls are a mixture of block-work rendered in plaster, and timber sheeting. All are painted off-white. There is a total 37 m of wall space available for hanging. Video work has been exhibited successfully. Lighting fixtures are a mixture of architectural fluorescent wall-lighters, and track spotlights. Limited storage. Loading doors 2.3 m high x 1.5 m wide space on first floor. Small lift available.

Access details: Mermaid's gallery is accessible by wheelchair via the lift.

Exhibitions policy / 'ethos' of gallery: The Mermaid gallery shows the best of national and international work which would otherwise not be seen in County Wicklow. It also provides an exhibition space for Wicklow based artists in the Mermaid Open Submission exhibition.

What should interested artists do?
Artists should send a CV plus slides to the attention of the Artistic Director. Mermaid charges 30% commission on work sold. Mermaid covers the cost of the opening reception and invitation design, printing and posting. Mermaid also undertakes the PR and marketing of each exhibition.

Management structure: Mermaid Arts Centre is a charity and a limited company with an independent voluntary Board. It is funded by Wicklow County Council, Bray Town Council and the Arts Council.

OS|B Art Gallery

Church Hill
Enniskerry Village
Tel: +353 (0) 1 286 2065

E-mail: info@osbgallery.com
www.osbgallery.com

Re-use of an historic building

Contact person: Ian Bewick, John O'Sullivan

Architects: Unknown

Formerly the Metatron, OS|B Art Gallery
is a commercial gallery on two floors in a
listed historic building in Enniskerry
village.

**Number of rooms / galleries; area in
square metres**: Approximately 213 square
metres in total.

Specifications: Gallery on two floors, airy
open space downstairs, work also hung on
the stairs and landings and and in the
large room upstairs. Wooden floors.

Access details: No disabled access.

Exhibitions policy / 'ethos' of gallery: The
gallery shows mainly contemporary Irish
art, including painting and sculpture.

What should interested artists do? Artists
should send material in whatever best suits
their medium, by post or by email. Gallery
commission on sales is by negotiation.

Management structure: Private.

Contributors

Barbara Dawson has been Director of Dublin City Gallery The Hugh Lane since 1991. Since then she has reorganised the Gallery's position and contemporary identity, bringing to it a greater international profile. Ongoing programmes of temporary exhibitions and educational projects, both in the gallery and off-site, complement the renowned permanent collection. The collection has been significantly enhanced by the donation of Francis Bacon's studio, which she secured in 1998 and, more recently, by a donation of nine works by Sean Scully as well as six unfinished paintings by Frnacis Bacon. Further recent ascquisitions include works by Jaki Irvine and Elizabeth Magill. The Gallery's new extension was approved by Dublin City Council in 2004 and is due to open in 2006. Barbara Dawson also writes essays and monographs for art publications.

Damien Coyle describes himself as an artist, writer, pseudo-bureaucrat and recovering Arts Council employee. He has worked in the area of arts, education and training and cultural management. During a diverse career he has exhibited locally, nationally and internationally, established artist-focussed projects such as Queen's Street Studios and the Artsite schemes and was responsible for developing the Cultural Management Training Programme at the University of Ulster. Damien Coyle is a former Chairperson of, and contributor to, *CIRCA* Art Magazine.

John Gerrard is an artist based in Dublin working in real-time 3D, photography and sculpture. Recent exhibitions include: *Touch and Temperature*, Bitforms Gallery, NY, USA, *Some Exhaust*, Lehmann Maupin Gallery, NY, USA, *The Ars Electronica Festival*, Austria and the *Liverpool Biennial*. He received a BFA (Sculpture) from the Ruskin School of Oxford University in 1997, an MFA (Art and Technology) from the Art Institute of Chicago and a MSc (Multimedia) from Trinity College Dublin in 2001.
See also www.johngerrard.net

Paul Harron is Architecture and Public Art Officer at the Arts Council of Northern Ireland. He sits on the N.I. Interdepartmental Architecture Policy Steering Group, is an advisor to the Board of PLACE, and is on the Editorial Committee of *Perspective*, to which he contributes regularly. With a background largely in art and architectural history, he was editor at Phaidon Press and senior editor at Laurence King Publishing working on the architecture and design lists; and has taught at QUB and the Open University. He is undertaking doctoral research at QUB into the work of the firm Young & Mackenzie.

Brian Kennedy is an artist based in Belfast, and a Contributing Editor to *CIRCA* Art Magazine. A founder member of ARE in Belfast, Brian has curated and exhibited widely in Ireland and internationally, and also writes on contemporary visual art and culture.

Fiona Kearney is a curator, academic and art critic. Currently Director of the Lewis Glucksman Gallery, University College Cork, she is a graduate of UCC where she was awarded a double first class honours in French and Philosophy. She went on to graduate first in her class at Trinity College Dublin with an M.Phil in Text and Image studies. She has received several distinguished awards including the NUI Prix d'Honneur from the French Government, a Fulbright Scholarship and several awards from the Arts Council of Ireland.

James Kerr is the Executive Director of the Verbal Arts Centre. He was previously Director of Kaleidoscope Arts Ltd and Context Gallery. He has worked for the Arts Council of Northern Ireland as Visual Arts Officer and Lottery Officer. He is a board member of *CIRCA* Art Magazine, Echo Echo Dance Company, Stage Beyond Theatre Company and a trustee of Artscare. He was previously a board member of the Arts Council of Northern Ireland.

Declan Long is an Assistant Lecturer in the Faculty of History of Art and Design and Complementary Studies at the National College of Art and Design, Dublin. He has written widely on contemporary art and related subjects.

Ciarán Mackel is a partner in Mackel + Doherty Architects and the immediate past president of the Royal Society of Ulster Architects. The practice is based in inner North Belfast and has gained a number of design awards and commendations for their work. Ciarán is a regular contributor to *Perspective* – the journal of the RSUA – writing reviews, editorials, and essays and submitting photographic essays to generate discussion on architecture and urbanism. He has been architect-assessor on a number of architectural competitions in recent years following his role as Arts Council Lottery panel member, Architectural Policy panel member, and as a creative advisor on the built environment to Imagine Belfast. Ciarán is currently part of the RSUA's PLACE project developed in co-operation with Belfast City Council to provide a city centre venue as an Architecture and Built Environment Centre.

Based in Dublin, **McCullough Mulvin Architects** is one of Ireland's most prestigious and award winning young architectural practices. It was established in the late 1980s by Valerie Mulvin and Niall McCullough and now includes a number of the country's best young architects. The buildings reflect the way in which architecture has begun to play an increasing part in the definition of culture in Ireland's changing society. The office has worked on major cultural projects like the Abbey Theatre, and in the Temple Bar regeneration area (where the practice designed Temple Bar Galleries, Black Church Print Studios and the Music Centre), and in the recently completed Model Arts and Niland Gallery in Sligo. The projects reflect the practice's interest in modern things; in trying to keep an open mind on how architecture might reflect thought about the way we live and work in Ireland; and in the opportunities that that offers to form new and unique public spaces, reflecting evolving attitudes to land, history and memory. Many of the projects are either in sensitive contexts, and reflect a specific response to site and place, or are modern interventions into existing buildings, an open-ended exploration of scale, materials and form.
See also www.mccolloughmulvin.com

Des McMahon is a founding Director of Gilroy McMahon Architects, one of Ireland's leading practices, who have designed some of the country's most interesting and challenging buildings. Current and recent projects demonstrate an immense diversity of successful work such as Croke Park Stadium, the Irish International Folk Music Centre in Ennis (Glór) and the conversion of Collins Barracks Dublin to the National Museum. They have won numerous awards of merit some at European level including the Gulbenkian Award for museum design, RIAI Triennial Gold Medal for excellence, and the Silver Medal for conservation. Currently working on the Hugh Lane Gallery extension, Des places emphasis on what he defines as the three most important priorities in gallery design: circulation, light and barely-visible architecture.

Patrick Murphy is Director of the RHA Gallagher Gallery. He began his career in 1980 as Visual Arts Officer at the Arts Council; from 1984 until 1989 Murphy was Director at the Douglas Hyde Gallery, Dublin, before moving to the US to take up the post of Director at

Philadelphia's Institute of Contemporary Art in 1990. He returned to Dublin and the RHA in 1999.

Peter Murray is Director of the Crawford Art Gallery in Cork, and deputy chair of the Cultural Relations Committee.

Ruairí Ó Cuív has worked in the arts since the early 1980's. He was lecturer of History of Art in Sligo RTC from 1980-82 and then worked as a specialist in the handling and installation of exhibitions. He was Exhibitions Officer in the Royal Hospital Kilmainham (1987-89), Curator of Exhibitions in the Douglas Hyde Gallery (1989-1991) and Director of Temple Bar Gallery and Studios (1991-1996). Since 1996 he has worked as an arts consultant, specialising in areas including curation of exhibitions, management of public art commissions, cataloguing of art collections and undertaking developmental and strategic studies for arts and heritage organisations. He writes catalogue essays and articles for journals. He is chairperson of CREATE and is on the editorial panel for *Contexts*, the journal of arts and practise in Ireland.

Brian O'Doherty is a renowned artist who has exhibited extensively internationally, always under the name Patrick Ireland. As an art critic, his book *Inside the White Cube* is a canonical text on the intersection of commerce, society and aesthetics. He has also been a Booker Prize nominee for his novel *The Deposition of Father McGreevy*. A retrospective of his work is planned for the Hugh Lane Gallery in 2006.

Irish-born artist **Eamon O'Kane** currently lives and works in Bristol. Memories, travel and the large-scale panoramas of the 19th century are recurrent themes in his work. In 2002 O'Kane began working on Anti-Mates, a project based around a group of fictional art assistants which has resulted in animations and large-scale installations exhibited at EV+A 2003 and in Frankfurt, Germany. O'Kane's current work has developed into an exploration of the 'ideal studio space'. His recent paintings consist of views of architectural interventions where the man-made meets with nature. These works further draw out O'Kane's conceptual concerns about art and architecture.

Marianne O'Kane is Curator of Cavanacor Gallery. She is a writer and critic and a regular contributor to the Irish Arts Review, *CIRCA* Magazine and Perspective Architecture Magazine. Marianne has been a member of the Editorial Board of *Perspective* for the past two years. She was a full faculty member of Boston University's Dublin Internship

Programme for four years and continues to lecture on Irish art. She has worked as Visual Arts Officer for the Arts Council of Northern Ireland. Marianne has authored a number of monographs on artists including Michael Kane and Adrian O'Connell.

Peter Richards is an Artist and Gallery Director of the Golden Thread Gallery, Belfast. He is also a freelance curator/facilitator based in Belfast. Richards graduated in 1994 from the University of Wales, Cardiff with a BA (Hons.) degree in Fine Art. He continued his education at the University of Ulster, Belfast, where he completed an M/Phil research degree "Reconstructing Representations of the Histories of Performance Art" in May 1999. As an artist, Richards has exhibited widely nationally and internationally, and is one of the artists selected to represent Northern Ireland at the 2005 Venice Biennale.

Noel Sheridan is an artist who has directed spaces for art: Experimental Art Foundation Adelaide South Australia; Perth Institute of Contemporary Arts Western Australia and the National College of Art and Design Dublin.

Jimi Shields graduated from DIT Bolton Street in 1991. He enjoyed an internationally acclaimed musical career between 1991 & 1999. He worked in New York city with John B. Murray Architect and is currently practising under the name thirtythreetrees with his wife Maria Vlahos (Head gardener at Mount Usher Gardens). Their current projects include garden design collaborations with de Paor Architects.

Gemma Tipton is a writer and critic of contemporary art and architecture. Based in Dublin, she contributes regularly to art and architectural publications, radio and television programmes. Formerly manager of *CIRCA* Art Magazine, she is currently Editor of *Contexts*, the journal of contemporary arts practice. Gemma is also a judge for the Museum of the Year Awards.

John Tuomey graduated from the School of Architecture University College Dublin in 1976, gaining a Master's degree in 2004. He worked in London for Stirling Wilford Associates 1976-1981. During this time he worked on the design of the Staatsgalerie in Stuttgart from design conception to construction. He worked as an architect in the Office of Public Works from 1981 to 1987, where he was responsible for the design and contract management for two award winning buildings: a Laboratory at Abbotstown (1985) and for a courthouse in Smithfield, completed in 1987, which was part of an Urban Design project for the Smithfield area. In 1988 he set up O'Donnell + Tuomey Architects with Sheila O'Donnell. Their work has won many national and international awards and has been widely published and exhibited in Europe, Japan and America. John Tuomey was managing director of Group 91 Architects, urban designers for the Temple Bar Development Plan and played a key role in liaising with Temple Bar Properties, with Government agencies and various interest groups. He was president of the Architectural Association of Ireland in 1992 and was elected a Fellow of RIAI in 1994. He was Visiting Critic at Princeton in 1987 and Harvard GSD in 1988, has taught at Syracuse, Cambridge and Oxford and has lectured at many schools of architecture in Europe, Japan and America. He has been external examiner at Oxford, Cambridge, UEL and AA London. He is a studio lecturer at the School of Architecture UCD.

In 1993, **Vittorio Urbani** founded the *Nuova Icona, Associazione Culturale per le Arti*, a non-profit organization dedicated to new art production in Venice. Nuova Icona has two exhibition venues, the Gallery on the Giudecca island and a little church, the Oratorio di San Ludovico. A curator of national and international exhibitions, Vittorio has also collaborated actively in the realization of the National Pavilions in the Biennale for Ireland (1995, 1996, 1999, 2001, 2003); Turkey (2001, 2003), Scotland (2003), Wales (2003).

Vox Pop contributions: Liz Aders, Chris Bailey, Charles Blanc & Tristan Surtees – Sans façon, Mark Cullen, Cora Cummins, Cian Donnelly, Oliver Dowling, Chérie Driver, Rita Duffy, Brian Duggan, Brendan Earley, Peter FitzGerald, Mike Fitzpatrick, Joy Gerrard, John Graby, Barbara Griffin, Brian Harten, Katie Holten, Alannah Hopkin, Allan Hughes, Megan Johnston, Enrique Juncosa, Fiona Killeen, Suzanne Lyle, Sean Lynch, Stephanie McBride, Roisín Mc Donough, Nóirín Mc Kinney, Dermot McLaughlin, Eoghan McTigue, Hugh Mulholland, Jason Oakley, Aisling O'Beirn, Sandra O'Connell, Jerome O Drisceoil, om lekha, Mark Orange, Garrett Phelan, Alison Pilkington, Jim Smyth, Allyson Spellacy, Gavin Weston.

Index of Architects, Artists and Arts Spaces